Mastering Internet of Things

Design and create your own IoT applications using
Raspberry Pi 3

Peter Waher

BIRMINGHAM - MUMBAI

Mastering Internet of Things

Commissioning Editor: Vijin Boricha
Acquisition Editor: Namrata Patil
Content Development Editor: Trusha Shriyan
Technical Editor: Naveenkumar Jain
Copy Editor: Laxmi Subramanian and Safis Editing
Project Coordinator: Kinjal Bari
Proofreader: Safis Editing
Indexer: Mariammal Chettiyar
Graphics: Jisha Chirayil
Production Coordinator: Nilesh Mohite

First published: March 2018

Production reference: 1230318

Published by Packt Publishing Ltd.
Livery Place
35 Livery Street
Birmingham
B3 2PB, UK.

ISBN 978-1-78839-748-3

www.packtpub.com

Today. while writing this, it has passed 11 months to the day since the work on this book began. A lot of time and effort has been dedicated to creating this book and its contents. If this book helps you, the reader, gain insights into the world of Internet of Things and the future Smart City, or Smart Society, this effort has been well spent. I would like to dedicate this book to the loving memory of my little brother, Viktor, who unfortunately passed away last year, only thirty-seven years old, leaving behind his wife and children. It was a difficult time for the entire family, and in many regards, it still is. This book wouldn't have been completed without the help, support, and understanding of my father, Jüri, who has dedicated a lot of time and effort to his grandchildren; and my wife, Katya; and daughters, Maria-Lorena and Ella-Pauline. Without their support and understanding, it wouldn't have been possible to dedicate all the late nights and weekends to this book. I would also like to thank the editors at Packt, who have had patience with all the many missed deadlines.

–Peter Waher

`mapt.io`

Mapt is an online digital library that gives you full access to over 5,000 books and videos, as well as industry leading tools to help you plan your personal development and advance your career. For more information, please visit our website.

Why subscribe?

- Spend less time learning and more time coding with practical eBooks and Videos from over 4,000 industry professionals

- Improve your learning with Skill Plans built especially for you

- Get a free eBook or video every month

- Mapt is fully searchable

- Copy and paste, print, and bookmark content

PacktPub.com

Did you know that Packt offers eBook versions of every book published, with PDF and ePub files available? You can upgrade to the eBook version at `www.PacktPub.com` and as a print book customer, you are entitled to a discount on the eBook copy. Get in touch with us at `service@packtpub.com` for more details.

At `www.PacktPub.com`, you can also read a collection of free technical articles, sign up for a range of free newsletters, and receive exclusive discounts and offers on Packt books and eBooks.

Contributors

About the author

Peter Waher is the founder of Little Sister®—a standards-based distributed social network—based on the principles of edge computing, privacy, and information ownership for humans and machines. Currently, he advises companies on topics such as privacy, the IoT, and Smart Cities. He has worked for 24 years with computers and device communication, including low-level development in assembler for resource-constrained devices to high-level system design and architecture. His award-winning applications have attracted global attention; he has also spoken at prestigious events.

About the reviewer

Pankaj Ganguly is currently working as an IoT architect with Wipro. Previously, he served Persistent for 12 years. He architected and delivered many IoT solutions using diverse technologies and cloud platforms.

He is an AWS certified solution architect and a ToGAF 9 certified enterprise architect who has published seven research papers in international conferences and journals. He also reviewed many journal and conference papers. He taught at NIT as a visiting faculty, and has been a part of the academic committee and external evaluators of many NITs in India.

Packt is searching for authors like you

If you're interested in becoming an author for Packt, please visit `authors.packtpub.com` and apply today. We have worked with thousands of developers and tech professionals, just like you, to help them share their insight with the global tech community. You can make a general application, apply for a specific hot topic that we are recruiting an author for, or submit your own idea.

Table of Contents

Preface

Hello and welcome to *Mastering Internet of Things*. This book will guide you through the very fascinating subject of Internet of Things, and the emerging concept of Smart Cities. If you're a novice to the subject, don't worry, you'll be introduced to it. You are assumed to know the basic principles of software development. Standard components such as Raspberry Pi, Arduino, and related peripherals will be used throughout the book. There is no need for knowledge of electronics, even though an understanding of the basic underlying principles will help. The book will guide you through many of the different problems each developer needs to face and master, using several practical projects. We've chosen to use C# in all the examples. It's a modern language that will allow us to reuse code efficiently between PCs, embedded devices, smart phones, and tablets. You can choose between using free or commercial development tools. By the end, you'll be an adept in the field, having mastered many of the fundamentals of Internet of Things and will be ready to join us in the effort in creating the next generation of Smart Cities and Smart Societies.

Defining the Internet of Things

The successful study of any subject begins with using good definitions. Without clear definitions, the boundaries become fuzzy and immediate consequences and implications become unclear. The term **Internet of Things** started as a visionary statement, a buzz word, rather than a definition. While the term has enjoyed exceptional media coverage, the visionary statement has been interpreted differently by different people.

The term is normally considered to be coined by Kevin Ashton in 1999 when he described a future where things such as barcode readers would be directly connected to the internet, without the interference of humans. Humans were likened to bad, slow, and error prone routers. While "things" had already been connected to the internet way before this statement, the term had not been coined yet. The utility sector, for instance, had long used connected meters to retrieve meting data automatically. This was first done using modems and the phone network already in the late 70s and 80s. When ISPs began providing internet access locally, switching to the internet became a way to reduce costs, since local phone calls could be used instead of long distance calls. Even the internet itself is a network of *things*. Computers and servers are naturally things that are connected. But here, *thing* has come to mean non-computer-thing, even though the *thing* must have a small computer inside, to be able to connect...confusing...

So, to avoid any further confusion, let's provide a clear definition of what the Internet of Things is.

 The **Internet of Things** is what you get when you connect things that are not operated by humans to the internet.

This definition has four clear areas of study that we will introduce in this book:

1. How to **connect** things; this is the study of communication protocols.
2. The study of **things**; this includes concepts such as sensors, actuators, controllers, concentrators, bridges, and so on.
3. Things are considered **not operated by humans;** do differentiate them from normal computers. This requires them to make their own decisions and act alone. This leads to the study of decision support, artificial intelligence, and so on.
4. Being connected to the **internet** means the things become neighbors with all the world's criminals, hackers, and curious teenagers at once. Since things are supposedly not operated by humans, and work possibly for years unsupervised, the study of security becomes acute. IoT inherits all security issues related to building information systems on the internet.

While the Internet of Things has seen a lot of development in the first two areas mentioned previously, the last two are underdeveloped and often omitted. This has lead people such as James Clapper, former Director of National Intelligence in the USA, to state that *America's Greatest Threat is the Internet of Things* (http://www.popsci.com/clapper-americas-greatest-threat-is-internet-things).

Competing terminology

As different companies and organizations strive to get attention, it's not surprising to find a myriad of similar buzz words being used, each one highlighting different aspects of the same underlying problem, or to boast of one's supposedly exceptional understanding of the subject. **Web of Things** (**WoT**), for instance, concerns itself with web-based technologies for the Internet of Things, such as the HTTP and Web Services. It forms a clear subset of the Internet of Things (IoT). A Connected Device is often used as a selling point. It normally refers to the internet connectivity of the device, and then falls under IoT or WoT. As an extension, the Connected Home, Connected Car, and so on, are specializations of this trend. Perhaps as an attempt to boast, **Internet of Everything** (**IoE**) was coined. But how do you connect something that is not a thing? Can you connect an emotion or a smell, without a thing in between doing the sensing? How do you connect space or water? How about abstract things, such as happiness, how do you connect that? Clearly, IoE comprises the same items and technologies as Internet of Things, but with a more bombastic title. The same can be said about Internet of People and Things. This term tries to include human interaction into the equation. But humans and their processes are already implicitly included in the original term "Internet"; it needs no further introduction. But there exists terminology that have clear differences in meaning, that are worth mentioning. **Machine-to-Machine** (**M2M**) communication relates to communication between machines, including devices and things. It doesn't presuppose the use of the IP protocol, and the internet. Many different types of protocols and technologies can be used in M2M solutions, including the IP protocol. But solutions are typically sealed or closed. The internet, if used, is used as a carrier of signals and not a platform for interoperability. **Cyber-Physical Systems** (**CPS**) is like M2M in the sense that it doesn't presuppose the use of the IP-protocol. In CPS, however, it's the interaction between algorithms running on machines with the physical environment that is of interest.

Envisioning the Smart City

For our purposes, since we aim at being able to build smart interoperable cities and societies, the term Internet of Things fits best. Taking the full definition of IoT given earlier, we could even say that we try to build an **Internet for Things**, by providing the necessary infrastructure for things to be able to make good decisions during their connected life-times. But what is a **Smart City**, or a **Smart Society**?

In a Smart City, or a Smart Society, you have:

- Ubiquitous access to interoperable sensors and things
- Ubiquitous access to data and information from society's authorities

- Access to smart services in all niches of society

When you've completed reading this book, you'll know how to accomplish this goal.

What this book covers

Chapter 1, *Preparing Our First Raspberry Pi Project*, introduces you to development for Raspberry Pi. You'll get an introduction to the Raspberry Pi and peripherals and how to prepare, start, and administer your device. You'll learn how to develop, compile, run, deploy, and test your application on your device.

Chapter 2, *Creating a Sensor to Measure Ambient Light*, shows you how to create a basic sensor firmware application for your device. This includes sampling, error correction, management of physical quantities, basic statistics, and data persistence.

Chapter 3, *Creating an Actuator for Controlling Illumination*, focuses on how to create a basic actuator firmware application. You'll learn how to define control parameters, use relays to control equipment, persist control states, and log important control events.

Chapter 4, *Publishing Information Using MQTT*, presents a simple way to publish your information on the internet. It introduces you to the MQTT protocol, the Publish/Subscribe communication pattern, how to connect to a broker, publish information, and subscribe to information. You'll learn to test and troubleshoot your communication and consider basic security issues.

Chapter 5, *Publishing Data Using HTTP*, introduces you to the HTTP protocol and the Request/Response communication pattern. This includes locating resources on the internet and basic protocol semantics. You'll also learn how to publish machine-readable web service interfaces and the fundamentals of encryption.

Chapter 6, *Creating Web Pages for Your Devices*, continues by focusing on human interfaces for your devices, and how they can be used to monitor and interact with them. You'll learn how to publish file-based content how to use Markdown to publish human-readable web content, how to interact with backend web services from JavaScript. You will also learn how to perform basic authentication using login pages and **Java Web Tokens (JWT)**.

Chapter 7, *Communicating More Efficiently Using CoAP*, shows you how to create interfaces for resource-constrained devices. You'll get an introduction to the CoAP protocol, how security is performed, how content is encoded, how data is published, and how to respond to control actions. You'll be introduced to a new Communication Pattern, the Event Subscription, and the Observe pattern. You'll learn how to test your CoAP-enabled devices and how to secure them using encryption.

Chapter 8, *Interoperability*, introduces the concept of application-level interoperability and how standardized technologies can help us in our work. You'll be introduced to **Constrained RESTful Environments (CoRE)**, the **Light-weight Machine-to-Machine (LWM2M)** enabler , and a standardized object model for the management of devices based on CoAP and CoRE. IPSO Smart Objects, a set of standardized object interfaces for sensors and actuators, will also be presented.

Chapter 9, *Social Interaction with Your Devices Using XMPP*, begins a series of chapters introducing a more advanced paradigm of communication with devices that will allow us to do much more interesting things with them in a more secure and interoperable, yet flexible manner. This chapter introduces the XMPP protocol and the basics of XMPP extensions. It introduces a trust-based model for communication and security in a social context. The chapter shows how the Request/Response, Event Subscription, and Publish/Subscribe patterns can be used in XMPP. It also shows how to build human-to-machine chat interfaces.

Chapter 10, *The Controller*, introduces a new type of device, the controller. It presents a way to register and discover things on the internet using Thing Registries. It will subscribe to data from sensors it finds and accepts and send control operation commands to appropriate actuators it finds and accepts.

Chapter 11, *Product Life Cycle*, highlights that managing devices in an IoT infrastructure is more complicated than just installing devices, finding them, and starting to communicate with them. You need to manage the devices over their entire life cycle. You also need to consider operating costs, without compromising on the security and integrity of the data and people involved. This chapter introduces a method of provisioning that takes all these aspects into account. It defines the concept of ownership of data, and how owners can claim their devices. It presents a decision support extension to XMPP that helps devices determine who can be their friends and who can do what with them, based on the wishes of their owners.

Chapter 12, *Concentrators and Bridges*, presents a method to encapsulate virtual devices inside one communicating entity called a concentrator seamlessly, as if they were standalone devices on the network. The same technique used to model embedded devices can be used to bridge between protocol islands, either using the same or different types of communication protocols, or to integrate backend systems into the network. You'll learn to create a concentrator embedding both your sensor and actuator functionality into one single physical device. You'll also learn how you can interact with these embedded devices and how they can be provisioned just as if they were standalone devices.

Chapter 13, *Using an Internet of Things Service Platform*, shows how an IoT Service Platform can help you with many of the repetitive tasks required to create a successful IoT application. It introduces the IoT Gateway project, its architecture and hardware abstraction layer, security infrastructure, and its management interfaces. You'll learn how to create services running on the IoT Gateway, how to use its databases for persistence, how to interface things, and use its hosting environment.

Chapter 14, *IoT Harmonization*, introduces a standardization effort to harmonize the wide range of technologies used in the field of Internet of Things, with the goal of creating an infrastructure for the Smart City. It reviews the vision of a Smart City and identifies the main driving forces and requirements for reaching the vision. The chapter gives an overview of the required new standards and new business roles.

Chapter 15, *Security for the Internet of Things*, motivates the reader to add security for the Internet of Things from the beginning, integrating it into the fabric of the design and architecture, and not adding it later, as an add-on, in case it is needed. It provides a general introduction to the problem, reviews common attack surfaces, and presents some common counter measures.

Chapter 16, *Privacy*, introduces privacy, and why it matters. It presents new modern privacy legislation, and how technology presented in this book can be used to protect the privacy.

What you need for this book

Apart from a computer running Windows, Linux, or Mac OS, you will need three Raspberry Pi 2 model B credit-card-sized computers or later, with 16 GB SD cards containing the Windows 10 IoT operating system installed. The first chapter lists the components used to build the circuits used in the examples presented in the book as well as the applications needed to build the projects. The source code for all the projects presented in this book is available for download from GitHub at `https://github.com/PeterWaher/MIoT`.

Who this book is for

This book is for students, developers, or electronics engineers who want an introduction to the Internet of Things, or for professionals who want to deepen their understanding and explore the possibilities of different technologies for the Internet of Things and the Smart City. With only a rudimentary understanding of electronics (high school level), Raspberry Pi or similar credit-card-sized computers, and some programming experience using managed code such as C# or Java or object-oriented languages such as C++, you will be taught to develop state-of-the-art solutions for the Internet of Things in an instant.

Conventions

In this book, you will find a number of text styles that distinguish between different kinds of information. Here are some examples of these styles and an explanation of their meaning.

Code words in text, database table names, folder names, filenames, file extensions, path names, dummy URLs, and user input are shown as follows: "Make sure the `serialCommunication` device capability is added."

A block of code is set as follows:

```
<Capabilities>
    <Capability Name="internetClient" />
    <DeviceCapability Name="serialcommunication">
        <Device Id="any">
            <Function Type="name:serialPort" />
        </Device>
    </DeviceCapability>
</Capabilities>
```

When we wish to draw your attention to a particular part of a code block, the relevant lines or items are set in bold:

```
<Capabilities>
    <Capability Name="internetClient" />
    <DeviceCapability Name="serialcommunication">
        <Device Id="any">
            <Function Type="name:serialPort" />
        </Device>
    </DeviceCapability>
</Capabilities>
```

Any command-line input or output is written as follows:

```
$ sudo apt-get udpate
$ sudo apt-get upgrade
$ sudo apt-get install mono-complete
```

New terms and `important words` are shown in bold. Words that you see on the screen, for example, in menus or dialog boxes, appear in the text like this: "Clicking the `Next` button moves you to the next screen."

 Warnings or important notes appear like this.

 Tips and tricks appear like this.

Reader feedback

Feedback from our readers is always welcome. Let us know what you think about this book—what you liked or disliked. Reader feedback is important for us as it helps us develop titles that you will really get the most out of.

To send us general feedback, simply e-mail `feedback@packtpub.com`, and mention the book's title in the subject of your message.

If there is a topic that you have expertise in and you are interested in either writing or contributing to a book, see our author guide at `www.packtpub.com/authors`.

Customer support

Now that you are the proud owner of a Packt book, we have a number of things to help you to get the most from your purchase.

Downloading the color images of this book

We also provide you with a PDF file that has color images of the screenshots/diagrams used in this book. The color images will help you better understand the changes in the output. You can download this file from `http://www.packtpub.com/sites/default/files/ downloads/MasteringInternetOfThings_ColorImages.pdf`.

Download the example code files

You can download the example code files for this book from your account at `www.packtpub.com`. If you purchased this book elsewhere, you can visit `www.packtpub.com/support` and register to have the files emailed directly to you.

You can download the code files by following these steps:

1. Log in or register at `www.packtpub.com`.
2. Select the **SUPPORT** tab.
3. Click on **Code Downloads & Errata**.
4. Enter the name of the book in the **Search** box and follow the onscreen instructions.

Once the file is downloaded, please make sure that you unzip or extract the folder using the latest version of:

- WinRAR/7-Zip for Windows
- Zipeg/iZip/UnRarX for Mac
- 7-Zip/PeaZip for Linux

The code bundle for the book is also hosted on GitHub at </span>`https://github.com/ PacktPublishing/Mastering-Internet-of-Things`. In case there's an update to the code, it will be updated on the existing GitHub repository.

We also have other code bundles from our rich catalog of books and videos available at `https://github.com/PacktPublishing/`. Check them out!

Errata

Although we have taken every care to ensure the accuracy of our content, mistakes do happen. If you find a mistake in one of our books—maybe a mistake in the text or the code—we would be grateful if you could report this to us. By doing so, you can save other readers from frustration and help us improve subsequent versions of this book. If you find any errata, please report them by visiting http://www.packtpub.com/submit-errata, selecting your book, clicking on the **Errata Submission Form** link, and entering the details of your errata. Once your errata are verified, your submission will be accepted and the errata will be uploaded to our website or added to any list of existing errata under the Errata section of that title.

To view the previously submitted errata, go to https://www.packtpub.com/books/content/support and enter the name of the book in the search field. The required information will appear under the **Errata** section.

Piracy

Piracy of copyrighted material on the Internet is an ongoing problem across all media. At Packt, we take the protection of our copyright and licenses very seriously. If you come across any illegal copies of our works in any form on the Internet, please provide us with the location address or website name immediately so that we can pursue a remedy.

Please contact us at copyright@packtpub.com with a link to the suspected pirated material.

We appreciate your help in protecting our authors and our ability to bring you valuable content.

Questions

If you have a problem with any aspect of this book, you can contact us at questions@packtpub.com, and we will do our best to address the problem.

1
Preparing Our First Raspberry Pi Project

In this chapter, we'll start getting our hands dirty and create our first Raspberry Pi project. You are surely eager to get started. This chapter covers:

- An introduction to the Raspberry Pi and peripherals
- How to install Windows 10 on your device
- How to start and administer your device
- How to create a simple C# project for Raspberry Pi
- How to download and run your application on your device
- How to debug your application remotely on your device

Getting what you need

For the purposes of this chapter, you will need the following:

- A Raspberry Pi 2 or 3 (you'll need three in total, throughout the book)
- A micro SD memory card (16 GB or greater) for each Raspberry Pi
- A shielded box, to avoid electrostatic damage to your device
- A laptop or PC running Windows 10, where you can insert the memory card
- An Ethernet network cable, if you use Raspberry Pi 2 or lack Wi-Fi
- An internet connection

The Raspberry Pi 2 or 3 will allow us to run .NET applications and control peripherals using digital input and output easily. It's also a great platform for creating connected distributed services. One of its weaknesses, however, is its lack of simple out-of-the-box analog interfaces. To do analog input and output, you must connect additional chips or equipment using either synchronous or asynchronous serial communication interfaces that converts analog signals to digital ones. To simplify this task, you can also use an **Arduino** board that you connect to the Raspberry Pi via USB. This has the added benefit of allowing you to use a wide range of standard Arduino peripherals and devices in your Raspberry Pi projects. So, you need to add to your list:

- Arduino shield for Raspberry Pi B+/2B/3B
- Short serial USB cable to connect the Arduino board to the Raspberry Pi
- Analog Arduino-compatible light sensor
- Digital motion detection PIR sensor
- Digital relay module

Most of the above equipment (and more) can be obtained in so-called **Starter Kits**. Such starter kits make for great fun, since they often include a wide variety of sensors and actuators for you to play with. For examples, refer to `https://www.dfrobot.com/category-173.html`.

You can use the Arduino Uno board as well. The advantage of the Arduino shield for Raspberry Pi is that it mounts easier on top of the Raspberry Pi.

Downloading the IoT Dashboard

Installing Windows 10 on a Raspberry Pi is both free and very easy. Microsoft has developed a tool for this purpose: the **IoT Dashboard**. Apart from allowing you to download and install Windows 10 on your devices, it also helps you manage your devices in the network. It's a very handy tool, and does not require you to learn any command-line syntax:

Download and install the IoT Dashboard from the following link: `https://developer.microsoft.com/en-us/windows/iot/docs/iotdashboard`

The IoT Dashboard is a Windows 10 app. Once running, you can choose to right-click on its icon and select **Pin to taskbar**, so that you can find it easier later.

If you don't want to use Windows 10, and want to use Linux instead, you can do so with the following modifications:

- You can use the Raspbian operating system instead. It's based on Debian. Follow the following instructions on how to download and install it:
  `https://www.raspberrypi.org/documentation/installation/installing-images/`.
- Instead of compiling your project as a **.NET Core** application, compile it as a standard **.NET Framework** application instead.
- Run the application using **Mono**. You can follow the following instructions on how to accomplish this:
  `http://www.raspberry-sharp.org/eric-bezine/2012/10/mono-framework/installing-mono-raspberry-pi/`.

> You can run .NET Core on Linux as well. For more information, see:
> `https://github.com/dotnet/core/blob/master/samples/RaspberryPiInstructions.md`

Installing Windows 10 on your Raspberry Pi

When you've installed and run the IoT Dashboard, a window appears:

1. Select **Set up a new device** in the left-hand menu. This will open a simple form. Select your device (**Raspberry Pi 2 & 3**) and the OS you want to download and install (**Windows 10 IoT Core**).

2. Also, insert the memory card into the computer and select the **Drive** letter it is assigned to. Other relevant information you need to provide include the **Device name** and an **Administrator password**:

Setting up a new device

Remember the password!

3. If you have access to Wi-Fi (**2.4 GHz**), and are programming a device with access to Wi-Fi, make sure the correct **Wi-Fi Network Connection** is also assigned:

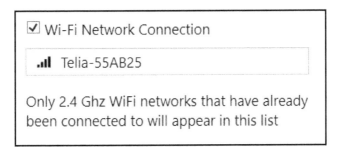

Configuring Wi-Fi connectivity

4. Finally, accept the license agreement, and press the **Download and install** button:

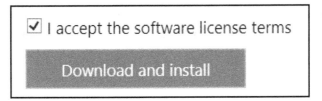

Installing Windows 10

You need to confirm you really want to format the memory card, and install Windows 10 on it. All previous data on the card will be lost. The IoT Dashboard then goes on to download the operating system and preparing the memory chip for you, including configuring the device, according to the settings you provided. This process includes performing some command-line tasks, so you will see a terminal window appear temporarily.

Starting your Raspberry Pi

When the card is ready, an Explorer window might appear, and the IoT Desktop window gives you instructions to remove the card and insert it into your device. Do so, and make sure you connect your device correctly. Then power it on. Meanwhile, go to the **My Devices** view in the IoT Dashboard. It might take a short while to boot the device up the first time. Don't worry, after first-time initialization, your Raspberry Pi, with Windows 10, should appear. This process can take from a couple of minutes to a quarter of an hour, depending on the memory card used:

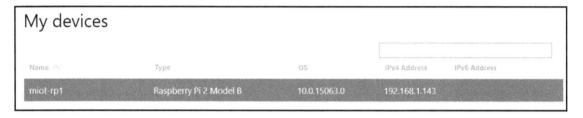

Name ⌃	Type	OS	IPv4 Address	IPv6 Address
miot-rp1	Raspberry Pi 2 Model B	10.0.15063.0	192.168.1.143	

Device ready for use

Connecting to your Raspberry Pi

When the device appears in your list of devices, right-click on it, and select **Open in Device Portal**. Your browser should open and prompt you to login. The username is **Administrator**. Enter the password you provided when you prepared your memory chip.

The Device Portal is a very handy and powerful web portal for your device. In it you can:

- Configure basic device settings (you should update your **time zone** at this point).
- Update your password.
- Remotely view what's on the screen. This will come in handy, especially for devices that are not connected to monitors. Press the **Capture Screenshot** button to try this out.
- Control installed apps.
- Access files.
- View processes and system performance.
- Access a command prompt.
- Access debugging tools.
- Control system devices.

- Manage network connectivity.
- Update Windows (make sure you have the latest version by clicking on the **Check for updates** button):

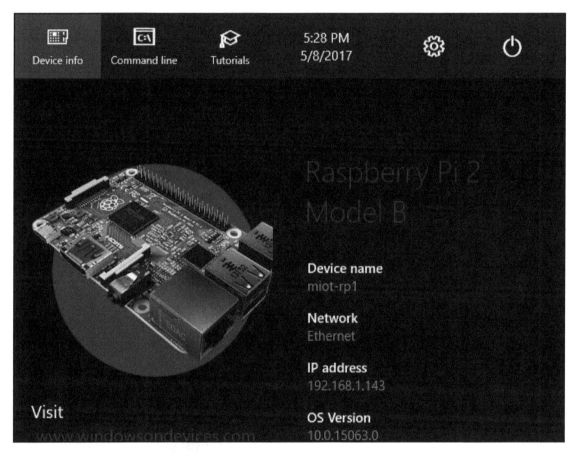

Windows 10 start screen

Since the **Device Portal** is so powerful and only protected by a simple username and password, of which the username is known beforehand, you need to take extra care by protecting it from outside access. Always keep your devices protected by firewalls. Don't allow anybody on the outside to connect to your devices, unless you have full control of what happens, and can make appropriate security decisions.

We will present methods in this book, allowing you to develop IoT applications that will allow outside access in a simple way, but not through connecting to the device directly. This is much more secure. Using these techniques avoids risking the device needlessly.

Downloading the Arduino IDE

In projects where you want to use the **Arduino** in conjunction with the Raspberry Pi, you typically use an Arduino board that is mounted on top of the Raspberry Pi. This board also needs to be prepared. You do this using the **Arduino IDE** software, which can be downloaded from this link: https://www.arduino.cc/en/Main/Software. There are setup applications for Windows, Linux, and MAC.

Installing Firmata on your Arduino board

To access analog sensors on a Raspberry Pi, you need to add circuitry supporting serial communication to your board since it's not supported by default. One way is to use I²C or SPI circuits with analog to digital converters. Another way, which we explore in this book, is to use an Arduino board. The Arduino is a programmable chip, and, as such, you can program your own firmware with your own serial protocol inside. A simpler method, is to use the well-used and battle-tested **Firmata** protocol. Software for this already exists, and is available in the Arduino IDE directly. Libraries for Firmata exist in many languages.

To install Firmata on your Arduino board, simply follow the following procedure:

1. Connect your Arduino board to your PC using a short USB cable.
2. Load the Firmata application into the IDE. This is done by selecting **File**, then **Examples**, **Firmata** and **Standard Firmata** from the menu in the Arduino IDE.
3. Specify the *serial port* you connected the Arduino board to. This is done under **Tools** and **Port** in the Arduino IDE.

4. Next you need to specify the type of Arduino you're using. If using an Arduino Starter Kit, the name should be listed in the specification. You select the board under **Tools** and **Board** in the Arduino IDE.

5. Finally, you upload the firmware to the Arduino board. You do this by clicking on the **Upload** button, formed as an arrow.

 If unsure about what type of Arduino you've connected, try the **Tools** and **Get Board Info** command.

Your Arduino board is now prepared with the Firmata firmware. You can close the Arduino IDE. You will not use it any more in this book.

Testing your Arduino board

Without disconnecting your Arduino board from your PC, you can test that it works as it should. Since the Firmata protocol is well known, there exist a lot of applications on varying operating systems, that can read sensors and control devices connected to the Arduino. Since we demonstrate Windows 10 in this book, you can use the **Windows Remote Arduino Experience App** for this purpose. It can be downloaded at
`https://www.microsoft.com/sv-se/store/p/windows-remote-arduino-experience/9nblg gh2041m`.

To test this software, we also need to connect some devices to it for testing. Let's connect our light sensor, PIR sensor, and relay module to it to see if we can access them. Make sure to connect ground, power and signal correctly. Also make sure to differentiate between digital pins and analog pins on your Arduino board. For the purposes of our example, I connected the PIR sensor to `digital pin 8,` and the relay to `digital pin 9`. The light sensor was connected to the `analog pin A0`.

In my Starter Kit, ground (GND or –) is always black, power (3.3V, 5V or +) is always red. Analog pins are colored blue, while digital are colored green.

 While digital pins 0 and 1 can be used on some Arduino boards for general purpose input and output, other boards use them for serial communication only. That's why we've selected pins 8 and 9 instead of 0 and 1.

Also, consider using an **antistatic wrist strap** to protect your hardware from electrostatic discharges.

When opening the Windows Remote Arduino Experience App, you must first choose how the app will communicate with your Arduino board. Since it's connected to a USB port, select **USB** in the **Connection** box, and select a communication speed of **57600 baud**. Next, the app makes a search, and a list of devices will be presented. The Arduino board should appear. Select it and click the **Connect** button.

You should now be able to interact with the hardware you connected. First go to the **Analog** tab. Set the **A0** pin to **Input**, and then watch how the value changes as you cover or illuminate the sensor accordingly:

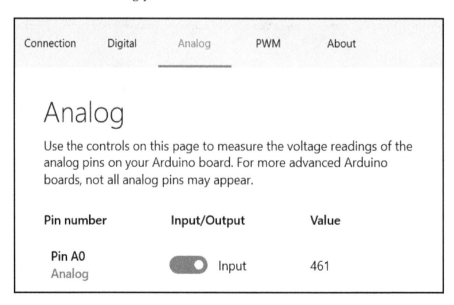

Analog peripherals

Similarly, on the **Digital** tab, set the **8** pin to **Input**. Move your hand in front of the PIR sensor to activate it, and watch how the value jumps to a high voltage level. Set the **9** pin to **Output** and control it by setting the value correspondingly. You should hear the relay clicking as it changes position:

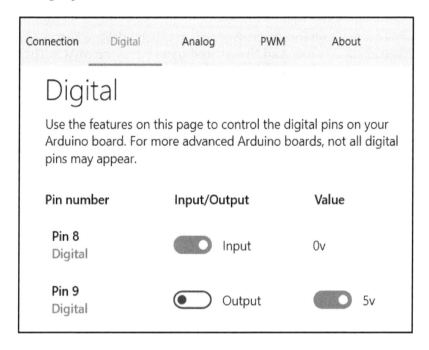

Digital peripherals

Now that you know your Arduino is programmed correctly, and that values are reported as they should be over the USB serial cable, you're ready to start programming.

Choosing a development environment

You're now ready to start actual coding. The first step is to choose a development environment. Since this book focuses on C# and .NET, including .NET Core 2, an obvious choice is to use Visual Studio. But it's not your only option.

For .NET Core development, you can also choose to use **Roslyn**, which, apart from being open source, can also be run directly on Windows 10 IoT Core, including the version we use on the Raspberry Pi. For more information about Roslyn, see
`https://msdn.microsoft.com/magazine/mt808499`.

Another option, is to use **Xamarin Studio**. It's a development tool focusing on cross platform development using C#. With Xamarin you can develop applications for IoT devices, smart phones and tablets, as well as PCs using the same code base. It runs on both Windows and MAC. The community-edition is free. For more information, see `https://www.xamarin.com/studio`.

Since Microsoft acquired Xamarin, its cross-platform capabilities are also available in Visual Studio. A free version also exists. And Visual Studio can be run on MACs. The examples published in this book have been developed using Visual Studio 2017. For more information, see `https://www.visualstudio.com/`.

Using the IoT Gateway project and libraries

The projects presented in this book are all available on GitHub at `https://github.com/PeterWaher/MIoT`. To simplify development and prototyping, these projects use several libraries. These are available as downloadable and updateable packages (**NuGets**), most of which are open source, available on GitHub in the **IoT Gateway** repository at `https://github.com/PeterWaher/IoTGateway`. The IoT Gateway repository is available free for personal or academic use, or for security analysis. Commercial use requires a commercial license. The repository includes communication libraries, an encrypted object database, event logging infrastructure, application hosting, web server, content management, scripting, runtime-tools, and so on. Things that are good to have, to prototype real-world embedded IoT applications easily and quickly.

Creating your first project

Let's begin. Since our Raspberry Pi now runs Windows 10 IoT Core, .NET Core applications will run on it, including **Universal Windows Platform** (**UWP**) applications. From a blank solution, let's create our first Raspberry Pi application. Choose **Add** and **New Project**. In the **Visual C#** category, select **Blank App (Universal Windows)**. Let's call our project `FirstApp`. Visual Studio will ask us for target and minimum platform *versions*. Check the screenshot and make sure the version you select is lower than the version installed on your Raspberry Pi.

In our case, the Raspberry Pi runs **Build 15063**. This is the March 2017 release. So, we accept **Build 14393** (July 2016) as the target version and **Build 10586** (November 2015) as the minimum version. If you want to target the Windows 10 Fall Creators Update, which supports .NET Core 2, you should select **Build 16299** for both.

In the Solution Explorer, we should now see the files of our new UWP project:

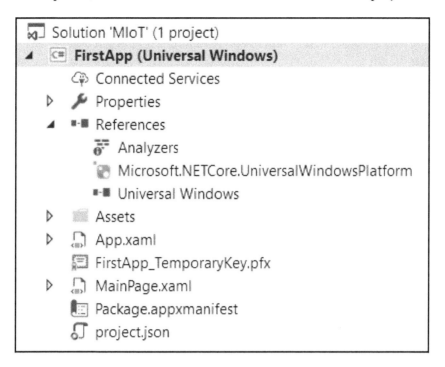

New project

Adding NuGet packages

We proceed by adding functionality to our app from downloadable packages, or **NuGets**. From the **References** node, right-click and select **Manage NuGet Packages**. First, go to the **Updates** tab and make sure the packages that you already have are updated. Next, go to the **Browse** tab, type `Firmata` in the search box, and press *Enter*. You should see the `Windows-Remote-Arduino` package. Make sure to install it in your project. In the same way, search for the `Waher.Events` package and install it.

Aggregating capabilities

Since we're going to communicate with our Arduino using a USB serial port, we must make a declaration in the `Package.appxmanifest` file stating this. If we don't do this, the runtime environment will not allow the app to do it. Since this option is not available in the GUI by default, you need to edit the file using the XML editor. Make sure the `serialCommunication` device capability is added, as follows:

```
<Capabilities>
   <Capability Name="internetClient" />
   <DeviceCapability Name="serialcommunication">
        <Device Id="any">
              <Function Type="name:serialPort" />
        </Device>
   </DeviceCapability>
</Capabilities>
```

Initializing the application

Before we do any communication with the Arduino, we need to initialize the application. We do this by finding the `OnLaunched` method in the `App.xml.cs` file. After the `Window.Current.Activate()` call, we make a call to our `Init()` method where we set up the application.

```
Window.Current.Activate();
Task.Run((Action)this.Init);
```

 We execute our initialization method from the *thread pool*, instead of the standard thread. This is done by calling `Task.Run()`, defined in the `System.Threading.Tasks` namespace. The reason for this is that we want to avoid locking the standard thread. Later, there will be a lot of asynchronous calls made during initialization. To avoid problems, we should execute all these from the thread pool, instead of from the standard thread.

We'll make the method asynchronous:

```
private async void Init()
{
   try
   {
        Log.Informational("Starting application.");
        ...
```

```
        }
    catch (Exception ex)
    {
            Log.Emergency(ex);
            MessageDialog Dialog =
new MessageDialog(ex.Message, "Error");
            await Dialog.ShowAsync();
    } IoT Desktop
    }
```

The static Log class is available in the `Waher.Events` namespace, belonging to the NuGet we included earlier. (`MessageDialog` is available in `Windows.UI.Popups`, which might be a new namespace if you're not familiar with UWP.)

Communicating with the Arduino

The Arduino is accessed using Firmata. To do that, we use the `Windows.Devices.Enumeration, Microsoft.Maker.RemoteWiring`, and `Microsoft.Maker.Serial` namespaces, available in the `Windows-Remote-Arduino` NuGet. We begin by enumerating all the devices it finds:

```
DeviceInformationCollection Devices =
    await UsbSerial.listAvailableDevicesAsync();
foreach (DeviceInformationDeviceInfo in Devices)
{
```

If our Arduino device is found, we will have to connect to it using USB:

```
if (DeviceInfo.IsEnabled&&DeviceInfo.Name.StartsWith("Arduino"))
{
    Log.Informational("Connecting to " + DeviceInfo.Name);

    this.arduinoUsb = new UsbSerial(DeviceInfo);
    this.arduinoUsb.ConnectionEstablished += () =>
        Log.Informational("USB connection established.");
```

Attach a remote device to the USB port class:

```
this.arduino = new RemoteDevice(this.arduinoUsb);
```

We need to initialize our hardware, when the remote device is ready:

```
this.arduino.DeviceReady += () =>
{
    Log.Informational("Device ready.");
```

```
this.arduino.pinMode(13, PinMode.OUTPUT);      // Onboard LED.
this.arduino.digitalWrite(13, PinState.HIGH);

this.arduino.pinMode(8, PinMode.INPUT);        // PIR sensor.
MainPage.Instance.DigitalPinUpdated(8,
        this.arduino.digitalRead(8));
this.arduino.pinMode(9, PinMode.OUTPUT);       // Relay.
this.arduino.digitalWrite(9, 0);               // Relay set to 0

this.arduino.pinMode("A0", PinMode.ANALOG);  // Light sensor.
MainPage.Instance.AnalogPinUpdated("A0",
        this.arduino.analogRead("A0"));
};
```

 Important: the analog input must be set to PinMode.ANALOG, not PinMode.INPUT. The latter is for digital pins. If used for analog pins, the Arduino board and Firmata firmware may become unpredictable.

Our inputs are then reported automatically by the Firmata firmware. All we need to do to read the corresponding values is to assign the appropriate event handlers. In our case, we forward the values to our main page, for display:

```
this.arduino.AnalogPinUpdated += (pin, value) =>
{
    MainPage.Instance.AnalogPinUpdated(pin, value);
};

this.arduino.DigitalPinUpdated += (pin, value) =>
{
    MainPage.Instance.DigitalPinUpdated(pin, value);
};
```

Communication is now set up. If you want, you can trap communication errors, by providing event handlers for the ConnectionFailed and ConnectionLost events. All we need to do now is to initiate communication. We do this with a simple call:

```
this.arduinoUsb.begin(57600, SerialConfig.SERIAL_8N1);
```

Testing the app

Make sure the Arduino is still connected to your PC via USB. If you run the application now (by pressing *F5*), it will communicate with the Arduino, and display any values read to the event log. In the GitHub project, I've added a couple of GUI components to our main window, that display the most recently read pin values on it. It also displays any event messages logged. We leave the relay for later chapters.

 For a more generic example, see the **Waher.Service.GPIO** project at `https://github.com/PeterWaher/IoTGateway/tree/master/Services/Waher.Service.GPIO`. This project allows the user to read and control all pins on the Arduino, as well as the GPIO pins available on the Raspberry Pi directly.

Deploying the app

You are now ready to test the app on the Raspberry Pi. You now need to disconnect the Arduino board from your PC, and install it on top of the Raspberry Pi. The power of the Raspberry Pi should be turned off when doing this. Also make sure the serial cable is connected to one of the USB ports of the Raspberry Pi. Begin by switching the target platform, from **Local Machine** to **Remote Machine**, and from **x86** to **ARM**:

Run on a remote machine with an ARM processor

Your Raspberry Pi should appear automatically in the following dialog. You should check the address with the IoT Dashboard used earlier, to make sure you're selecting the correct machine:

Select your Raspberry Pi

You can now run or debug your app directly on the Raspberry Pi, using your local PC. The first deployment might take a while, since the target system needs to be properly prepared. Subsequent deployments will be much faster. Open the Device Portal from the IoT Dashboard, and take a Screenshot, to see the results. You can also go to the **Apps Manager** in the **Device Portal**, and configure the app to be started automatically at startup:

D8:

LOW

A0:

969

Events:
Device ready.
USB connection established.
Connecting to Arduino Leonardo
Starting application.

App running on the Raspberry Pi

Summary

In this chapter, you've been given an introduction on how to develop apps for the Raspberry Pi using C#. You've learned how to prepare the hardware and how to use the IoT Dashboard to install and configure Windows 10 IoT on the device. You've used the Device Portal to control the applications running on it. You've learned how to extend the functionality of the Raspberry Pi by using Arduino boards. You've configured these with Firmata using the Arduino IDE. You've learned how to create a Universal Windows Platform application to run on the Raspberry Pi, and how to use NuGet packages to add existing software components to your application. You also successfully tested and deployed your application. In the next chapter, you will learn the basics of creating a working sensor.

 There are many excellent blog posts on the internet that provide tutorials concerning C# development on the Raspberry Pi. One example of such an article is https://msdn.microsoft.com/magazine/mt808503.

2
Creating a Sensor to Measure Ambient Light

In the previous chapter, you learned how to create a Universal Windows Platform application and execute it on the Raspberry Pi. You also learned how to do basic I/O with your Arduino board and connected peripherals.

In this chapter, we'll focus more on how to build a real sensor firmware, and prepare it for use in the Internet of Things. The chapter covers:

- Sampling
- Error correction
- Physical quantities
- Basic statistics
- Data persistence

Preparing our project

Following the same steps as outlined in the previous chapter, we will create a new Universal Windows Platform application project. This time, we call it `Sensor`. We can use the same hardware setup as in the previous chapter, even though we will only use the light sensor and motion detector (PIR sensor) in this project. We will also add the latest version of a new `NuGet` package, the `Waher.Persistence.FilesLW` package. This package will help us with data persistence. It takes our objects and stores them in a local object database. We can later load the objects back into the memory and search for them. This is all done by analyzing the metadata available in the class definitions, so there's no need to do any database programming. Go ahead and install the package in your new project.

The `Waher.Persistence.Files` package contains similar functionality, but it performs data encryption and dynamic code compilation of object serializes as well. These features require **.NET standard v1.5**, which is not compatible with the Universal Windows Platform in its current state. That is why we use the Light Weight version of the same library, which only requires **.NET standard 1.3**. The Universal Windows Platform supports .NET Standard up to 1.4. For more information, visit `https://docs.microsoft.com/en-us/dotnet/articles/standard/librar y#net-platforms-support`.

Initializing the inventory library

The next step is to initialize the libraries we have just included in the project. The persistence library includes an inventory library (`Waher.Runtime.Inventory`) that helps with dynamic type-related tasks, as well as keeping track of available types, interfaces and which ones have implemented which interfaces in the runtime environment. This functionality is used by the object database defined in the persistence libraries. The object database figures out how to store, load, search for, and create objects, using only their class definitions appended with a minimum of metadata in the form of *attributes*. So, one of the first things we need to do during startup is to tell the inventory environment which assemblies it and, by extension, the persistence library can use. We do this as follows:

```
Log.Informational("Starting application.");
Types.Initialize(
    typeof(FilesProvider).GetTypeInfo().Assembly,
    typeof(App).GetTypeInfo().Assembly);
```

Here, `Types` is a static class defined in the `Waher.Runtime.Inventory` namespace. We initialize it by providing an array of assemblies it can use. In our case, we include the assembly of the persistence library, as well as the assembly of our own application.

Initializing the persistence library

We then go on to initialize our persistence library. It is accessed through the static `Database` class, defined in the `Waher.Persistence` namespace. Initialization is performed by registering one **object database provider**. This database provider will then be used for all object database transactions. In our case, we register our local files object database provider, `FilesProvider`, defined in the `Waher.Persistence.Files` namespace:

```
Database.Register(new FilesProvider(
```

```
Windows.Storage.ApplicationData.Current.LocalFolder.Path +
    Path.DirectorySeparatorChar + "Data",
"Default", 8192, 1000, 8192, Encoding.UTF8, 10000));
```

The first parameter defines a folder where database files will be stored. In our case, we store database files in the `Data` subfolder of the application local data folder. Objects are divided into **collections**. Collections are stored in separate files and indexed differently, for performance reasons. Collections are defined using attributes in the class definition. Classes lacing a collection definition are assigned the **default collection**, which is specified in the second argument.

Objects are then stored in **B-tree** ordered files. Such files are divided into blocks into which objects are crammed. For performance reasons, the **block size**, defined in the third argument, should be correlated to the sector size of the underlying storage medium, which is typically a power of two. This minimizes the number of reads and writes necessary. In our example, we've chosen 8,192 bytes as a suitable block size. The fourth argument defines the number of blocks the provider can **cache** in the memory. Caching improves performance, but requires more internal memory. In our case, we're satisfied with a relatively modest cache of 1,000 blocks (about 8 MB).

Binary Large Objects (**BLOBs**), that is, objects that cannot efficiently be stored in a block, are stored separately in BLOB files. These are binary files consisting of doubly linked blocks. The fifth parameter controls the block size of BLOB files. The sixth parameter controls the *character encoding* to use when serializing strings. The seventh, and last parameter, is the maximum time the provider will wait, in milliseconds, to get access to the underlying database when an operation is to be performed.

Sampling raw sensor data

After the database provider has been successfully registered, the persistence layer is ready to be used. We now continue with the first step in acquiring the sensor data: **sampling**. Sampling is normally done using a short regular time interval. Since we use the Arduino, we get values as they change. While such values can be an excellent source for event-based algorithms, they are difficult to use in certain kinds of statistical calculations and error-correction algorithms. To set up the regular sampling of values, we begin by creating a `Timer` object from the `System.Threading` namespace, after the successful initialization of the Arduino:

```
this.sampleTimer = new Timer(this.SampleValues,
    null, 1000 - DateTime.Now.Millisecond, 1000);
```

This timer will call the `SampleValues` method every thousand milliseconds, starting the next second. The second parameter allows us to send a state object to the timer callback method. We will not use this, so we let it be `null`. We then sample the values, as follows:

```
privateasync void SampleValues(object State)
{
    try
    {
        ushort A0 = this.arduino.analogRead("A0");
        PinState D8= this.arduino.digitalRead(8);
        ...
    }
    catch (Exception ex)
    {
        Log.Critical(ex);
    }
}
```

We define the method as *asynchronous* at this point, even though we still haven't used any asynchronous calls. We will do so, later in this chapter. Since the method does not return a `Task` object, exceptions are not propagated to the caller. This means that they must be caught inside the method to avoid unhandled exceptions closing the application.

Performing basic error correction

Values we sample may include different types of errors, some of which we can eliminate in the code to various degrees. There are **systematic errors** and **random errors**. Systematic errors are most often caused by the way we've constructed our device, how we sample, how the circuit is designed, how the sensors are situated, how they interact with the physical medium and our underlying mathematical model, or how we convert the sampled value into a physical quantity. Reducing systematic errors requires a deeper analysis that goes beyond the scope of this book.

Random errors are errors that are induced stochastically and are often unbiased. They can be induced due to a lack of resolution or precision, by background noise, or through random events in the physical world. While background noise and the lack of resolution or precision in our electronics create a noise in the measured input, random events in the physical world may create spikes. If something briefly flutters past our light sensor, it might register a short downwards spike, even though the ambient light did not change. You'll learn how to correct for both types of random errors.

Canceling noise

Since the digital PIR sensor already has error correction built into it, we will only focus on how to cancel noise from our analog light sensor. Noise can be canceled electronically, using, for instance, low-pass filters. It can also be cancelled algorithmically, using a simple averaging calculation over a short window of values. The averaging calculation will increase our resolution, at the cost of a small delay in the output.

If we perform the average over 10 values, we effectively gain one power of 10, or one decimal, of resolution in our output value. The value will be delayed 10 seconds, however. This algorithm is therefore only suitable for input signals that vary slowly, or where a quick reaction to changes in the input stimuli is not required.

Statistically, the expected average value is the same as the expected value, if the input is a steady signal overlaid with random noise.

The implementation is simple. We need the following variables to set up our averaging algorithm:

```
privateconstintwindowSize = 10;
privateint?[] windowA0 = new int?[windowSize];
privateint nrA0 = 0;
privateint sumA0 = 0;
```

We use nullable integers (int?), to be able to remove bad values later. In the beginning, all values are null.

After sampling the value, we first shift the window one step, and add our newly sampled value at the end. We also update our counters and sums. This allows us to quickly calculate the average value of the entire window, without having to loop through it each time:

```
if (this.windowA0[0].HasValue)
{
    this.sumA0 -= this.windowA0[0].Value;
    this.nrA0--;
}

Array.Copy(this.windowA0, 1, this.windowA0, 0, windowSize - 1);
this.windowA0[windowSize - 1] = A0;
this.sumA0 += A0;
this.nrA0++;

double AvgA0 = ((double)this.sumA0) / this.nrA0;
```

```
int? v;
```

Removing random spikes

We now have a value that is 10 times more accurate than the original, in cases where our ambient light is not expected to vary quickly. This is typically the case, if ambient light depends on the sun and weather. Calculating the average over a short window has an added advantage: it allows us to remove bad measurements, or spikes. When a physical quantity changes, it normally changes continuously, slowly, and smoothly. This will have the effect that roughly half of the measurements, even when the input value changes, will be on one side of the average value, and the other half on the other side. A single **spike,** on the other hand, especially in the middle of the window, if sufficiently large, will stand out alone on one side, while the other values remain on the other. We can use this fact to remove bad measurements from our window. We define our middle position first:

```
private const int spikePos = windowSize / 2;
```

We proceed by calculating the number of values on each side of the average, if our window is sufficiently full:

```
if (this.nrA0 >= windowSize - 2)
{
    int NrLt = 0;
    int NrGt = 0;

    foreach (int? Value in this.windowA0)
    {
        if (Value.HasValue)
        {
            if (Value.Value < AvgA0)
                NrLt++;
            else if (Value.Value > AvgA0)
                NrGt++;
        }
    }
}
```

If we only have one value on one side, and this value happens to be in the middle of the window, we identify it as a spike and remove it from the window. We also make sure to adjust our average value accordingly:

```
if (NrLt == 1 || NrGt == 1)
{
    v = this.windowA0[spikePos];
```

```
if (v.HasValue)
{
        if ((NrLt == 1 && v.Value < AvgA0) ||
        (NrGt == 1 && v.Value > AvgA0))
        {
                this.sumA0 -= v.Value;
                this.nrA0--;
                this.windowA0[spikePos] = null;

                AvgA0 = ((double)this.sumA0) / this.nrA0;
        }
    }
}
```

Since we remove the spike when it reaches the middle of the window, it might pollute the average of the entire window up to that point. We therefore need to recalculate an average value for the half of the window, where any spikes have been removed. This part of the window is smaller, so the resolution gain is not as big. Instead, the average value will not be polluted by single spikes. But we will still have increased the resolution by a factor of five:

```
int i, n;

for (AvgA0 = i = n = 0; i < spikePos; i++)
{
    if ((v = this.windowA0[i]).HasValue)
    {
            n++;
            AvgA0 += v.Value;
    }
}

if (n > 0)
{
    AvgA0 /= n;
```

Converting to a physical quantity

It is not sufficient for a sensor to have a numerical **raw** value of the measured quantity. It only tells us something if we know something more about the raw value. We must therefore convert it to a known **physical unit**. We must also provide an estimate of the **precision** (or **error**) the value has.

 A sensor measuring a **physical quantity** should report a *numerical value,* its *physical unit,* and the corresponding *precision,* or *error* of the estimate.

To avoid creating a complex mathematical model that converts our measured light intensity into a known physical unit, which would go beyond the scope of this book, we convert it to a percentage value. Since we've gained a factor of five of precision using our averaging calculation, we can report two decimals of precision, even though the input value is only 1,024 bits, and only contains one decimal of precision:

```
double Light = (100.0 * AvgA0) / 1024;
MainPage.Instance.LightUpdated(Light, 2, "%");
}
```

Illustrating measurement results

Following image shows how our measured quantity behaves. The light sensor is placed in broad daylight on a sunny day, so it's saturated. Things move in front of the sensor, creating short dips. The thin blue line is a scaled version of our raw input A0. Since this value is event based, it is being reported more often than once a second. Our red curve is our measured, and corrected, ambient light value, in percent. The dots correspond to our second values. Notice that the first two spikes are removed and don't affect the measurement, which remains close to 100%. Only the larger dips affect the measurement. Also, notice the small delay inherent in our algorithm. It is most noticeable if there are abrupt changes:

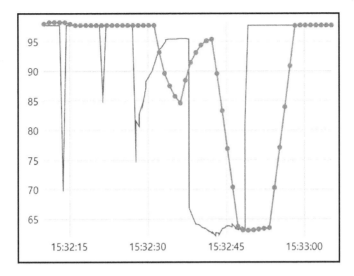

Removal of spikes

If we, on the other hand, have a very noisy input, our averaging algorithm helps our measured value to stay more stable. Perhaps the physical quantity goes below some sensor threshold, and input values become uncertain. In the following image, we see how the floating average varies less than the noisy input:

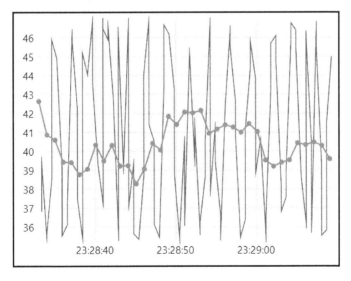

Removal of noise

Calculating basic statistics

A sensor normally reports more than the measured momentary value. It also calculates basic statistics on the measured input, such as peak values. It also makes sure to store measured values regularly, to allow its users to view historical measurements. We begin by defining variables to keep track of our peak values:

```
private int? lastMinute = null;
private double? minLight = null;
private double? maxLight = null;
private DateTime minLightAt = DateTime.MinValue;
private DateTime maxLightAt = DateTime.MinValue;
```

We then make sure to update these after having calculated a new measurement:

```
DateTime Timestamp = DateTime.Now;

if (!this.minLight.HasValue || Light < this.minLight.Value)
{
   this.minLight = Light;
   this.minLightAt = Timestamp;
}

if (!this.maxLight.HasValue || Light > this.maxLight.Value)
{
   this.maxLight = Light;
   this.maxLightAt = Timestamp;
}
```

Defining data persistence

The last step in this chapter is to store our values regularly. In later chapters, when we present different communication protocols, we will show how to make these values available to users. Since we will use an object database to store our data, we need to create a class that defines what to store. We start with the class definition:

```
[TypeName(TypeNameSerialization.None)]
[CollectionName("MinuteValues")]
[Index("Timestamp")]
public class LastMinute
{
   [ObjectId]
   public string ObjectId = null;
}
```

The class is decorated with a couple of attributes from the
`Waher.Persistence.Attributes` namespace. The `CollectionName` attribute defines the
collection in which objects of this class will be stored. The `TypeName` attribute defines if we
want the type name to be stored with the data. This is useful, if you mix different types of
classes in the same collection. We plan not to, so we choose not to store type names. This
saves some space. The `Index` attribute defines an index. This makes it possible to do quick
searches. Later, we will want to search historical records based on their timestamps, so we
add an index on the `Timestamp` field. We also define an **Object ID** field. This is a special
field that is like a **primary key** in object databases. We need it to be able to delete objects
later.

> You can add any number of indices and any number of fields in each
> index. Placing a hyphen (–) before the field name makes the engine use
> descending sort order for that field.

Next, we define some member fields. If you want, you can use properties as well, if you
provide both getters and setters for the properties you wish to persist. By providing default
values, and decorating the fields (or properties) with the corresponding default value, you
can optimize storage somewhat. Only members with values different from the declared
default values will then be persisted, to save space:

```
[DefaultValueDateTimeMinValue]
public DateTime Timestamp = DateTime.MinValue;

[DefaultValue(0)]
public double Light = 0;

[DefaultValue(PinState.LOW)]
public PinState Motion= PinState.LOW;

[DefaultValueNull]
public double? MinLight = null;

[DefaultValueDateTimeMinValue]
public DateTime MinLightAt = DateTime.MinValue;

[DefaultValueNull]
public double? MaxLight = null;

[DefaultValueDateTimeMinValue]
public DateTime MaxLightAt = DateTime.MinValue;
```

Storing measured data

We are now ready to store our measured data. We use the `lastMinute` field defined earlier to know when we pass into a new minute. We use that opportunity to store the most recent value, together with the basic statistics we've calculated:

```
if (!this.lastMinute.HasValue)
    this.lastMinute = Timestamp.Minute;
else if (this.lastMinute.Value != Timestamp.Minute)
{
    this.lastMinute = Timestamp.Minute;
```

We begin by creating an instance of the `LastMinute` class defined earlier:

```
LastMinute Rec = new LastMinute()
{
    Timestamp = Timestamp,
    Light = Light,
    Motion= D8,
    MinLight = this.minLight,
    MinLightAt = this.minLightAt,
    MaxLight = this.maxLight,
    MaxLightAt = this.maxLightAt
};
```

Storing this object is very easy. The call is asynchronous and can be executed in parallel, if desired. We choose to wait for it to complete, since we will be making database requests after the operation has completed:

```
await Database.Insert(Rec);
```

We then clear our variables used for calculating peak values, to make sure peak values are calculated within the next period:

```
    this.minLight = null;
    this.minLightAt = DateTime.MinValue;
    this.maxLight = null;
    this.maxLightAt = DateTime.MinValue;
}
```

Removing old data

We cannot continue storing new values without also having a plan for removing old ones. Doing so is easy. We choose to delete all records older than 100 minutes. This is done by first performing a search, and then deleting objects that are found in this search. The search is defined by using filters from the `Waher.Persistence.Filters` namespace:

```
foreach (LastMinute Rec2 in await Database.Find<LastMinute>(
    new FilterFieldLesserThan("Timestamp",
    Timestamp.AddMinutes(-100))))
{
    await Database.Delete(Rec2);
}
```

You can now execute the application, and monitor how the `MinuteValues` collection is being filled.

Summary

In this chapter, you've been shown how to create a simple sensor app for the Raspberry Pi using C#. You've learned how to sample data, correct for common sampling errors, work with physical quantities, and calculate basic statistics. You've also learned how to use a local object database for persisting this data, and delete it when it's considered old. In the next chapter, you will learn the basics of creating a working actuator.

3
Creating an Actuator for Controlling Illumination

In the previous chapter, you learned how to create a sensor app that runs on Raspberry Pi. You also learned some basic principles of sampling and error correction and how to persist your sensed data.

In this chapter, we'll focus more on how to build an actuator, and prepare it for use in the Internet of Things. The chapter will cover:

- The basics of control parameters
- Using relays to control equipment
- Persisting control states
- Logging important control events

Preparing our project

Let's create a new Universal Windows Platform application project. This time, we'll call it Actuator. We'll follow the same steps outlined in the previous two chapters. We can also use the same hardware, even though we will only use the relay in this project. To make persistence of application states even easier, we'll also include the latest version of the NuGet package Waher.Runtime.Settings in the project. It uses the underlying object database defined by Waher.Persistence to persist application settings. We initialize the application in a similar manner as in the previous two cases. But we don't need to handle incoming pin measurement events from the Arduino or sampling. We make sure to terminate the application in the same way as we did in previous applications.

Defining control parameters

Actuators come in all sorts, types, and sizes, from the very complex to the very simple. While it would be possible to create a proprietary format that configures the actuator in a bulk operation, such a method is doomed to fail if you aim for any type of interoperable communication. Since the internet is based on *interoperability* as a core principle, we should consider this from the start, during the design phase.

Interoperability means devices can learn to operate together, even if they are from different manufacturers. To achieve this, devices must be able to describe what they can do, in a way that each participant understands. To be able to do this, we need a way to break down (*divide and conquer*) a complex actuator into parts that are easily described and understood. One way is to see an actuator as a *collection* of **control parameters**. Each control parameter is a named parameter with a simple and recognizable **data type**. (In the same way, we can see a sensor as a *collection* of sensor data **fields**.) We will delve deeper into interoperability in later chapters:

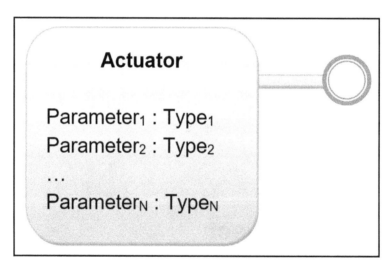

Actuator as a collection of control parameters

For our example, we will only need one control parameter: A Boolean control parameter controlling the state of our relay. We'll just call it *Output,* for simplicity.

Understanding relays

Relays, simply put, are electric switches that we can control using a small output signal. They're perfect for small controllers, like Raspberry Pi, to switch other circuits with higher voltages on and off. The simplest example is to use a relay to switch a lamp on and off. We can't light the lamp using the voltage available to us in Raspberry Pi, but we can use a relay as a switch to control the lamp.

The principal part of a normal relay is a coil. When electricity runs through it, it magnetizes an iron core, which in turn moves a lever from the **Normally Closed** (**NC**) connector to the **Normally Open** (**NO**) connector. When electricity is cut, a spring returns the lever from the NO connector to the NC connector. This movement of the lever from one connector to the other causes a characteristic clicking sound. This tells you that the relay works. The lever in turn is connected to the **Common Ground** (**COM**) connector.

The following figure illustrates how a simple relay is constructed. We control the flow of the current through the coil (**L1**) using our output **SIGNAL** (**D1** in our case). Internally, in the relay, a resistor (**R1**) is placed before the base pin of the transistor (**T1**), to adapt the signal voltage to an appropriate level. When we connect or cut the current through the coil, it will induce a reverse current. This may be harmful for the transistor when the current is being cut. For that reason, a fly-back diode (**D1**) is added, allowing excess current to be fed back, avoiding harm to the transistor:

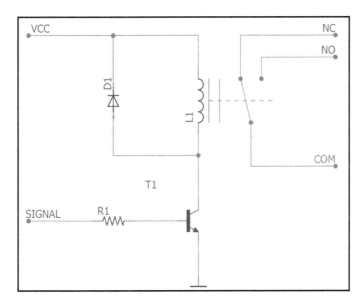

Simplified schematic of a relay

Connecting our lamp

Now that we know how a relay works, it's relatively easy to connect our lamp to it. Since we want the lamp to be illuminated when we turn the relay on (set **D1** to HIGH), we will use the NO and COM connectors, and let the NC connector be. If the lamp has a normal two-wire AC cable, we can insert the relay into the AC circuit by simply cutting one of the wires, inserting one end into the NO connector and the other into the COM connector, as is illustrated in the following figure:

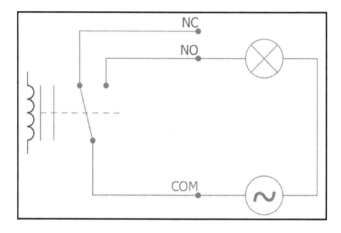

Connecting a lamp

 Be sure to follow appropriate safety regulations when working with electricity.

Connecting an LED

An alternative to working with the **alternating current** (**AC**) is to use a low-power **direct current** (**DC**) source and an LED to simulate a lamp. You can connect the **COM** connector to a resistor and an LED, and then to **ground** (**GND**) on one end, and the **NO** directly to the 5V or 3.3V source on the Raspberry Pi on the other end. The size of the resistor is determined by how much current the LED needs to light up, and the voltage source you choose. If the LED needs 20 mA, and you connect it to a 5V source, Ohms Law tells us we need an $R = U/I = 5V/0.02A = 250\ \Omega$ resistor. The following figure illustrates this:

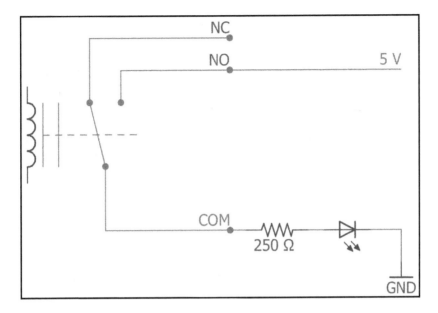

Connecting a LED

Controlling output

The relay is connected to our digital output pin 9 on the Arduino board. As such, controlling it is a simple call to the digitalWrite() method on our arduino object. Since we will need to perform this control action from various locations in code in later chapters, we'll create a method for it:

```
internal async Task SetOutput(bool On, string Actor)
{
    if (this.arduino != null)
    {
        this.arduino.digitalWrite(9,
            On ? PinState.HIGH : PinState.LOW);
```

The first parameter simply states the new value of the control parameter. We'll add a second parameter that describes who is making the requested change. This will come in handy later, when we allow online users to change control parameters.

Persisting control parameter states

If the device reboots for some reason, for instance after a power outage, it's normally desirable that it returns to the state it was in before it shut down. For this, we need to persist the output value. We can use the object database defined in `Waher.Persistence` and `Waher.Persistence.Files` for this. But for simple control states, we don't need to create our own data-bearing classes. That has already been done by `Waher.Runtime.Settings`. To use it, we first include the NuGet, as described earlier. We must also include its assembly when we initialize the runtime inventory, which is used by the object database:

```
Types.Initialize(
    typeof(FilesProvider).GetTypeInfo().Assembly,
    typeof(App).GetTypeInfo().Assembly,
    typeof(RuntimeSettings).GetTypeInfo().Assembly);
```

Depending on the build version selected when creating your UWP application, different versions of .NET Standard will be supported. Build 10586 for instance, only supports .NET Standard up to v1.4. Build 16299, however, supports .NET Standard up to v2.0.

The `Waher.Runtime.Inventory.Loader` library, available as a NuGet package, provides the capability to loop through existing assemblies in a simple manner, but it requires support for .NET Standard 1.5. You can call its `TypesLoader.Initialize()` method to initialize `Waher.Runtime.Inventory` with all assemblies available in the runtime. It also dynamically loads all permitted assemblies available in the application folder that have not been loaded.

Saving the current control state is then simply a matter of calling the `Set()` or `SetAsync()` methods on the static `RuntimeSettings` class, defined in the `Waher.Runtime.Settings` namespace:

```
await RuntimeSettings.SetAsync("Actuator.Output", On);
```

During the initialization of the device, we then call the `Get()` or `GetAsync()` methods to get the last value, if it exists. If it does not exist, a default value we define is returned:

```
bool LastOn = await RuntimeSettings.GetAsync("Actuator.Output",
    false);
this.arduino.digitalWrite(1, LastOn ? PinState.HIGH :
    PinState.LOW);
```

Logging important control events

In distributed IoT control applications, it's vitally important to make sure unauthorized access to the system is avoided. While we will dive deeper into this subject in later chapters, one important tool we can start using is to log everything of security interest in the event log. We can decide what to do with the event log later, whether we want to analyze or store it locally, or distribute it in the network for analysis somewhere else. But unless we start logging events of security interest directly when we develop, we risk forgetting logging certain events later. So, let's log an event every time the output is set:

```
Log.Informational("Setting Control Parameter.",
    string.Empty, Actor ?? "Windows user",
    new KeyValuePair<string, object>("Output", On));
```

If the `Actor` parameter is `null`, we assume the `control` parameter has been set from the Windows GUI. We use this fact, to update the window, if the change has been requested from somewhere else:

```
if (Actor != null)
    await MainPage.Instance.OutputSet(On);
```

Using Raspberry Pi GPIO pins directly

The Raspberry Pi can also perform input and output without an Arduino board. But the **General-Purpose Input/Output** (**GPIO**) pins available only supports digital input and output. Since the relay module is controlled through a digital output, we can connect it directly to the Raspberry Pi, if we want. That way, we don't need the Arduino board. (We wouldn't be able to test-run the application on the local machine either, though.)

Checking whether GPIO is available

GPIO pins are accessed through the `GpioController` class defined in the `Windows.Devices.Gpio` namespace. First, we must check that GPIO is available on the machine. We do this by getting the default controller, and checking whether it's available:

```
gpio = GpioController.GetDefault();
if (gpio != null)
{
    ...
}
else
```

```
Log.Error("Unable to get access to GPIO pin " +
    gpioOutputPin.ToString());
```

Initializing the GPIO output pin

Once we have access to the controller, we can try to open exclusive access to the GPIO pin we've connected the relay to:

```
if (gpio.TryOpenPin(gpioOutputPin, GpioSharingMode.Exclusive,
out this.gpioPin, out GpioOpenStatus Status) &&
Status == GpioOpenStatus.PinOpened)
{
    ...
}
else
    Log.Error("Unable to get access to GPIO pin " +
        gpioOutputPin.ToString());
```

Through the `GpioPin` object `gpioPin`, we can now control the pin. The first step is to set the operating mode for the pin. This is done by calling the `SetDriveMode()` method. There are many different modes a pin can be set to, not all necessarily supported by the underlying firmware and hardware. To check that a mode is supported, call the `IsDriveModeSupported()` method first:

```
if (this.gpioPin.IsDriveModeSupported(GpioPinDriveMode.Output))
{
    This.gpioPin.SetDriveMode(GpioPinDriveMode.Output);
    ...
}
else
    Log.Error("Output mode not supported for GPIO pin " +
        gpioOutputPin.ToString());
```

There are various output modes available: `Output`, `OutputOpenDrain`, `OutputOpenDrainPullUp`, `OutputOpenSource`, and `OutputOpenSourcePullDown`. The code documentation for each flag describes the particulars of each option.

Setting the GPIO pin output

To set the actual output value, we call the `Write()` method on the `pin` object:

```
bool LastOn = await RuntimeSettings.GetAsync("Actuator.Output",
    false);
this.gpioPin.Write(LastOn ? GpioPinValue.High : GpioPinValue.Low);
```

We need to make a similar change in the `SetOutput()` method.

The Actuator project in the MIOT repository uses the Arduino use case by default. The GPIO code is also available through conditional compiling. It is activated by uncommenting the GPIO switch definition on the first row of the `App.xaml.cs` file.

You can also perform Digital Input using principles similar to the preceding ones, with some differences. First, you select an input drive mode: `Input`, `InputPullUp` or `InputPullDown`. You then use the `Read()` method to read the current state of the pin. You can also use the `ValueChanged` event to get a notification whenever the input pin changes value.

Summary

In this chapter, you've looked at how to create a simple actuator app for the Raspberry Pi using C#. You've learned how to divide an actuator into a set of control parameters. You've also learned the basics of how relays work and how you can control them using the Arduino board. You've persisted control states and logged important security-related control events. As an alternative to using Arduino, you've also learned how to work directly with General Purpose input/output on the Raspberry Pi. In the next chapter, you'll learn how to use the MQTT protocol to publish sensor data and control the actuator over the internet.

4
Publishing Information Using MQTT

In the previous chapter, you learned how to create an actuator app that runs on the Raspberry Pi. You also learned how to do basic I/O directly using your Raspberry Pi.

In this chapter, we'll start publishing data we collect on the internet. The first protocol we'll study is the MQTT protocol. This chapter covers:

- An introduction to the MQTT protocol
- The Publish/Subscribe communication pattern
- Connecting to a broker
- Publishing information
- Subscribing to information
- Testing and troubleshooting communication
- Basic security considerations

Introducing the MQTT protocol

One of the most popular protocols to use for **Machine-to-Machine** (**M2M**) communication, and the **Internet of Things** (**IoT**), is the **MQ Telemetry Transport** (**MQTT**) protocol. The MQ refers to IBM's MQ series product line, even though MQTT was not part of that series in the beginning. Since its inception in 1999, the MQTT protocol is implemented in a large array of tools, servers, and libraries in many different languages.

MQTT has drawn interest for various reasons. It is very simple and easy to use, and it is TCP/IP-based. It also includes a new communication pattern that has become popular for efficient distribution of data to multiple consumers: the **Publish/Subscribe pattern**. That pattern allowed for efficient syndication of news and has become a great tool for efficiently distributing other kinds of information as well, such as sensor data.

Most IP communication patterns before this were focused on either direct *asynchronous messaging* or the *request/response* pattern. While it is possible to mass-distribute data using the **Internet Group Messaging Protocol** (**IGMP**), on which *UDP multicast* is based, that method is often very crude, and hence not always suitable for M2M and IoT, which require more detail. IGMP requires a unique IP address for each type of conversation.

Understanding the Publish/Subscribe pattern

The Publish/Subscribe pattern solves the problem of detail, by introducing a new concept: a **topic**, or a **node**. A **broker** is used to distribute messages from **publishers** to **subscribers**. Each message that is being published, is published on a given topic (or node). In turn, subscribers let the broker know which topics (or nodes) they are interested in. The broker matches incoming publications with the requests of the subscribers, and forwards messages accordingly. Using such message filtering makes sure participants avoid receiving unnecessary messages. In MQTT, publishers can also be subscribers.

Topics (or nodes) can also be formed into trees, with topics, sub-topics, and so on. This allows for a great amount of detail. In MQTT, topics are simple string names, where nodes are separated by the forward slash character (/). MQTT also allows subscribers to subscribe to any node in the tree. Using **wildcards**, subscribers can even subscribe to entire branches of the tree, or even the entire tree itself. MQTT defines two types of wildcards: a node wildcard (+), and a branch wildcard (#). The node wildcard matches any node on a given level. The branch wildcard matches any number of nodes.

Using a broker also allows machines to overcome the problem of network topology, where the publishers and subscribers normally reside behind **firewalls**. Since both publishers and subscribers *connect* to the broker, only the broker needs to be accessible. The others can reside behind firewalls. The following figure illustrates the basic Publish/Subscribe communication pattern, where solid lines represent connections, dashed lines represent the flow of information, and the grey boxes represent possible local networks protected by firewalls:

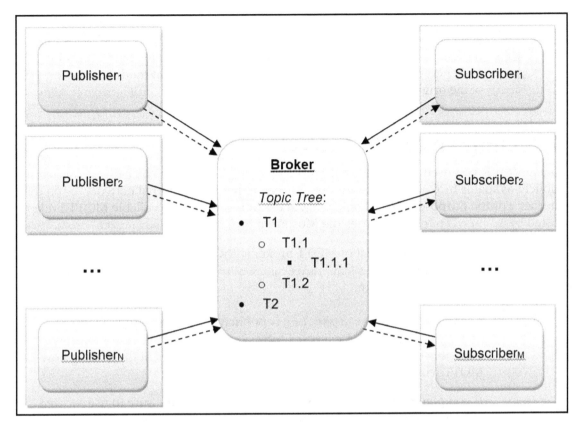

Publish/Subscribe pattern

Preparing our project

We create a new Universal Windows Platform application project, based on the `Sensor` project described in chapter 2. This time, we call it `SensorMqtt`. We use the same hardware setup and sensor code developed earlier. In this chapter, we will focus on how to publish the information we've sampled on the internet, and how to receive it. We begin by adding a new **NuGet** package, the `Waher.Networking.MQTT.UWP` package. This package contains a simple MQTT client we can use to communicate using the MQTT protocol. We also add the `Waher.Runtime.Settings` package introduced in the previous chapter.

For.NET standard, .NET Core, or traditional .NET Framework projects, you can use the `Waher.Networking.MQTT`NuGet instead. UWP apps use different libraries and runtime binaries when it comes to communication and encryption. For this reason, it requires a somewhat modified version of the original library.

Selecting an MQTT broker

To use MQTT, you need to decide what MQTT broker you will use. You can either select a publicly-available broker, or host your own broker, either in an internal network, or on the Internet. For the purposes of this book, we will use a free, publicly-available MQTT broker, hosted by `iot.eclipse.org`. It uses the Mosquitto broker(`http://mosquitto.org/`).

A non-exhaustive list of MQTT broker software is available at `https://github.com/mqtt/mqtt.github.io/wiki/servers`. There are many to choose from.

The broker at `iot.eclipse.org` is publicly accessible, and it allows anonymous access and wildcard subscriptions. Any data you publish will be visible to anybody on the internet. For the purposes of illustrating how MQTT works, it serves its purpose.

If you plan to publish sensitive or personal data, make sure to use secured brokers. To secure a broker, make sure it only accepts encrypted connections, only authenticates clients using certificates (not passwords), and authorizes access using **access-control lists** (**ACL**). It must also be updated regularly, to make sure security patches are installed in a timely fashion.

Creating a Device ID

The Internet contains a huge number of devices. To be able to distinguish our device from the rest, we must make sure to create a persistent **Device ID** for it, and make sure it's unique:

```
private string deviceId;
```

After having started the Arduino initiation, we need to check whether we have a `deviceId` created. We use our runtime settings library for this:

```
this.deviceId = await RuntimeSettings.GetAsync(
    "DeviceId", string.Empty);
```

If you haven't created one yet, let's do so. A simple way to generate a globally unique `deviceId` is to create a `Guid`. We also remove any hyphens:

```
if (string.IsNullOrEmpty(this.deviceId))
{
    this.deviceId = Guid.NewGuid().ToString().
            Replace("-", string.Empty);
    await RuntimeSettings.SetAsync("DeviceId", this.deviceId);
}
```

Log the `deviceId` to the log. This will allow us to see it in the user interface:

```
Log.Informational("Device ID: " + this.deviceId);
```

Connecting to the broker

Once we have our Device ID and know which broker we want to use, it's easy to connect to it. We begin by defining an MQTT client variable for our application:

```
private MqttClient mqttClient = null;
```

We then create the corresponding `MqttClient` object (defined in the `Waher.Networking.MQTT` namespace). Creating the object will automatically connect to the broker:

```
this.mqttClient = new MqttClient("iot.eclipse.org", 8883, true,
    this.deviceId, string.Empty);
```

The first parameter defines the host name or IP address of the broker. The second defines the port to connect to. The `iot.eclipse.org` broker supports unencrypted MQTT communication on port `1883` and encrypted communication on `8883`. We choose the encrypted version (third parameter) for some minimal form of security, due to MQTT's inherent vulnerabilities. The last two parameters are the username and password to use. Since the broker accepts anonymous connections, we use our Device ID as the username, and an empty string as the password.

An overload to the constructor accepts a certificate parameter instead of the username and password. It is only used with encryption. If such a client certificate is used, it can also be used to authenticate the client, by the server.

We must also make sure to close the connection when we're done. This is done by disposing the connection object:

```
if (this.mqttClient != null)
{
    this.mqttClient.Dispose();
    this.mqttClient = null;
}
```

Monitoring connection events

Connecting to a broker is an asynchronous process that is error-prone and can take time. Applications should always strive to provide relevant feedback to their users as quickly as possible. For asynchronous communication processes, such relevant feedback can be showing the state of the process. The MqttClient object allows us to monitor this state, through the OnStateChanged event. For our example, we log each state change as an event:

```
this.mqttClient.OnStateChanged += (sender, state) =>
    Log.Informational("MQTT client state changed: " +
        state.ToString());
```

Recovering from lost connections

Since MQTT uses TCP, it requires a live socket connection to work. Since a socket connection may fail for different reasons over time, we need to build a recovery mechanism into our device. The simplest such mechanism is to check the state of the connection at regular intervals, and reconnect if we detect that the connection has been lost. We can use our sampling timer for this. Once a minute, we check the connection state, and initiate a reconnection if it is offline or in an error state. The reconnection itself fails, if the network is not available at the time. In that case, new reconnection attempts will be performed every minute:

```
if (Timestamp.Second == 0 && this.mqttClient != null &&
    (this.mqttClient.State == MqttState.Error ||
    this.mqttClient.State == MqttState.Offline))
{
```

```
        this.mqttClient.Reconnect();
}
```

The `MqttClient` class has a basic mechanism for keeping the connection alive. `PING` messages are regularly sent every 15 seconds, which is half of the *keep-alive time* configured by default. If a message is not received within the keep-alive time interval, the broker will assume the connection to be lost.

The client can choose to register a last **will** and testament to the broker when it connects. The will and testament will be published by the broker itself on the topic specified by the will, if the connection is lost. You can set the will in the constructor of the `MqttClient` class. Gracefully terminating the connection by disposing the `MqttClient` class, will not trigger the will to be published.

Publishing sensor data

Now that we have a live connection, we're ready to publish sampled sensor data. We will first need some member variables. These will store last values, last-published values, and the timestamps of last-published values:

```
private double? lastLight = null;
private bool? lastMotion = null;
private double? lastPublishedLight = null;
private bool? lastPublishedMotion = null;
private DateTimelastLightPublishTime = DateTime.MinValue;
private DateTimelastMotionPublishTime = DateTime.MinValue;
```

From our sampling and event methods where we receive and calculate our most recent sensor data, we call two new methods: `PublishLight()` and `PublishMotion()`. To illustrate different ways of publishing data, these two methods will publish the corresponding sensor data fields on individual topics, as strings. They will then individually call `PublishLastJson()`, which will publish both fields on one topic, as a JSON object string.

Choosing relevant values

Before we publish the data, we need to consider what data is *relevant* to publish. We want to avoid spamming the broker, or any subscribers. We define relevant to mean values that show a significant change (more than one percentage point), or values after significant silence (at least 15 seconds):

```
private void PublishLight(double Light)
{
    DateTime Now = DateTime.Now;

    this.lastLight = Light;

    if ((!this.lastPublishedLight.HasValue ||
        Math.Abs(this.lastPublishedLight.Value-Light) >= 1.0 ||
        (Now-this.lastLightPublishTime).TotalSeconds >= 15.0) &&
        this.mqttClient != null &&
        this.mqttClient.State == MqttState.Connected)
    {
        this.lastPublishedLight = Light;
        this.lastLightPublishTime = Now;
```

What *relevant* means should be configurable. In following chapters, when discussing the *event subscription pattern*, a method will be demonstrated where the subscriber defines what *relevant* means.

We then proceed by creating the string we want to publish. Our goal is to publish this string on the `Waher/MIOT/[DEVICE_ID]/Light` topic, where `[DEVICE_ID]` is replaced by the real device ID:

```
string ValueStr = ToString(Light, 2) + " %";
```

Choosing a quality of service

We then need to choose a **Quality of Service**. There are three to choose from: *At most once*, *At least once*, and *Exactly once*. **At most once** is the simplest, and requires only one MQTT packet to be sent for each publication. But the publication is not guaranteed to be received; it can be lost in transit. Since we regularly update our sensor data, we choose this service. It doesn't negatively affect system performance a great deal if packets are lost, and we avoid unnecessary control packets.

If you want to safeguard against accidental losses, you can use the **At least once** service instead. When such a packet is received, an **Acknowledgement** is returned as a receipt. The original packet is resent until an acknowledgement is received, or the process is aborted. Since the acknowledgement message can also be lost, this method makes sure the original packet is delivered, but not that it is delivered only once to each destination. This quality of service is perfect for important, nonrepetitive messages, especially **idempotent** commands. Idempotent commands are commands that can be applied any number of times, giving the same result. Examples include setting control parameters to absolute values. *Turn the light on* is an idempotent command. It only causes a change if the light is off. If you issue the command a hundred times, the light will still only be turned on once.

If you need to avoid repetitive reception of a packet, you can use the **Exactly Once** quality of service. The MQTT layer divides such a packet into two acknowledged packet transmissions, one that transports the content, and one that delivers it-both *idempotent* operations. The transport packet can be sent multiple times without affecting the state of the receiver. The content is never delivered to the overlying application; it is only stored in a cache. The delivery takes the packet from the cache, and removes it, before delivering it to the overlying application. If the delivery packet is received again, the original packet is not found in the cache, and hence, not delivered again to the application. The *Exactly Once* service model is perfect for any non-idempotent commands, such as relative control commands (for example *Increase light 10%*), or messages that need to be counted.

 Sending a packet using the *At most once* service requires one MQTT packet to be transmitted. Sending a packet using the *At least once* service requires at least two MQTT packets to be transmitted. Sending a packet using the *Exactly once* service requires at least four MQTT packets to be transmitted. Only the original packet contains the content payload however.

Publishing the light field

When we have chosen the quality of service, we need to decide whether the content should be retained by the broker on the given topic. In our example, we choose not to. A new subscriber will be updated anyway if the sensor is connected. If the sensor is not connected, we don't want to give new subscribers obsolete sensor data.

The last parameter of the PUBLISH() method contains the actual payload of the packet we want to publish. Payloads in MQTT are always binary! There are no rules for how the content is encoded. We choose to encode our string using UTF-8:

```
this.mqttClient.PUBLISH(
    "Waher/MIOT/" + this.deviceId + "/Light",
    MqttQualityOfService.AtMostOnce, false,
    Encoding.UTF8.GetBytes(ValueStr));

this.PublishLastJson();
}

MainPage.Instance.LightUpdated(Light, 2, "%");
}
```

 Care must be taken when decoding data received on MQTT, to avoid unexpected decoding errors. You should always assume data received can be erroneously encoded.

Publishing data on the Motion and JSON topics is done in a similar way. Refer to the code in the GitHub project for details.

Checking encrypted communication

If you're interested in what is being communicated, you normally use a network **sniffer**, or **network protocol analyzer**. One of the better ones is called Wireshark (https://www.wireshark.org/). But external sniffers, or network protocol analyzers, have, for obvious reasons, difficulty monitoring encrypted communication. You are left with two options: either you turn off encryption while you use the external tool to examine your communication, or you monitor the communication internally before it is encrypted or after it has been decrypted.

Which method to use depends on the use case. It might be necessary to retain encryption, or something in the communication chain will not work, or work differently. In this case, you are left with only one option: you need to monitor the communication internally.

To facilitate this, the `MqttClient` class accepts a set of **sniffer objects**. These are objects implementing the `ISniffer` interface, defined in the `Waher.Networking.Sniffers` namespace. Anything received or sent over the connection will be reported to these sniffer objects. Any relevant communication events will also be reported to these objects. The `SensorMqtt` app in the GitHub project defines a very simple sniffer, that redirects anything reported to it, to the event log. Since we already have a simple display of logged events, we can easily see what is being communicated, in realtime, even when the connection is being encrypted. To enable such internal sniffing, we simply modify the constructor of the MQTT client, as follows:

```
this.mqttClient = new MqttClient("iot.eclipse.org", 8883, true,
    this.deviceId, string.Empty, new LogSniffer());
```

The following figure shows an example of how such MQTT communication can look in our log:

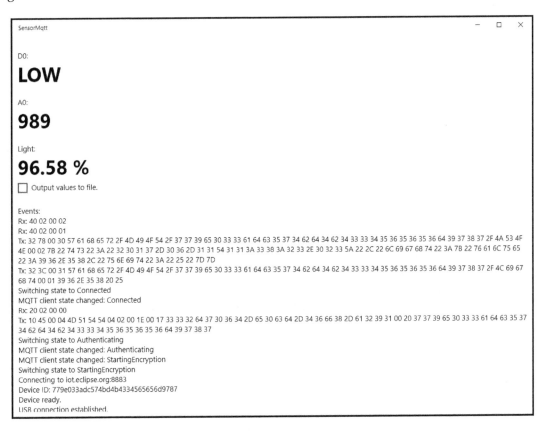

Using the log to display contents of encrypted communication.

Adding MQTT support to the actuator

To add MQTT support to our actuator, we create a new UWP app project and name it `ActuatorMqtt`. We copy the actuator logic from our `Actuator` project, and the preceding procedures to create and maintain an MQTT connection to the broker. Even though it's an actuator, we want to publish sensor data for it, representing the current state of the actuator. If it changes state, we want the new state to be published. But since the value will not be updated using a regular interval, as in the sensor case, we will ask the broker to **retain** our latest value. We will also use a different *Quality of Service* level: *At Least Once*. This is to make sure that the most recent value is propagated correctly. We don't need to use the *Exactly Once* level, since the operation is *idempotent*:

```
this.mqttClient.PUBLISH(
    "Waher/MIOT/" + this.deviceId + "/On",
    MqttQualityOfService.AtLeastOnce, true,
    Encoding.UTF8.GetBytes(On.ToString()));

StringBuilder Json = new StringBuilder();

Json.Append("{\"ts\":\"");
Json.Append(DateTime.Now.ToUniversalTime().ToString(
    "yyyy-MM-ddTHH:mm:ss.fffZ"));
Json.Append("\",\"on\":");
Json.Append(On ? "true" : "false");
Json.Append('}');

this.mqttClient.PUBLISH(
    "Waher/MIOT/" + this.deviceId + "/JSON",
    MqttQualityOfService.AtLeastOnce, true,
    Encoding.UTF8.GetBytes(Json.ToString()));
```

When publishing data using JSON, you should include a timestamp. This is especially important if the data is being retained by the broker. This allows subscribers to determine when the data was published and how valid it is. The Date and Time format to use should conform to **ISO-8601** and be in **Coordinated Universal Time**, as in the preceding above. This is especially important if you publish the data on the Internet for global consumption. This ensures it is portable and easy to decode.

Subscribing to topics

Subscribing to topics is easy. You call the SUBSCRIBE method with one or more topics you're interested in. For each topic, you can also provide the maximum *Quality of Service* level you want to support on your end. Anything published with a higher *Quality of Service* will be downgraded on your connection. You can also use the wildcard characters, + (node) and # (branch), in your subscription request. In our example, we choose to subscribe to the Waher/MIOT/[DEVICE_ID]/Set/+ topic. Through it, publishers can execute generic set commands on actuator properties. The name of the actual property is defined by the sender, in the last subtopic node. We update the OnStateChanged event handler as follows:

```
this.mqttClient.OnStateChanged += (sender, state) =>
{
    Log.Informational("MQTT client state changed: " +
        state.ToString());

    if (state == MqttState.Connected)
        this.mqttClient.SUBSCRIBE(
            "Waher/MIOT/" + this.deviceId + "/Set/+",
            MqttQualityOfService.AtLeastOnce);
};
```

 You can use different wildcards on different levels of the topic tree to achieve interesting effects. To subscribe to a specific parameter named On, you subscribe to Waher/MIOT/[DEVICE_ID]/Set/On. To subscribe to any of the parameters on a given device you subscribe to Waher/MIOT/[DEVICE_ID]/Set/+. To subscribe to the On parameter on any device, subscribe to Waher/MIOT/+/Set/On. To subscribe to anything that is sent to a device, subscribe to Waher/MIOT/[DEVICE_ID]/#, and so on.

Handling incoming commands

As soon as the MQTT client receives data on any of the topics it has subscribed to, it raises the OnContentReceived event. We provide an event handler to parse incoming data.

Extra care must be taken, considering we don't know who sent the data, how the data has been encoded, or even if it is correctly encoded.

 Also remember that the maximum size of an MQTT packet is 256 MB, which may create temporary memory problems for small devices.

In the new MQTT v5 specification published by Oasis on December 25 2017, a client can specify a maximum packet size. This would mitigate this problem if supported. There is also a possibility to control the flow of packets, by stating the amount of concurrent packages requiring acknowledgements that the client can process.

Since we used a node-level wild-card in the subscription, we first check the last part of the topic, to figure out what parameter has been requested to change. If it is the On parameter, we proceed by parsing it. Note that the `bool` type uses **Pascal casing** in its string representation of Boolean values. Before we parse it, we must make sure to convert it to Pascal casing first. We also make sure to catch any unforeseen errors in a try-catch statement:

```
this.mqttClient.OnContentReceived += async (sender, e) =>
{
    try
    {
        if (e.Topic.EndsWith("/On"))
        {
            string s = Encoding.UTF8.GetString(e.Data);
            s = s.Substring(0, 1).ToUpper() +
                s.Substring(1).ToLower();

            if (bool.TryParse(s, out bool On))
                await this.SetOutput(On, "MQTT");
        }
    }
    catch (Exception ex)
    {
        Log.Critical(ex);
    }
};
```

Testing MQTT

You now have both a sensor and an actuator that speaks MQTT! Great. But they still don't communicate with anyone. To test your communication interfaces, there are many client tools available for download on the Internet. Some will allow you to publish and subscribe to data through interactive GUIs. The following screenshot shows how **mqtt-spy** (`https://github.com/eclipse/paho.mqtt-spy/wiki/Downloads`) can be used to interact with our actuator and monitor general MQTT activity:

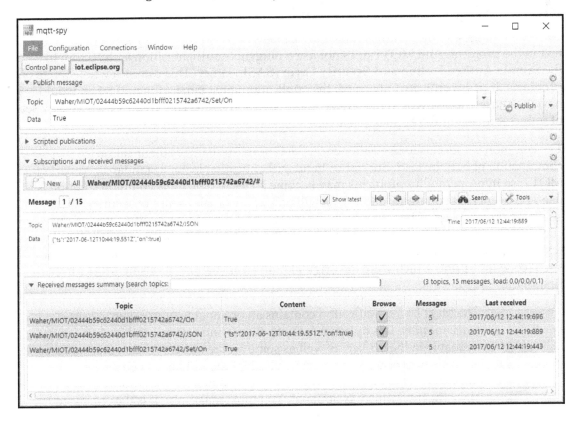

Using mqtt-spy to interact with our Actuator.

Security considerations

Since MQTT is very simple to get started with, both from an application user perspective and a protocol developer perspective, it has become very popular for use in IoT. But the simplicity has its drawbacks. MQTT has some serious vulnerabilities that any developer using it must be made aware of.

Managing authentication

One of the biggest vulnerabilities is its management of passwords. They are sent in clear text in the protocol. And MQTT does not use a pluggable authentication architecture like the **Simple Authentication and Security Layer** (**SASL**) either. This causes a whole range of problems. If passwords are to be used, the application must persist them. If SASL would have been used, a *hash* would most likely have been sufficient. This creates a whole new set of vulnerabilities for the application layer.

The common solution is to use either encryption or out-of-band authentication, or a combination of both instead. But out-of-band authentication is not a standardized part of MQTT, so interoperability problems may become an issue. The most common solution is to use TLS to encrypt communication. This will only create a false sense of security, since you still have the problem of how to persist the password. To avoid passwords, you can use client certificates, and use them to authenticate the user out of band. This avoids the clear text password. But you are left with a solution that is no longer small and simple with a small code foot-print, which were the original motivators behind choosing MQTT in the first place.

The MQTT v5 specification contains an optional feature called *enhanced authentication*. It is optional for both clients and servers. If this option is available in the broker, as well as some secure authentication mechanisms, and this option is enforced, this vulnerability will have been partly mitigated. The solution is still susceptible to man-in-the-middle attacks, since the mechanism is optional. You must make sure it is the enhanced authentication mechanism that is used during authentication and not its vulnerable predecessor.

Managing privacy

Lack of privacy in MQTT is another big vulnerability. Due to the ability to subscribe using wildcards, you can also subscribe to data you're not supposed to have access to. There is no management of access control built into MQTT. Publishers cannot negotiate with subscribers who should have access to what. There are no identities at all available to clients, regarding other actors in the network.

Privacy is difficult to manage in MQTT. The most common solution to this problem is to use **Access Control Lists** (**ACL**) to control who can subscribe to what topics. But these are completely out-of-band, and hence not interoperable between brokers. Solutions depending on ACLs may have serious problems migrating to other types of brokers.

Another way to solve privacy is by using **End-to-end encryption(E2E)**. E2E encryption not only makes sure the broker is incapable of decoding the content payload, it also makes sure eavesdroppers in MQTT cannot either. But E2E encryption is not trivial in a Publish/Subscribe environment, where you have the one-to-many transmission of data.

In single-casting point-to-point communication, E2E encryption can be relatively easily implemented using encryption based on a **Public Key Infrastructure** (**PKI**), such as **RSA**. Everybody can distribute their own public key. But since the private key is required to decrypt data, you need to encrypt it specifically for each recipient. Therefore, Publish/Subscribe complicates matters. To solve this, you would have to divide the problem in two. First, you could use point-to-point PKI-encrypted communication to exchange keys for a symmetric cipher, like the **Advanced Encryption Standard** (**AES**). When everybody knows the shared symmetric key, Publish/Subscribe with one-to-many communication can be encrypted, using the symmetric cipher, instead of the PKI cipher.

Managing interoperability

The lack of *content metadata* in MQTT is problematic for **interoperability**. If all participants in the network are developed and controlled by the same entity, this might not be a problem. But if actors from different companies are to cooperate on the same network, interoperability becomes a big problem.

Since payloads are binary, there is no standardized way of knowing what type of content it contains, or how it is encoded. Each recipient must try as best it can. This may open a wide array of vulnerabilities, related to quality assurance, possibility of injection, resilience, localization, and so on. Traditionally, this problem has been solved on the Internet by providing some form of **Content Type**. This is missing in MQTT. And there is no good way to solve the problem, except by making backwards incompatible changes to the protocol.

 In the MQTT v5 specification, you can provide a content type string and application-specific user properties with the published payload. This provides some form of way to describe the data that is being transmitted.

Managing authorization

Authorization is the ability to determine who has access to what or who can do what. Authorization requires authenticated identities. MQTT does not forward the identities of publishers. This makes authorization a big problem. How do you know if a packet is valid, or if the sender is authorized to send it? Since anybody can publish packets on any topic, by default, **injection** a great problem.

As with the problem of privacy, this vulnerability can be solved using ACL. It can also be solved by cryptographic means, for instance by signing packets using a PKI encryption method, such as RSA. Signatures using PKI work well in a Publish/Subscribe setting. It is only the sender that needs the private key. Recipients only require the public key of the sender to validate the signature.

The same PKI method can be used to achieve privacy in point-to-point communication or used to distribute shared symmetric keys. But implementation is far from simple, and the chances of achieving interoperability is slim.

The authorization problem, perhaps the most important problem to solve, is not solved in the MQTT v5 specification. Due to the serious vulnerabilities inherent in the MQTT protocol, it is better used in controlled environments, and then only with equipment that is programmed using the same proprietary data protection measures. Achieving secure, open, and interoperable internet-based solutions using MQTT is far from simple, if at all practically possible. For this reason, it might be better to view MQTT as a good M2M protocol, and not a suitable IoT protocol.

If interoperability is important to your solution, there are other protocols that you can use to solve these issues. More on these protocols in later chapters.

Summary

In this chapter, you've been shown how you can use MQTT to publish sensor data and interact with actuators on the internet. You've learned the basic principles behind the MQTT protocol, how to connect and maintain a connection with an MQTT broker, how to publish data on topics as well as how to subscribe to topics to receive published data. You've also learned how to test and troubleshot your interfaces. In the end, you were introduced to the basic vulnerabilities inherent in the protocol, and what you must do to protect your solutions. In the next chapter, you'll learn how you can use the HTTP protocol to include your things into the *Web of Things*.

5
Publishing Data Using HTTP

In the previous chapter, you learned how to use the MQTT protocol to communicate with your devices. You also learn the pros and the cons of the protocol and how to use it in a secure manner.

In this chapter, we'll introduce the HTTP protocol, and how it can be used to communicate with your connected things. The chapter covers:

- An introduction to the HTTP protocol
- The Request/Response communication pattern
- How to locate resources on the web
- Basic principles of the HTTP protocol semantics
- Publishing machine-readable web service interfaces
- Encryption fundamentals

Introducing the HTTP protocol

The **Hypertext Transfer Protocol**, or **HTTP**, is one of the best known and most used internet protocols today. It was originally designed in 1989 by Tim Berners-Leeas a means to publish *hypertext* documents on a distributed set of servers, today called **web servers**. Clients, for example **web browsers**, would be able to fetch these documents using the HTTP protocol. Hyper, meaning beyond in the word *hypertext*, literally means beyond the text, signifying the possibility to link to other hypertext documents from within the text itself. These referenced documents may in turn reside on other servers. To achieve this, each document, or **resource**, is assigned a **Uniform Resource Locator** or **URL**. This URL is treated as a simple string but contains all the information the client needs to find and download the contents of the resource.

Resources on the web are not necessarily hypertext documents. They can be images, audio, video, binary applications, or more generally, any type of data that can be encoded. Originally, hypertext documents were written in **HTML**, and could include basic formatting and simple media content, such as images. Later developments allowed for the separation of the overall design of the hypertext document into **Cascading Style Sheet**, or **CSS**, documents. Hypertext documents, or **web pages** as they are now called, would soon be made dynamic with the inclusion of **JavaScript** documents and the standardization of a **Document Object Model**, or **DOM**. Data can be represented in **eXtensible Markup Language** or **XML** documents, as **JavaScript Object Notation** or **JSON** documents, or any number of different formats.

All technologies related to HTTP in some way are often referred to as **web technologies**. All resources accessible using HTTP are likewise called the web, the **World Wide Web**, or **WWW**. When we talk of **web services**, we talk of services made available using the HTTP protocol somehow. Popular methods include **Simple Object Access Protocol** (**SOAP**) and **Representational State Transfer**, or **REST**, sometimes called **RESTful** web services.

 Don't confuse the internet with the web. The internet is standardized by the **Internet Engineering Task Force**, or **IETF**, and concerns itself with all IP-related protocols and technologies; HTTP is just one of many. The IETF publishes standards in documents called **Request For Comments** or **RFCs**. The web is standardized by the **World Wide Web Consortium** or **W3C**. They produce standards that are called **Recommendations**.

Locating a resource

All these resources, whether they are static files or dynamically generated in real-time, must be identified using URLs, one for each resource, if they are to be accessible on the web. A URL is a string with the following basic format:

```
scheme ":" authority[ path ] [ "?" query ] [ "#" fragment ]
```

The `scheme` part describes how to interpret the rest of the URL. For communication purposes, you can see this as the means to access and retrieve the resource, or simply put, what *communication protocol* is being used. For HTTP, this part would be `http`. For encrypted HTTP, or **HTTPS**, it would be `https`.

The `authority` describes the entity hosting the resource. For HTTP, this would typically be the **domain name** or **IP address** of the web server, prefixed by `//`. The authority also determines the **port number** to use when connecting to the web server. As the HTTP protocol is based on the TCP protocol, a TCP connection to a given port on the server needs to be performed. This port number is by default `80` for traditional HTTP, and `443` for HTTPS. If any other port number is used, it must be specified in the authority. This is done by appending a colon, `:`,after the domain name or IP address, followed by the port number to use.

> Historically, you could also provide user credentials directly in the URL for authentication purposes. This is not a recommended way to do authentication on the web.

The optional `path` portion can be empty or contain a semicolon,`/`, followed by an optional series of sub-paths (delimited by semicolons: `/`), and finally a resource name. It is like a path in a filesystem. Originally, the resources were actual static files in an actual filesystem. Today, resources can be dynamically generated or fetched from a database by the underlying services.

The optional `query` portion contains a set of parameters that can be used to customize the resource. Normally, queries consist of a set of `name"="value` pairs, separated by `&` characters. The optional `fragment` part is typically used for secondary client-side referencing and is normally not part of the server-side processing of a resource. It can be used to identify a section in an article, for instance.

Following are some URL examples:

- `http://example.com`
- `http://example.com:8080/Folder1/Folder2/Resource.ht`
- `https://example.com/Page?Article=12345&Cat=678#Section2`

> URLs, or the more general URIs, are defined in RFC 3986:
>
> `https://tools.ietf.org/html/rfc3986`

Understanding the Request/Response pattern

The HTTP protocol is based on a client/server architecture, where clients know what they want to do and request documents (or data or services) from a server. The client is active, the server is reactive. For this purpose, HTTP is built around a simple **Request/Response** mechanism. Clients connect to servers, pose their requests, and servers respond with one response per request. The connection can be dropped by any of the clients or servers:

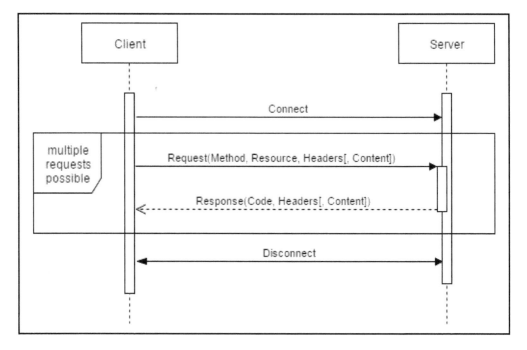

Request/Response pattern in HTTP

 Most HTTP servers today allow for multiple requests over the same connection to improve performance. This feature, called persistent connections, was not specified in HTTP 1.0. Support for it is required in HTTP 1.1, unless explicitly disabled, but only one request can be served at a time. In HTTP 2.0 multiple requests can be processed simultaneously over the same connection.

Handling sessions

The underlying connection is **stateless**. This means the HTTP layer does not remember anything about the client between requests. All information relevant to the request must be transmitted in the actual request. The purpose of this is to allow for **scalability**. The client should not rely on a particular server being able to handle the request. In reality, the server might actually be a set of servers in a cluster, taking turns to respond to incoming requests.

To add states to the communication, such as providing a **session**, the concept of a **cookie** was introduced. Cookies are named strings corresponding to the domain, stored on the client. Cookies can be embedded in requests, as HTTP headers, and allow the server application to process requests according to states read from the cookies. Creating sessions is one example of how cookies can be used. A session can be seen as a short-lived bag of states maintained by the server, referred to by a session identifier, or a session cookie.

 How session cookies are handled is important from a security perspective. Access to the cookie gives you access to the session, the corresponding login, and potentially the data it contains and refers to.

Limiting connectivity

One of the limitations of the HTTP protocol is that only the client can initiate communication over a connection. If both actors are reachable from each other, both can connect to each other and perform requests on each other over two different connections. But typically, web clients reside behind **firewalls**. These protect private **Local Area Networks**, or **LANs**, from incoming connections. While this is a good solution to protect private computers in cases where people navigate the web using web clients, it poses a problem for the Internet of Things.

In the traditional sense, the web server contains the interesting information (the pages), and clients consume them from their private network. The server resides publicly on the internet, and clients connect to it to retrieve the information they want to consume. For the Internet of Things, the roles are reversed: the entity that contains the interesting information is typically a device residing in the local private network. The information has to be transported somehow to an entity on the internet or beyond, be it a server, another thing, or perhaps an application running on a phone or other device in some other private network. But these cannot typically connect to your device in your private network.

Choosing a connection direction

There are two basic solutions to this problem if HTTP is to be used:

- Make the device public or reachable by interested parties. This means making the device into a web server. A sensor can return momentary values immediately as responses to GET method calls, and actuators can react directly on control state POST requests. Latency is minimized.
- Emulate a Publish or Subscribe pattern, constantly pushing new sensor information to the server using POST requests, and at the same time polling the server, perhaps using the same POST request, for any new control actions to execute. In this case, the device is a web client, and the server is responsible for pushing the information to interested parties.

In this book, we've chosen the first approach, for the following reasons:

- Real-time communication with devices, especially in control applications, is of paramount importance. The first method avoids unnecessary latency.
- The Publish/Subscribe pattern (the second approach) is better solved using other protocols rather than HTTP.
- We want to avoid building our own back-end server software or use proprietary platforms on the web. The more we can use standard software components, the less time we need to spend on proprietary non-reusable code that does not deliver added value. Instead, we can focus on developing the functionality we wish to achieve.
- The second pattern is too limited in its communication patterns. It is best suited for sensor data collection on centralized servers. This use case is too narrow. We aim for distributed real-time applications. It's easier to do centralized data collection in distributed real-time environments than it is to do distributed real-time operations in an architecture based on centralized data collection.
- We want to publish local pages on the device anyway, making it possible to configure it locally using a browser. This requires us to make the device into a web server anyway, albeit available perhaps only in the local network.
- Privacy should be paramount to any IoT solution. Decentralized architecture can protect privacy better than centralized ones operated by third parties.

HTTP 2.0 and **Web Sockets** are technologies that attempt to solve the above problem, but only do so halfway. Still, only the client can connect to the server, but once a HTTP/2 or Web Socket connection is established, the server can use that connection to push information to the client. But the problem of network topology and firewalls remain. It is not possible for a server to connect to a device residing behind a firewall.

Understanding methods

Each request specifies one HTTP method to call. The HTTP method is a simple string provided in the request. Even though web servers are technically free to invent their own methods, the HTTP 1.1 specification only defines nine methods, of which you typically only use five: GET, HEAD, POST, PUT and DELETE. A sixth method OPTIONS can be used to request information from a resource what communication options it supports. Use OPTIONS to learn what methods are supported by a resource.

 The HTTP method should be seen as a method on the web server. It should not be confused with a method on an underlying service hosted by the web server, which is more related to the resource path than the HTTP method.

The GET method retrieves the contents of a resource. The HEAD method performs the same operation as a GET method call, but only returns the headers, not the corresponding content. The HEAD method can be used to quickly assess the existence of resources, how they are encoded, and their sizes, or checks cache status without the risk of starting content downloads. This can be useful in multimedia scenarios, for example when the application needs to evaluate what a resource represents to be able to choose the type of application or receptor needed to handle the content, before starting the download. Both the GET and HEAD methods are considered **safe** methods, meaning they don't affect the resources themselves or perform an action other than retrieval.

 When publishing resources accessible using the GET method, you must always assume responses are being *cached*. If you publish information that changes in real-time, you must always consider how long information can be stored in caches, if allowed at all.

Updating resources

Updating the contents of a resource is done using the PUT method. The content provided in the request is supposed to be stored under the supplied resource. To delete a resource, the DELETE method is used.

The PUT and DELETE methods, together with the GET and HEAD methods, are considered **idempotent**. This means that any number of identical requests made to the server, in sequence, results in the same server or resource state. This property is used by caches in clients, web proxies, and the server itself, to optimize performance. For idempotent method calls, cached responses can be returned.

 An *idempotent operation I(x)* is such that $I^n(x)=I(x)$ for all $n \in \mathbb{Z}^+$.

Interacting with resources

Any other type of interaction with resources that are not safe nor idempotent, such as submitting data to a resource, or performing resource-specific actions, should be done using the POST method. We will use the POST method extensively for control actions or for web form submissions, to name a couple of examples. The POST method is not safe nor idempotent. This means proxies and web servers relay the request all the way to the underlying service for processing every time a POST request is received and accepted.

 Technically, you could implement idempotent control actions using the PUT method. But that would require knowledge of impotence from the client on a control-parameter basis. It's simpler to just assume no control operations are idempotent at the HTTP level and use the POST method for all.

 An example of an idempotent control action is the setting of absolute parameter values. Changing a control parameter using relative values, such as a change in percent, or toggling a digital output, is not idempotent. Counting operations are not idempotent either.

The following table summarizes the most common methods in HTTP:

Method	Safe	Idempotent
HEAD	✓	✓
GET	✓	✓
PUT		✓
DELETE		✓
POST		

Encoding content

To distinguish between the different types of content possible to transport using HTTP, an interoperability layer has been built into the protocol. The encoding of any payload is identified using an **Internet Content Type** or **Media Type**. By always including this type of information with the payload, the receiver can always determine if it can decode the payload, and how. Today, Media Types are managed by the **Internet Assigned Numbers Authority** or **IANA**.

 These Media Types were originally designed for use with email, and are therefore also called **Multipurpose Internet Mail Extensions**, or **MIME** types. The format of Media Types is defined by the IETF in RFC 2046: `https://tools.ietf.org/html/rfc2046`

The basic structure of a Media Type is as follows:

```
top_level_type "/" subtype [ ";" parameters ]
```

The `top_level_type` defines the general category of the content. This may include `application`, `audio`, `image`, `text`, `video`, and so on. To further classify the encoding, a `subtype` is needed. For files, this often corresponds to the file format used. When the `top_level_type` and `subtype` are not sufficient to determine how the content is encoded, as is typically the case for text-based content, additional parameters can be added. Following are some examples of some common Internet Content Types:

```
text/html; charset=utf-8
image/png
application/xml
```

For a list of registered Media Types, with links to reference documentation, see: `https://www.iana.org/assignments/media-types/media-types.xhtml`.

Applying headers

Both requests and responses contain HTTP headers. These consist of sets of key-value pairs. Normally, clients do not need to set these headers explicitly. It is typically done by the HTTP clients being used. But sometimes, you need to set some of these headers manually, to customize a request according to your needs. Following is a shot list of useful headers:

Header	Description
Accept	If the resource supports multiple content type encodings, you can specify your preference using the `Accept` header.
Cache-Control	Controls how the response may be cached.
Content-Type	The media type of the content payload.
ETag	An `entity` tag is a string identifying the content. It can be a hash value of the content, or an ordinal number, as long as it changes when the content changes. Entity tags can be used for caching purposes.
Expires	Describes when the content expires. Is used by caches to remove old entries.
Last-Modified	A timestamp for the content. It can be used for caching purposes.
User-Agent	A string describing the software of the client making the request.

For a complete list of headers, their syntax, and what they mean, see section 14 of RFC 2616, defining the HTTP 1.1 protocol: `https://tools.ietf.org/html/rfc2616#page-100`

Optimizing requests

Other headers can be used to optimize HTTP performance. HTTP supports **conditional requests**. Conditional requests are typically used together with some form of cache or previous knowledge of a resource. You can use the `If-` headers to perform actions, such as getting a resource if it is newer (`Last-Modified`) or different (`ETag`) from the resource you already have. You can upload new content only if you have a newer (`Last-Modified`) or different (`ETag`) version:

Header	Description
Expect	Can be used to break a Request/Response into two requests/responses. First, only the header of the request is sent, and secondly, only the content, and only if the server is ready to accept it. While this might be counter-intuitive as a means to optimize communication, it might increase performance if uploading content using conditional requests. It avoids the transfer of the content in cases where it is not necessary.
If-Match	Only executes the method if the current entity tag of a resource matches any of the entity tags provided in this header. Typically used with `PUT` and `DELETE`.
If-Modified-Since	Checks the current timestamp of the content of the resource, and only executes the method if the resource has a later timestamp compared to the value provided in the header. Typically used with `GET`.
If-None-Match	The opposite of `If-Match`. Only executes the method if the current entity tag of a resource does not match any of the entity tags provided in this header. Typically used with `GET`.
If-Unmodified-Since	Executes the method only if the content timestamp is older than the timestamp provided. Typically used with `PUT` and `DELETE`.

Sending content

After sending the header, the content portion is sent, if expected. Content can be sent both in requests and responses. Both static content, where the size is known, and dynamic content, whose size is not known at the beginning of transmission, can be sent. This is controlled by the Content-Length and Transfer-Encoding header fields. These fields are typically managed by the HTTP client used.

The actual content is then sent in binary form. The actual encoding and decoding should be properly defined using the Content-Type header field and might have to be performed by the application itself. If using the Waher.Content NuGet library,with additions, encoding and decoding can be done for you.

Understanding status codes

All requests in HTTP return a response. The response begins with a status code, followed by a set of HTTP headers, followed by optional content. First, the status code needs to be understood. The code is first divided into sections:

Range	Meaning
1xx	*Informational response.* The request is acknowledged, and processing continues. This is used when dividing a Request/Response into more than one.
2xx	*Success response.* The request has been received, understood, and accepted.
3xx	*Redirection response.* The client is requested to redirect the original request to a new source.
4xx	*Client error.* The client has done something wrong.
5xx	*Server error.* The server has done something wrong.

Some of the more common status codes include:

Range	Meaning
200	*OK*. Request executed successfully.
301	*Moved Permanently*. The resource has moved permanently to another location. The new URL should be used in future requests.
303	*See Other*. The server requests the client to continue to a new location. This code is normally used in the **Post-Redirect-Get**, or **PRG-pattern**, a pattern that should be implemented by all resources accepting POST requests from browsers. The PRG-pattern avoids accidentally resending POST requests when going backwards in browser histories. When sending a POST request containing a form to a server, it processes the form, but should respond with a 303 See Other response instead of a 200 OK response, alerting the browser to perform a GET on the new location. When backtracking locations using the Back button, it is this GET that is remembered, not the previous POST, thus avoiding the accidental reposting of obsolete information to the server.
304	*Not Modified*. Used together with conditional requests to signify that the operation was not performed since the condition failed.
307	*Temporary Redirect*. The resource has moved temporarily to another location. Retry using the new URL. Future requests can be made to the original URL.
400	*Bad Request*. The request was badly formed and should be corrected before attempting again.
401	*Unauthorized*. The request has not been authorized. Authentication should ensue before attempting the request again.
403	*Forbidden*. Authentication failed, or user account lacks sufficient privileges to access resource.
404	*Not Found*. Resource was not found on the server.
406	*Not Acceptable*. Resource does not support the representations requested by the client.
500	*Internal Server Error*. Something went wrong inside the server, and the request could not be p roperly served.

For a more complete list of status codes, see RFC 2616, Section 6.1.1: `https://tools.ietf.org/html/rfc2616#page-39`

Using encryption

Encryption is the means to hide your content from access by unauthorized individuals. Only individuals with the correct set of keys or secrets should in theory be able to view the unencrypted content. Encryption is extremely important on the internet, which abounds with malicious users, teenage hackers, criminals, curious neighbors or co-workers, journalists, and state-sponsored surveillance apparatuses (not all mutually exclusive). Encryption is not only important to use, but it is important to do right.

Encryption in HTTP is called **HTTPS**, or HTTP Secure. It does not change the semantics of HTTP, it just requires the TCP connection to be encrypted before HTTP communication can take place. After the TCP connection has been established from the client to the server, an encryption handshake phase begins. During this phase, an encryption protocol is chosen, either **Secure Socket Layer** (**SSL**) or **Transport Layer Security** (**TLS**). Then the client and server agree on ciphers to use, and exchange keys, such as a server certificate, and optionally a client certificate. When the handshake is complete, normal HTTP semantics is possible, over the encrypted line. The following figure shows a simplified diagram of the communication taking place:

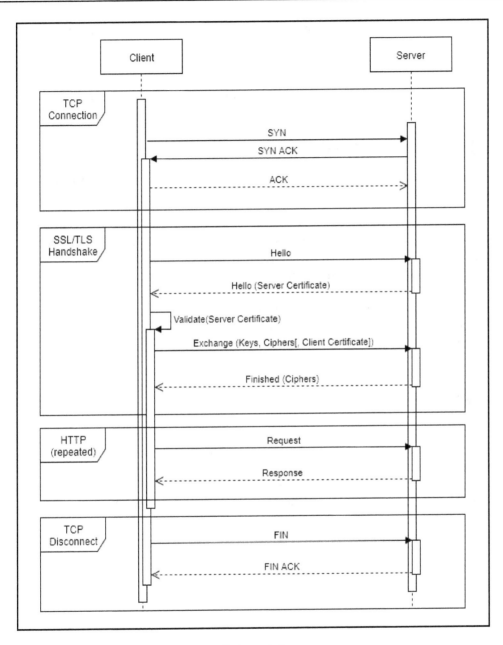

HTTPS communication

Secure Socket Layer, or SSL, is obsolete and deemed insecure. SSL should be disabled on all clients and servers in operating systems, as well as explicitly in code, to avoid **downgrade attacks**, where a malicious entity pretends it only knows SSL, and thus becomes able to utilize known vulnerabilities to decipher communication.

Validating certificates

An encryption scheme contains a chain of events and is no more secure than its weakest link. For HTTPS, the weakest links are certificate validation and the choice of ciphers.

Many developers deceive themselves by using self-signed certificates. These are easy to produce and do not cost anything, but they don't validate either. To avoid problems, certificate validation is disabled in software. Perhaps these developers think that it's enough not to be able to directly view what is being communicated by a sniffer. This is not correct. When you disable certificate validation, you also lose the ability to verify whether a malicious user is pretending to be the expected remote party, using a **man-in-the-middle** or **MITM** attack. Using an MITM attack, the attacker can freely access your communication as if it was unencrypted.

Don't disable proper certificate validation features.

Proper certificate validation includes two checks. One is to check that the certificate has not been **revoked**. If a certificate is compromised, it can be revoked by the **Certificate Authority**, or **CA**, that issued the certificate. Self-signed certificates do not have a CA, so they cannot be revoked. Revoked certificates fail validation. The other check is to make sure the **subject name** in the certificate corresponds to the domain name you used to form the connection, or that the domain name is listed in the *subject name* of the certificate. Any valid certificate will not do. The certificate must also have been created to protect the resource you want to connect to.

The full security features of HTTPS can only be used with domain names. If using the IP address to address a resource, you are not able to verify that the remote party is who it claims to be.

 Always make sure the subject name of the certificate corresponds to the corresponding domain name of the remote entity you connect to.

There are several cost-effective, and even free, alternatives providing valid certificates for your domains.

Redefining the web

The web, which is all based on the HTTP protocol, consists of an enormous set of technologies. To give you an overview of these goes beyond the scope of this book. But it might be good for the reader to know that many of the original ideas, definitions, and abstractions have been loosened and remade.

Originally, resources on the web were considered to be **web pages**, that is, pages for human consumption. Resources were identified using **Uniform Resource Locators**, or **URLs**. It was quickly realized that this was not a good abstraction. The URL construct was redefined into a **Uniform Resource Identifier**, or **URI**. Not all identifiers point to actual resources that can be found on the web. An example could be namespaces in XML, for instance. Furthermore, resources do not need to be pages. They can be data items, as is the case within the realms of the **Semantic Web** and **Linked Data**, where each data subject can be identified using an URI.

We can also access dynamic content and **Application Programming Interfaces** (or **APIs**) using URLs. The first popular web service architecture, **Simple Object Access Protocol**, or **SOAP**, focused on semantics rather than content. It was one of the cornerstones of the emerging new paradigm that came to be known as **Service-Oriented Architecture**, or **SOA**.

Today, a new service-oriented architecture, based on **Representational State Transfer**, or **REST**, has become very popular. One of the reasons is that RESTful interfaces are more loosely coupled than SOAP interfaces. This means they are easier to extend and adapt to. Another reason is that representation is separated from resource. This basically means you can extend the service to support multiple content types or representations of data, without modifying the interface itself. This permits the use of JSON, which simplifies their use from JavaScript clients. RESTful APIs focus more on content and resources than semantics, and URLs play an important part in this. RESTful interfaces also enforce server statelessness and require the client request to contain all required information to process the request. The reason this is done, is to be able to scale by allowing multiple servers to process incoming requests. To facilitate interacting with resources, each response is assumed to be self-describing and contain a set of links specifying operations that can the client can perform on the corresponding resource.

 Earlier models focusing on relational, or linked content models, were RSS and ATOM. Based on syndication principles, and closely related to semantic web technologies, they use URLs to link to related data content, a mix between machine-readable and human-readable content.

Authentication is another field where the web is seeing rapid restructuring. *Authentication is the means to make sure a claim is true, particularly claims of identity.* Originally, servers were considered to be aware of which users had the right to access which content, and so client authentication could be done locally on each server. This model worked when content providers published their own content and wanted to control who had access to it in their local environment. But the model failed in modern architecture that required interoperability between different online entities. This is especially the case for the Internet of Things, where servers are small and typically unaware of external entities, and transactions span a multitude of servers. Clients need to be able to identify themselves in the same manner regardless of server. New, distributed authentication methods such as **JSON Web Tokens**, or **JWT**, and **OAuth2** are being defined for this purpose. A distributed authorization framework is also being worked on, under the name **User-Managed Access** or **UMA**.

Optimization and security are other fields where great change is occurring. The traditional Request/Response mechanism is limiting in many regards. This has been addressed in efforts such as **Web Sockets** or **HTTP/2**. Web Sockets involve a HTTP connection being negotiated to become more like a normal full-duplex socket. *HTTP/2*, which is a standard from IETF, removes the limitation of being able to only pose one question at a time, greatly enhancing HTTP performance.

The topology problem of HTTP is still a major obstacle. Clients can connect to servers, but servers can normally not connect back to clients, since most of these reside behind firewalls. It is even more difficult for actors behind separate firewalls to interconnect. **Web RTC** aims to provide interconnectivity between actors behind separate firewalls using web technologies. Other alternatives, such as using **HTTP over XMPP**, instead of TCP, also solves this problem.

Preparing our project

As in the previous chapter, we will create a new project based on our Sensor project. Let's call it SensorHttp. We use the same hardware and software setup as in previous chapters. But this time, we add the Waher.Networking.HTTP.UWP NuGet package instead. It will allow us to host a web server on Raspberry Pi and publish web resources, both static and dynamic ones.

 For .NET standard, .NET Core, or traditional .NET Framework projects, you can use the Waher.Networking.HTTP NuGet instead. Universal Windows Platform apps use different libraries and runtime binaries when it comes to communication and encryption. For this reason, it requires a somewhat modified version of the original library.

Since we will accept incoming connections to our app, we also need to provide sufficient capabilities to do so. If we don't, the framework will throw an exception if we try. We add the internetClientServer capability to our set of capabilities in the Package.appxmanifest file:

```
<Capability Name="internetClientServer" />
```

Creating an HTTP server

The HTTP library defines a HttpServer class that we will use to set up our server. Creating an HTTP server is easy:

```
privateHttpServerhttpServer = null;
...
this.httpServer = new HttpServer();
```

Add a reference to a sniffer in the constructor, such as the `LogSniffer` available in the GitHub project, to view communication passing through the server.

You can also specify port numbers you want to use when hosting the web server. If you don't specify port numbers, the default HTTP port will be used.

The UWP version of the `HTTP` library does not support server-side encryption at the current time. The reason is that the underlying UWP framework does not support it. When .NET Standard 2.0 is released and available for Raspberry, this will be solved automatically, since the `Waher.Networking.HTTP` library can be used instead of the UWP version. In that version of the library, you just specify a server-side certificate to the `HttpServer` class, to enable server-side encryption (HTTPS):

```
X509Certificate2 Certificate =
Waher.Content.Resources.LoadCertificate(
"SensorHttp.certificate.pfx", "password");
This.httpServer = new HttpServer(Certificate);
```

Likewise, we must make sure to close the server properly when the application ends. This is simply done by disposing of the object:

```
if (this.httpServer != null)
{
    this.httpServer.Dispose();
    this.httpServer = null;
}
```

Adding dynamic synchronous resources

To publish resources through our web server, we just call the `Register` method on the `HttpServer` object. We can choose between two methods: either we provide resource objects, inherited from the `HttpResource` class, such as the `HttpSynchronousResource` or `HttpAsychronousResource` classes, or we use lambda expressions or delegates for simple `GET` and `POST` resources.

We first demonstrate the latter to publish a resource for reading momentary sensor data. We provide a lambda expression, taking a request and response parameter. This expression will be executed when a GET method is received on the /Momentary resource:

```
this.httpServer.Register("/Momentary", (req, resp) =>
{
    ...
});
```

The resource will be added as a **synchronous resource**. This means that the response must be generated completely before returning from the expression. We don't have to worry about exceptions or explicitly sending the response. The web server will do that for us if we forget.

To access query variables in the request, you can call the req.Header.TryGetQueryParameter() method.

Choosing representation

Instead of only providing a fixed format of the content we return from our resource, HTTP allows us to use the Accept header in the request to figure out what format the client desires. This makes it possible to use the resource seamlessly in different types of applications and for different use cases. Returning XML, JSON, or an image, based on client preference, allows us to use the resource in automation and mobile phone apps, or embed it in image tags. If the client wants something we cannot provide, we return a 406 Not Acceptable error back to the client. We do this by throwing an HTTP exception object. If no Accept header is available, we chose to return XML. Note that we also must specify an HTTP header in the response, to make sure any proxies and clients understand that the response should not be cached:

```
if (req.Header.Accept != null)
{ resp.SetHeader("Cache-Control",
"max-age=0, no-cache, no-store");
 switch (req.Header.Accept.GetBestContentType("text/xml",
        "application/xml", "application/json", "image/png",
        "image/jpeg", "image/webp"))
  {
        case "text/xml":
        case "application/xml":
            this.ReturnMomentaryAsXml(req, resp);
            break;
```

```
        case "application/json":
            this.ReturnMomentaryAsJson(req, resp);
            break;

        case "image/png":
            this.ReturnMomentaryAsPng(req, resp);
            break;

        case "image/jpg":
            this.ReturnMomentaryAsJpg(req, resp);
            break;

        case "image/webp":
            this.ReturnMomentaryAsWebp(req, resp);
            break;

        default:
            throw new NotAcceptableException();
    }
}
else
    this.ReturnMomentaryAsXml(req, resp);
```

 The ability to differentiate between the contents of a resource and its representation, and therefore have a natural way of allowing the client to choose representation without changing the resource name, is one of the properties of RESTful interfaces.

Returning an XMLresponse

Returning text-based responses is easy. The `HttpResponse` class derives from `TextWriter`. There are some things you need to keep in mind, however:

- Specify the Content Type properly.
- Don't confuse text encodings. If the text format contains references to the encoding to use, make sure the text encoding matches the Content Type encoding, which will be used for the binary transfer.
- XML and HTML are examples of text formats normally containing encoding specification as part of the text body.

We begin our response as follows:

```
private void ReturnMomentaryAsXml(HttpRequest Request,
    HttpResponse Response)
{
    Response.ContentType = "application/xml";

    Response.Write("<?xml version='1.0' encoding='");
    Response.Write(Response.Encoding.WebName);
    Response.Write("'?>");
```

Adding a schema reference

If you work with XML, you should also work with **XML Schema**. The XML Schema specifies the layout of the XML document. It can also be used to specify data types for content embedded in the document. XML Schemas make working with XML more predictable, since it is possible to validate XML against it and perform certain processes automatically. XML Schemas separate elements and their attributes using **namespaces**. These are typically URLs. In XML, the namespace of an element and its children are defined by using the `xmlns` attribute. Typically, for short XML responses, we only need to set it on the root element. In our case, we will use a local schema and define the namespace to be the URL of the sensor itself, with `/schema.xsd` appended to it:

```
string SchemaUrl = Request.Header.GetURL();
int i = SchemaUrl.IndexOf("/Momentary");
SchemaUrl = SchemaUrl.Substring(0, i) + "/schema.xsd";

Response.Write("<Momentary timestamp='");
Response.Write(DateTime.Now.ToUniversalTime().
    ToString("yyyy-MM-ddTHH:mm:ss.fffZ"));
Response.Write("' xmlns='");
Response.Write(SchemaUrl);
Response.Write("'>");
```

Adding momentary values

Adding content to the XML response is not straightforward. We add each value, if available, as a child element. At the end, we close the root element:

```
if (this.lastLight.HasValue)
{
    Response.Write("<Light value='");
    Response.Write(ToString(this.lastLight.Value, 2));
```

```
            Response.Write("' unit='%'/>");
    }

    if (this.lastMotion.HasValue)
    {
            Response.Write("<Motionvalue='");
            Response.Write(this.lastMotion.Value ?
                    "true" : "false");
            Response.Write("'/>");
    }

    Response.Write("</Momentary>");
}
```

Since the method is called from a synchronous resource, the response will be sent automatically. The GitHub project also contains the JSON method, which is implemented in the same manner and which returns the same type of JSON as in the MQTT project.

Returning an image response

To return a dynamic image we need to be able to draw it. **SkiaSharp** is a powerful cross-platform two-dimensional drawing engine. It will allow us to draw graphs and create images. Add the SkiaSharp NuGet package to the project. The `SensorHttp` project, in the GitHub repository for this book, contains a `GenerateGauge()` method that draws a gauge using SkiaSharp, based on the current momentary values. The method returns an object of type `SKImage`. Returning the image to the requester can be done very simply, as follows:

```
private void ReturnMomentaryAsPng(HttpRequest Request,
    HttpResponse Response)
{
    Response.Return(this.GenerateGauge(Request.Header));
}
```

What happens when you return an object is that the web server checks if there are any registered encoders for the type of object you're returning. A content encoder is a class implementing the `IContentEncoder` interface from the `Waher.Content` library. To encode the image, we simply add the `Waher.Content.Images` NuGet package. Since the `Waher.Runtime.Inventory` package introduced earlier is used to find encoders, we must also make sure to include the two assemblies during the initialization of the application. This is done by referencing the assemblies of the `IContentEncoder` interface and the `ImageCodec` class:

```
    Types.Initialize(
```

```
typeof(FilesProvider).GetTypeInfo().Assembly,
typeof(RuntimeSettings).GetTypeInfo().Assembly,
typeof(IContentEncoder).GetTypeInfo().Assembly,
typeof(ImageCodec).GetTypeInfo().Assembly,
typeof(App).GetTypeInfo().Assembly);
```

By implementing your own encoders using the `IContentEncoder` interface, you can return any type of data easily from your web resources.

Explicitly encoding your content

You can also choose to explicitly encode your content. The image encoder, for instance, encodes images to PNG files. If you want to encode the image to another file format, you can explicitly do so, as follows:

```
private void ReturnMomentaryAsJpg(HttpRequest Request,
    HttpResponse Response)
{
    SKImage Gauge = this.GenerateGauge(Request.Header);
    SKData Data = Gauge.Encode(SKEncodedImageFormat.Jpeg, 90);
    byte[] Binary = Data.ToArray();

    Response.ContentType = "image/jpeg";
    Response.Write(Binary);
}
```

Here you must explicitly set the content type of the response and then write the binary encoded data to the response stream.

You can now run the application and test it by typing in the URL of your new resource.

To test different representations of the same resource, you can download plugins to several of the web browsers available that allow you to customize HTTP headers in requests. This allows you to modify the `Accept` header and see how you get different responses depending on the values you provide.

Adding dynamic asynchronous resources

The actuator project (`ActuatorHttp` in the GitHub repository) also needs a `/Momentary` resource that returns the current state of the output in XML or JSON. The implementation is similar to that of the sensor, so it's straightforward to do. But we also need a way to control the output. We do that by adding a `/Set` resource. Since we will call asynchronous methods, we take this opportunity to add this resource as an asynchronous `POST` resource. This means we must explicitly handle errors and exceptions, as well as explicitly sending the response when it is ready:

```
this.httpServer.Register("/Set", null, async (req, resp) =>
{
    try
    {
        // Process resource here

        resp.SendResponse();    // Sends response.
    }
    catch (Exception ex)
    {
        resp.SendResponse(ex);  // Sends error response.
    }
}, false);
```

The first parameter defines the relative URL of the resource. The second is `null`, which means the resource does not accept `GET` method calls. The third contains a lambda expression that will be called when the `POST` method is called on the resource. Note the keyword `async`, which defines the expression as an asynchronous function. The fourth argument tells the web server that the resource is not synchronous, which is the same as saying it is asynchronous.

Decoding content

The `POST` request will have some content with it. Decoding this data is simple; we just call the `DecodeData()` method on the request object. The `Content-Type` HTTP header determines which decoder will be used when decoding the payload. We will assume plain text will be sent (`Content-Type` equal to `text/plain`). This will be decoded into a normal string:

```
if (!req.HasData)
    throw new BadRequestException();
string s = req.DecodeData() as string;
```

You can easily create your own content decoders. This is done by creating a class with a default constructor, implementing the `Waher.Content.IContentDecoder` interface, and making sure the assembly is initialized in the runtime inventory.

We then use the static `Waher.Content.CommonTypes` to help us with parsing the Boolean value. The `TryParse` method will accept `1`, `true`, `yes`, or `on` as true values, and `0`, `false`, `no`, and `off` as false values, using case insensitive comparison. If the content is not plain text, or not correctly formatted, we return a `400 Bad Request` error back to the client:

```
if (s == null || !CommonTypes.TryParse(s, out bool OutputValue))
    throw new BadRequestException();
```

Performing control action

As in the case for the `/Momentary` resource, we check the `Accept` header to see how the client wants the response to be represented. If no such header is available, we will assume XML is requested. If an unrecognized content type is requested, we make sure to return a `406 Not Acceptable` response before we perform the control action:

```
if (req.Header.Accept != null)
{
    switch (req.Header.Accept.GetBestContentType("text/xml",
        "application/xml", "application/json"))
    {
        case "text/xml":
        case "application/xml":
            await this.SetOutput(OutputValue,
                req.RemoteEndPoint);
            this.ReturnMomentaryAsXml(req, resp);
            break;

        case "application/json":
            await this.SetOutput(OutputValue,
                req.RemoteEndPoint);
            this.ReturnMomentaryAsJson(req, resp);
            break;

        default:
            throw new NotAcceptableException();
    }
}
else
{
```

```
        await this.SetOutput(OutputValue, req.RemoteEndPoint);
        this.ReturnMomentaryAsXml(req, resp);
}
```

Here, we reuse the content serialization methods defined for the `/Momentary` resource. But since the resource is defined as an *asynchronous* resource, it will actually not be sent, or completely sent, until the `resp.SendResponse();` is called.

Summary

In this chapter, you've been shown how you can use HTTP to publish sensor data and interact with devices on the internet. You've learned the basic principles of the HTTP protocol and how to publish resources and interact with them using HTTP. You've also learned to separate resource, state and representations of data, which is a requirement for making RESTful web services. In the next chapter, we will delve deeper into the world of the HTTP protocol by showing you how human interfaces can be built to interact with the machine-based web services created in this chapter.

6
Creating Web Pages for Your Devices

In the previous chapter, you learned how to use the HTTP protocol to publish your data dynamically from your devices. But HTTP is so much more. No HTTP implementation is complete without a human interface as well. This chapter continues the presentation of the HTTP protocol.

In this chapter, you'll learn how to add human user interfaces to your devices, and how you can monitor and interact with them. The chapter covers:

- How to publish file-based content
- The power of Markdown
- Publishing human-readable web content
- How to interact with backend web services from JavaScript
- Authentication on the web
- How to protect your pages using a user login
- How to protect your web services using **JSON Web Tokens (JWT)**

Adding file-based resources to your projects

Adding dynamic web service interfaces to publish our sensor data is not sufficient. To complete the web interface, we also want to publish some static resources, in the form of files, to provide a simple web page interface the user can view in a browser. To do this, we add a `HttpFolderResource` resource to our web server. It publishes all files available in a folder and its subfolders.

In **UWP** (**Universal Windows Platform**) applications, content files to be used can be stored under the `Assets` project folder. They should be marked as content files, but not be copied to the output directory. When deploying the application, these asset files will be deployed into the corresponding assets folder on the device. To find this folder at runtime, we can do as follows: create a `Root` subfolder in the `Assets` folder, to keep our web content files in, and put a `favicon.ico` file there, to provide our website with an icon. We can get the path of the file as follows, and then get the path to the folder by removing the filename (which is 11 characters long):

```
StorageFile File = await
    StorageFile.GetFileFromApplicationUriAsync(
    new Uri("ms-appx:///Assets/Root/favicon.ico"));
string Root = File.Path;
Root = Root.Substring(0, Root.Length - 11);
```

We then register a `HttpFolderResource` with our web server object, pointing to this `Root` folder. The first parameter defines the resource under which the folder will become public. We use the empty string to make the files accessible directly on the root. The second parameter is the disk folder containing the files. We then say that the `PUT` and `DELETE` methods are not allowed, making sure external users cannot change the contents of the files. We will accept anonymous `GET` requests and require user sessions. This will come in handy later, to keep track of user states, such as whether the user has logged in:

```
this.httpServer.Register(new HttpFolderResource(
    string.Empty, Root, false, false, true, true));
```

When running your application, any files you put in the `Root` folder will now be available from your browser as well.

 Apart from the `favicon.ico` file, you should place a `schema.xsd` file, containing the schema used in the XML representation of your sensor data. You can also include any web content you like, such as HTML files, CSS files, JavaScript files, images, and so on. You can also create a directory structure that will be logically mapped to the corresponding URLs on the web. The `SensorHttp` and `ActuatorHttp` projects in the GitHub repository contain several examples.

Converting Markdown to HTML in real time

Writing web content in HTML is time-consuming and laborious. Modern content management systems prefer simpler methods to edit and publish content. One such method is to use **Markdown**, which is a simple plain text format for writing content. Markdown, as opposed to markup (HTML), is made to be simple to use. It is easily parsed, and good-looking web pages can be generated from it.

 Markdown was originally invented by John Gruber at `daringfireball.net`. Since he allowed anybody to use the specification and extend it, it has become popular, and many extensions exist.

If you want to work with Markdown instead of HTML when you publish web content in your projects, you can do so easily. All you need to do is add two NuGet packages. The `Waher.Content.Markdown` package contains a Markdown parser that can generate HTML, XAML, and plain text from an extended version of Markdown with multimedia extensions and server-side script support. The `Waher.Content.Markdown.Web.UWP` package includes a real-time conversion module that the web server can use to convert Markdown files to HTML files in real time, if the browser accepts HTML but not Markdown. All we need to do is add these two packages and include them in the type inventory initialization call at the beginning of the app:

```
Types.Initialize(
    typeof(FilesProvider).GetTypeInfo().Assembly,
    typeof(RuntimeSettings).GetTypeInfo().Assembly,
    typeof(IContentEncoder).GetTypeInfo().Assembly,
    typeof(ImageCodec).GetTypeInfo().Assembly,
    typeof(MarkdownDocument).GetTypeInfo().Assembly,
    typeof(MarkdownToHtmlConverter).GetTypeInfo().Assembly,
    typeof(App).GetTypeInfo().Assembly);
```

 You would use the `Waher.Content.Markdown.Web` package instead if not developing a UWP application.

 You can extend the web server with any number of real-time converters. Each converter can convert one internet content type to another. A converter is a class with a default constructor implementing the `Waher.Content.IContentConverter` interface. The web server can, furthermore, combine converters dynamically to find conversion paths and more advanced conversion capabilities.

Adding simple Markdown content to the sensor project

Now that we can publish information using Markdown, let's add a new content file called `Index.md` to the web content `Root` folder in our sensor project. Let us add the following simple Markdown:

```
Title: Momentary
Author: Peter Waher
Description: This page displays the current state of the sensor.
Cache-Control: max-age=0, no-cache, no-store
CSS: Main.css
Javascript: UpdateGauge.js

Current state
============================

The following table contains the current state of the sensor.

| Sensor    | Value                     |
|:----------|:--------------------------|
| Light     | {SensorHttp.App.Light}    |
| Motion    | {SensorHttp.App.Motion}   |

![Light Gauge is green, if motion is detected.](/Momentary)
```

 Even though you normally see the HTML version of the content in a browser, you can still access the original Markdown document using the `Accept` header in the request. For this reason, never put any sensitive information in the document, such as passwords required to access databases or web services.

The first part of the Markdown file contains metadata about the file. This information will be used to set up the page, control caching, include related content (such as CSS files and JavaScript files), and publish information for simple **Search Engine Optimization** (**SEO**). After the first empty row, the content of the page begins. Simple rules allow you to add basic formatting, including a header, a table, and an image. Script between curly braces allows us to call methods or get values from properties in the underlying code. The `SensorHttp` project in the GitHub repository contains the CSS and JavaScript files referenced. They provide basic styles to make the page pleasant to view, and dynamic features, by updating the values in the table and the gauge every 2 seconds, repeatedly calling our web service interface. The application also contains the simple static properties referenced previously.

For a reference of the Markdown syntax supported, including multi-media extensions, metadata header fields, and so on, see http://waher.se/Markdown.md.

Calling our sensor API from JavaScript

We will call our /Momentary API in two ways. First, we will update the gauge on the screen. This is done by resetting the src property on the IMG tag of the gauge. To make sure the browser reloads the image, we add a query parameter that is unique, but not used by the API. Since it is an IMG tag, the browser will automatically add an Accept header field, telling the resource it wants an image. Code is straightforward:

```
var Images = document.getElementsByTagName("IMG");
Images[0].src = "/Momentary?TP=" + Date();
```

For updating the table, we use an XMLHttpRequest object. Here, we must manually set the Accept header to make sure we get the representation we desire. We need to follow the process. When we detect a successful response, we update the table with the received values:

```
var xhttp = new XMLHttpRequest();
xhttp.onreadystatechange = function ()
{
    if (xhttp.readyState == 4)
    {
            if (xhttp.status == 200)
            {
                    var Data = JSON.parse(xhttp.responseText);
                    var Cells = document.getElementsByTagName("TD");

                    Cells[1].firstChild.innerHTML =
                        Data.light.value + Data.light.unit;
                    Cells[3].firstChild.innerHTML =
                        Data.motion ? "Detected" : "Not detected";
            }

            delete xhttp;
    }
};

xhttp.open("GET", "/Momentary", true);
xhttp.setRequestHeader("Accept", "application/json");
xhttp.send("");
```

Note that we use the same resource for updating both information in the table and the gauge. This is one of the benefits of using RESTful interfaces.

We are now ready to test our page. If you run the application, you can view the page by navigating to `http://IP_ADDRESS/Index.md`. Note that UWP applications do not support the loopback interface, so you cannot view the page from the same machine you're running the app on. If you deploy it to Raspberry Pi, you can view it from your workstation or laptop. If you run it locally, you need to use another machine, phone, or tablet to connect to your machine and to view the page. The following image shows what your page might look like:

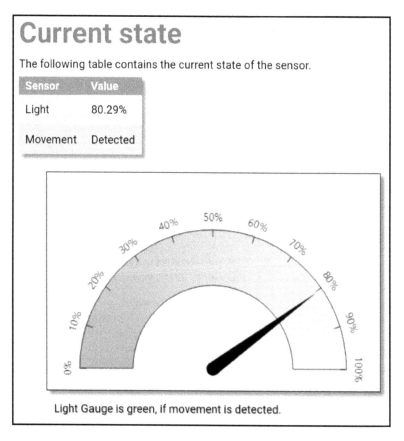

Sensor Markdown document, converted to HTML

Adding simple Markdown content to the actuator project

We also want to add a simple web interface to the actuator. It will just display the current state and provide a button we can use to toggle the state of the output. Note that we can embed HTML seamlessly into the Markdown to accomplish this. We embed the current value in a SPAN element with an id attribute, so that we can access it easily from JavaScript:

```
Title: Actuator
Author: Peter Waher
Description: This page displays the current state of the actuator.
Cache-Control: max-age=0, no-cache, no-store
CSS: Main.css
Javascript: ToggleOutput.js

Current state
=============================

Output is currently turned **<span
id='OutputState'>{ActuatorHttp.App.Output}</span>**

<button onclick='ToggleOutput();'>Toggle Output</button>
```

Calling our actuator API from JavaScript

Calling the actuator API is done slightly differently, since we use the POST method instead of the GET method. We need to send some content with the request. Sending text-based content is easy. We only need to send a string in the send() method. But we still need to set the Content-Type header to describe what type of text-based content we want to send. In our example, we use plain text:

```
var Span = document.getElementById("OutputState");
var CurrentState = Span.innerHTML;
var xhttp = new XMLHttpRequest();
xhttp.onreadystatechange = function ()
{
    if (xhttp.readyState == 4)
    {
        if (xhttp.status == 200)
        {
            var Data = JSON.parse(xhttp.responseText);
            Span.innerHTML = Data.output ? "ON" : "OFF";
        }
```

```
                delete xhttp;
    }
};

xhttp.open("POST", "/Set", true);
xhttp.setRequestHeader("Accept", "application/json");
xhttp.setRequestHeader("Content-Type", "text/plain");
if (CurrentState == "ON")
    xhttp.send("OFF");
else
    xhttp.send("ON");
```

The following image shows what our very simple user interface might look like in a browser:

Actuator Markdown document, converted to HTML

Adding default redirections

Users normally don't remember syntax, so we can't assume they will remember the URL for the device. The IP address should be sufficient. To solve this, we want to create a default resource that redirects to our default page if only the IP address is provided. This is easily done as follows:

```
this.httpServer.Register("/", (req, resp) =>
{
    throw new TemporaryRedirectException("/Index.md");
});
```

Plotting graphs

No sensor application is complete without plotting graphs. We can do this directly from the web interface hosted on the sensor itself. We have already defined a web page for it: `/History.md`. We first need to add the `Waher.Script.Graphs` NuGet package to the project. It adds graph plotting functions to our scripting engine. It uses the cross-platform `SkiaSharp` two-dimensional drawing package to do the actual drawing. We must just make sure to add the corresponding assemblies of `Waher.Script` and `Waher.Script.Graphs` to the types inventory when we initialize the application.

 For a list of script syntax supported, including some extension libraries, see `http://waher.se/Script.md`.

Reading historical values from the database

To plot historical values, we first need to read them from the database. We can use the `Find<T>()` method on the static `Database` class to find, filter, and sort objects in the database. It returns an enumerable set of objects of type `T` (`IEnumerable<T>`). We want to plot all values that are available, so we don't filter them. However, we want to get them in time order. To accessing the values from the script easier, we also convert our enumerable set of objects to an array. Database access is asynchronous, so we make our method asynchronous too:

```
public static async Task<LastMinute[]> GetLastMinutesAsync()
{
    List<LastMinute> Result = new List<LastMinute>();

    foreach (LastMinute Rec in
            await Database.Find<LastMinute>("Timestamp"))
    {
            Result.Add(Rec);
    }

    return Result.ToArray();
}
```

Script runs synchronously, so we add a second method calling the first, and then wait for the operation to complete:

```
public static LastMinute[] GetLastMinutes()
{
    Task<LastMinute[]> T = GetLastMinutesAsync();
    T.Wait();
    return T.Result;
}
```

Plotting historical values

We are now ready to plot the values. We create a new Markdown page called `History.md`. In it, we create a script block in which we call the static method, extract the corresponding values, and then create the plot. We will want to reuse the same type of graph for all our historical values (minutes, hours, and days), so we first create a function, `DrawGraph`, which calculates the plot, and then call it with the results received from the static method we called:

```
Title: History
Author: Peter Waher
Description: This page displays historical values of the sensor.
Cache-Control: max-age=0, no-cache, no-store
CSS: Main.css

Historical values
=============================

The following graphs display historical values of the sensor.

Minutes
-------------

{
DrawGraph(Records):=
(
    MinTP:=Records.MinLightAt;
    Min:=Records.MinLight;
    MaxTP:=Records.MaxLightAt;
    Max:=Records.MaxLight;
    TP:=join(MinTP, reverse(MaxTP));
    Values:=join(Min, reverse(Max));
    plot2darea(Records.Timestamp, Records.AvgMotion,
            rgba(0,255,0,64))+
            polygon2d(TP, Values, rgba(0,0,255,32))+
```

```
                plot2dline(Records.Timestamp, Records.AvgLight, "Red");
    );
    DrawGraph(SensorHttp.App.GetLastMinutes());
    }
```

The script works with **canonical extensions**. This means, for example, that
if a property is not available on an array `V=[E1, ..., En]`, as is the case
here, but on the elements of the array `E1, ..., En`, then the property is
automatically canonically extended to the array, as follows:
V.Property = [E1.Property, ..., En.Property]
This saves a lot of time in terms of not having to write code loops. For
more information, see
`http://waher.se/Script.md#canonicalExtensions`.
In the IoT Gateway repository on GitHub, you can compile and execute
the `Waher.Script.Lab` application. It allows you to experiment with
script live. With it you can experiment with different types of plots, data,
and combinations. You can also download an executable version
(compiled for the x86 processor) at
`https://github.com/PeterWaher/IoTGateway/blob/master/Executables`
`/Waher.Script.Lab.x86.zip?raw=true`.

Displaying the plot

We can now run the application and navigate to the `/History.md` resource. It might look
something like the following image. If you look at the script, you will notice that the
expression that returns the plot (the last statement in the function) is a sum of three separate
graphs. First, an area chart shows how much average motion has occurred during the
period. A polygon then paints an area, where the upper border represents the largest light
values, and the lower the smallest light values during each period. The red line corresponds
to the average light value during each period.

Adding graphs is done using the addition operator:

Plot of historical data

Generalizing the page

When we understand how the first plot works, it's easy to generalize the page and create similar plots for the other time bases we have: hours and days. First, we need to create analogous static methods in our code to read hourly and daily historical values from our persistence layer. We call these methods `GetLastHours()` and `GetLastDays()`. We then simply add the following sections to our Markdown page.

The `DrawGraph` script function defined earlier will draw the corresponding graphs:

```
Hours
-------------

{DrawGraph(SensorHttp.App.GetLastHours());}


Days
-------------

{DrawGraph(SensorHttp.App.GetLastDays());}
```

Creating a menu system

We now have two pages on the sensor that we would like to navigate between, using some kind of menu system. Instead of having to insert this menu structure manually into each page, the Markdown engine we use allows us to define a master/detail view of our page. We can create a **master** Markdown document that contains the menu, and that embeds **detail** documents in it.

Creating the master document

We begin by creating a new Markdown document in the `Root` folder and call it `Menu.md`. In it, we add the headers that we want all detail pages to have. We, therefore, move the CSS file to the `Menu.md` file, since we want all pages to have the same design. We can also define an `Icon` header.

We then go on to provide the general disposition of the page, using the HTML5 elements `header`, `nav`, `main`, and `footer`. We define the menu using a bullet-point list. This list is rendered to `ul` and `li` tags respectively. We can use the CSS file to transform this bullet-point list into a nicer-looking menu system. If a bullet contains a single link, pointing to the detail file being viewed, it will be marked using the `active` class name in HTML. This allows us to provide special styling for those elements dynamically in CSS.

Finally, we use the special `[%Details]` metadata reference on the location in the file where we want the detail Markdown page to be inserted. The result may look as follows. Note that we need the empty rows to allow the Markdown parser to separate the corresponding blocks into logical blocks:

```
CSS: Main.css
Icon: /favicon.ico

<header id="header">
<nav>

* [Momentary](/Index.md)
* [History](/History.md)
* [%Title]
* [Mastering IoT](https://github.com/PeterWaher/MIoT)
* [IoT Gateway](https://github.com/PeterWaher/IoTGateway)

</nav>
</header>
<main>

[%Details]

</main>

<footer>
This application is part of the [Mastering Internet of
Things](https://github.com/PeterWaher/MIoT) book.
</footer>
```

Referencing the menu

Now that we have the menu defined, we enter all our earlier detail pages, and add the following reference in the metadata section at the top of each document:

```
Master: Menu.md
```

We also make sure to remove the superfluous `CSS` tags, since we have one in the master document. If we run the application now and view the `Index.md` page in a browser, it might look as shown in the following image. Clicking on the links in the menu allows you to navigate your small website:

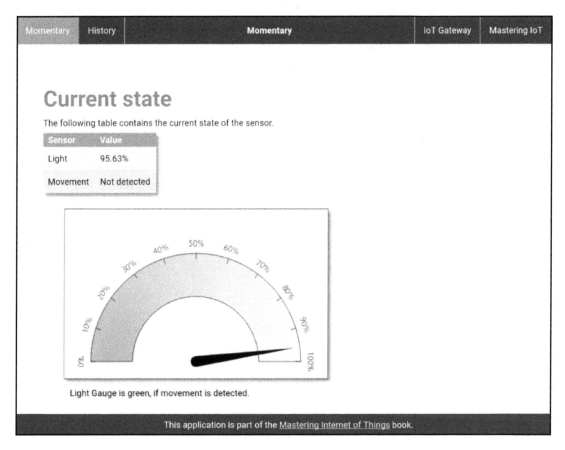

Menu system

Authenticating users

Our last task before the web page is complete is to provide some minimum form of protection by providing a login page. A user must be logged in to be able to view the data of the device or control its output.

The Markdown engine allows us to implement simple login pages. It is done by providing two header fields, `Login` and `UserVariable`. What they do is tell the parser that the page can only be viewed if a `Waher.Security.IUser` object is defined in the current session, with the variable name defined by the `UserVariable` header. If no such variable is found, the client is redirected to a new page, defined by the `Login` header. So, we begin by adding the following two rows to the `Index.md` and `History.md` files in the sensor project (the work for the controller is analogous):

```
UserVariable: User
Login: Login.md
```

Adding a login page

We now create a new Markdown page in the web `Root` asset folder, called `Login.md`. This page will display a simple login form to the user. When the user is redirected to this page, a query parameter called `from` will be available to inform the application where the redirection came from. A similar `from` variable will also be available in the session. After a successful login, the idea is to redirect the user back to this page. We begin by providing the simple contents of the form:

```
Title: Login
Description: Login page to the device.
Author: Peter Waher
Master: Menu.md
Parameter: from

Login
=============

<form id="LoginForm" action="/Login" method="post">

Please login by providing a user name and password:

User Name:
<input id="UserName" name="UserName" type="text" autofocus="autofocus"
style="width:20em" />

Password:
<input id="Password" name="Password" type="password" style="width:20em" />

{{if exists(LoginError) then]]
<div class='error'>
((LoginError))
</div>
```

```
[[;}}
```

```
<button id="LoginButton" type="submit">Login</button>
```

```
</form>
```

 `User Name:` and `Password:` should be followed by two spaces. These are invisible in print. Two spaces at the end of a row is transformed into a hard-line break in the generated output.

As we have done before, we can mix HTML with Markdown. What is new is that we use a new type of script in our Markdown file: **pre-processed script**. Embedded script, within single curly braces { . . . }, is executed when the page is rendered, and the result is displayed in the corresponding location. Pre-processed script is different. It allows you to change the structure of the actual document before it is parsed and rendered. Pre-processed script is written between double curly braces {{ . . . }}. Furthermore, the script can emit Markdown between [[. . .]], inserted anywhere in the pre-processed script. We use this to add an error label, if one is available in a session.

 For more information about pre-processed script, see `https://waher.se/Markdown.md#preProcessedScript`.

If we start the application and go to the main page, we are now confronted with something like in the following image:

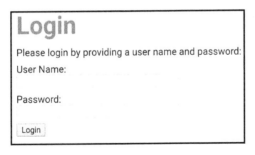

Login form

Creating our user

To authenticate users, we need a user database. `Waher.Security` defines two interfaces that we will use: `IUser` and `IUserSource`. Each user implements the first, and the user database implements the second. We will implement a very simplistic database with only one user. Full user management goes beyond the scope of this book, but such an implementation should be straightforward, using the persistence layer presented in this book.

We begin by defining our user. It will have the username `MIoT` and password `rox`:

```
public class User : IUser
{
    public string UserName => "MIoT";
    public string PasswordHash =>instance.CalcHash("rox");
    public string PasswordHashType => "SHA-256";

    public bool HasPrivilege(string Privilege)
    {
        return false;
    }
}
```

 Always use **salted** hashes when persisting credentials. Never persist passwords. This reduces the risk should the database get leaked. Salted hashes avoid the possibility of them being reused in other systems. Adding salt means the password is combined with some information that is unique to the installation of the application, for instance, a random number generated the first time the application is run.

Creating a very simple user database

The user database will only contain our one user. We leave it to the reader to create a more dynamic user database:

```
private IUserSource users = new Users();

public class Users : IUserSource
{
    public bool TryGetUser(string UserName, out IUser User)
    {
        if (UserName == "MIoT")
            User = new User();
        else
```

```
        User = null;

    return User != null;
    }
}
```

We also define our salted hash function as follows, using the unique device identity as the salt:

```
private string CalcHash(string Password)
{
    return Waher.Security.Hashes.ComputeSHA256HashString(
        Encoding.UTF8.GetBytes(Password + ":" + this.deviceId));
}
```

Posting login form

After filling out the form in a browser, and pressing the **Login** button, the contents will be sent to the server resource /Login using the POST method. We need to add such a resource to the server:

```
this.httpServer.Register("/Login", null, (req, resp) =>
{
    // Code comes here
}, true, false, true);
```

Here we've registered only a POST handler. The first true parameter tells the server the resource is synchronous. The following false tells the server that we only serve the /Login resource, and not any sub-resources. The last true tells the server the resource requires a user session.

 If sending the form over an unencrypted line, as is the case if you use UWP, the password will be readable by anybody sniffing the network traffic.

Parsing the form

The form will be sent using a `Content-Type` of `application/x-www-form-urlencoded`. This type is recognized by `Waher.Content`, and so decoding is simple. The form will be parsed into a string dictionary. All we need to do is to check that we get what we expect, and that the form has the correct parameters:

```
if (!req.HasData || req.Session == null)
    throw new BadRequestException();

object Obj = req.DecodeData();
Dictionary<string, string> Form =
    Obj as Dictionary<string, string>;

if (Form == null ||
    !Form.TryGetValue("UserName", out string UserName) ||
    !Form.TryGetValue("Password", out string Password))
{
    throw new BadRequestException();
}
```

We also need to check the source of the original request, in case we want to redirect the user back there after a successful login:

```
string From = null;

if (req.Session.TryGetVariable("from", out Variable v))
    From = v.ValueObject as string;

if (string.IsNullOrEmpty(From))
    From = "/Index.md";
```

Redirecting the user

Now that we have the credentials, we need to check them against our user database. We will define a method for this, `bool Login(UserName, Password)`, returning whether the credentials were authenticated or not. If successful, we set the session variable `User`, which we defined in the Markdown documents, to the corresponding user object. This tells the application that the user is logged in, and will stay logged in, while the session is maintained:

```
IUser User = this.Login(UserName, Password);
if (User != null)
{
```

```
        Log.Informational("User logged in.", UserName,
                req.RemoteEndPoint, "LoginSuccessful",
                EventLevel.Minor);

        req.Session["User"] = User; req.Session.Remove("LoginError");

        throw new SeeOtherException(From);
    }
    else
    {
        Log.Warning("Invalid login attempt.", UserName,
                req.RemoteEndPoint, "LoginFailure", EventLevel.Minor);
        req.Session["LoginError"] =
                "Invalid login credentials provided.";
    }

    throw new SeeOtherException(req.Header.Referer.Value);
```

The last thing we do in the method is to return a 303 See Other HTTP response, instead of the normal 200 OK, followed by some new content to display. This is called the **PRG pattern**, or POST-Redirect-GET pattern. This redirects the client to the page we want them to see and provides a better user experience in the browser.

 It's important to log login attempts to the event log. These **audit-logs** are the main source for detecting intrusion attempts in systems. Without them, it is virtually impossible to evaluate threats and any damage after breaches have been detected.

Authenticating the user

The authentication method used in our application is simple. It checks the user database to see if a user with the given name is available. Then it checks the password hash method used and calculates the corresponding hash of the provided password. If the hashes match, credentials are authenticated. If not, or if the hash method is not recognized, authentication fails:

```
private IUser Login(string UserName, string Password)
{
    if (this.users.TryGetUser(UserName, out IUser User))
    {
        switch (User.PasswordHashType)
        {
            case "":
                if (Password == User.PasswordHash)
```

```
                                  return User;
                          break;

                  case "SHA-256":
                          if (this.CalcHash(Password) ==
                                  User.PasswordHash)
                                          return User;
                          break;

                  default:
                          Log.Error("Unsupported Hash function: " +
                                  User.PasswordHashType);
                          break;
                  }
          }

          return null;
      }
```

You can now test the application. The first time you view any of your pages, the login page will be displayed. A successful login will then redirect you back to the original page you wanted to view.

Protecting our web services

The login page described earlier only protects our Markdown content, not our dynamic web services. If you know the resource names of the web services, you can still extract all sensor data and control the actuator output, unauthenticated. To avoid this, we need to add an authentication layer on top of our web services. We can do this by using **JWT (Java Web Tokens)**. These tokens are simple strings that are cryptographically signed by a server, and that can be easily transported in any type of machine-to-machine communication where you want to avoid sessions and login forms. The server can then validate the token by checking the signature. By adding the Waher.Security.JWT.UWP NuGet package to our SensorHttp and ActuatorHttp projects, we can use JWT to protect our web services.

 For .NET standard, .NET Core, or traditional .NET Framework projects, you can use the Waher.Security.JWT NuGet instead.

Getting a session token

We begin by creating a token factory. It will allow us to create tokens:

```
private JwtFactory tokenFactory = new JwtFactory();
```

We then add a resource that allows a web page, after having logged in, to get a session token:

```
this.httpServer.Register("/GetSessionToken", null, (req, resp) =>
{
    IUser User;

    if (!req.Session.TryGetVariable("User", out Variable v) ||
            (User = v.ValueObject as IUser) == null)
    {
            throw new ForbiddenException();
    }

    string Token = this.tokenFactory.Create(
            new KeyValuePair<string, object>("sub", User.UserName));

    resp.ContentType = JwtCodec.ContentType;
    resp.Write(Token);
}, true, false, true);
```

When you create a token, you provide a set of **claims**. One of the most important is `sub`, which means **subject**, and relates to the entity that the token is about. You can add any number of claims here, standard as well as custom. Try adding a custom claim containing the client IP address. You can then use that information inside your method, to make sure that future requests are only accepted if they are made from the same IP address. Other authorization claims can also be added. Care must be taken, however, since you don't want to leak sensitive personal information through the tokens.

For a list of public claim names, see IANA's list at
`https://www.iana.org/assignments/jwt/jwt.xhtml`.

Validating tokens

The `Waher.Security.JWT.UWP` library also contains the `JwtAuthentication` class that authenticates web requests based on JWT tokens. We first need to define a variable for it:

```
private JwtAuthentication tokenAuthentication;
```

When we've established the device identity, which we will use as a realm, we create an instance of this authenticator (the realm allows browsers to isolate credentials between sites):

```
this.tokenAuthentication = new JwtAuthentication(this.deviceId,
    this.users, this.tokenFactory);
```

The authenticator references our `users` database to check that subjects match users in the database. It also references the token factory to validate that tokens are correctly signed. We then simply add the reference to the authenticator as the last parameter to all the web service resource registrations that we want to protect.

Using tokens in JavaScript

Now that our web services are protected, we need to update our JavaScript to match this change. We begin by getting the current session token, as follows:

```
var SessionToken = null;

function GetSessionToken()
{
    var xhttp = new XMLHttpRequest();
    xhttp.onreadystatechange = function ()
    {
        if (xhttp.readyState == 4)
        {
            if (xhttp.status == 200)
            {
                SessionToken = xhttp.responseText;
                window.setInterval(RefreshGauge, 2000);
            }

            delete xhttp;
        }
    };

    xhttp.open("POST", "/GetSessionToken", true);
    xhttp.send("");
```

```
    }

    GetSessionToken();
```

When we have the token, we only need to add it to requests being made, using the Bearer**Authorization** header, to pre-empt the **WWW-authentication** step, as follows:

```
    xhttp.open("GET", "/Momentary", true);
    xhttp.setRequestHeader("Accept", "application/json");
    xhttp.setRequestHeader("Authorization", "Bearer " + SessionToken);
    xhttp.send("");
```

If you run the application now, it will still work. Try to access the /Momentary resource as before, without logging in first, and you'll see the resource is blocked.

 Unfortunately, since we cannot add custom headers to requests being made from IMG tags on the page, we cannot control the authorization mechanism being used for images on the momentary page. But such requests still send relevant cookies, so we can secure images being shown in IMG tags by using session state variables. The SensorHttp project in the GitHub page has, therefore, created a parallel resource, /MomentaryPng, which only returns a PNG image of the momentary value if the user has logged in and the corresponding session variable is defined.

Summary

In this chapter, you've been shown how you can use HTTP to publish a human interface to interact with your sensor data and actuator on the internet. You've learned how to publish file-based content and dynamic web services. You've also learned how to interact with your web services from JavaScript, how to plot graphs, and how to update your pages dynamically. You've built a menu system for your pages and secured them using JWT.

In the next chapter, you will learn how you can use the CoAP protocol as an efficient alternative to HTTP for constrained devices.

7
Communicating More Efficiently Using CoAP

In the previous two chapters, you learned how to use the HTTP protocol to publish your data and to interact with your devices. But HTTP has some limitations when it comes to resource-constrained devices: it is very verbose and consumes a lot of bandwidth compared to the amount of data being transported.

In this chapter, you'll learn how to use the **Constrained Application Protocol**, or **CoAP**, to create interfaces for resource-constrained devices, typically devices in networks where bandwidth is an issue. The chapter covers:

- An introduction to the CoAP protocol
- Security in CoAP
- Content encoding in CoAP
- Publishing data using CoAP
- The Observe or Event Subscription communication pattern
- Responding to control actions using CoAP
- Testing your CoAP devices
- Encrypting your CoAP devices

Introducing CoAP

There are several problems with using HTTP for resource-constrained devices. HTTP is verbose and requires a lot of bytes for headers. These headers are in plain text, and since HTTP has grown over time, there are a lot of headers that need to be supported to achieve compliance with the standards. This forces implementations to become large, which might be a problem if the device has limited memory. CoAP is much simpler and has less options, and therefore has a smaller *code footprint* than HTTP.

 CoAP is an **Internet Engineering Task Force** (**IETF**) standard and is defined in RFC 7252: `https://tools.ietf.org/html/rfc7252`.

At the same time, the amount of data in the payload is often small. A sensor value can be encoded in just a few bytes. The great difference between number of bytes sent and number of content bytes sent implies a great waste. This waste of *bandwidth* is particularly noticeable in resource-constrained networks, such as the **IPv6** radio-based network **6LoWPAN** (**IPv6 over Low-Power Wireless Personal Area Networks**). In such networks, datagrams have been reduced in size to be a maximum of 127 bytes, leaving only about 70-80 bytes for encrypted payload per datagram, depending on cipher used, before payload must be fragmented. This space must contain both headers and content. The need to compress headers is obvious. For this reason, CoAP employs *binary headers*. This not only reduces message size, but also reduces code footprint even further.

 If you're required to send content that exceeds the amount of data possible to embed in a datagram, CoAP allows you to divide your content into **blocks**. Whenever you send data using CoAP, you can also provide a **block size**. If the content exceeds this block size, the CoAP layer divides it into blocks and transmits them individually, while the receiving end assembles the blocks and delivers the complete payload to its application at the other end. Block-wise transfers using CoAP is defined in RFC 7959: `https://tools.ietf.org/html/rfc7959`.

The design of HTTP is also not well suited for the use case of transporting sensor data or performing small quick control actions. HTTP is based on TCP and on the Request/Response pattern. This means that each transfer of sensor data using HTTP is doubly acknowledged; it requires *at least* four messages. If we ignore TCP's connection establishment and TLS handshakes, each request is acknowledged, and each response is also acknowledged, resulting in four messages minimum. It doesn't matter if the client requests the data from the sensor, or if the sensor pushes the data.

CoAP reduces the set of methods endpoints can use somewhat, by converting the method to a 6-bit integer. But only seven methods are defined by IANA: GET, POST, PUT, DELETE, FETCH, PATCH, and iPATCH. In a similar manner, the number of response or result codes available have been somewhat reduced to facilitate implementations. Typically, response codes in CoAP have similar response codes in HTTP, with similar meanings.

The preceding image shows the flow of IP messages between a **Client** and a **Server** based on the Request/Response pattern using TCP:

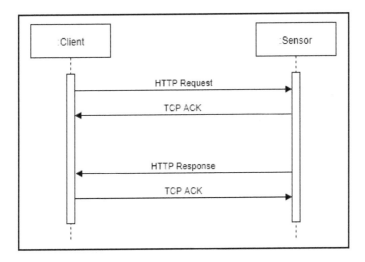

Transfer of a sensor value using HTTP requires a minimum of four IP packets

Using UDP

CoAP optimizes this drastically, changing two things. First, it uses **UDP** instead of TCP. In UDP, IP packets, called **datagrams**, are not acknowledged or ordered as they are in TCP. This means that datagrams can get lost or be received in a different order compared to when they were sent. Such considerations must be handled by CoAP implementations. While CoAP manages acknowledgements also, it is optional. This means that the application has the option of using the **unacknowledged** service when sending data. This saves a lot of network traffic, especially in cases where loss of datagrams is acceptable.

This is typically the case, for instance, with sensors measuring analog ambient values that regularly report their status. If a value gets lost, it gets replaced automatically by the next. And previous values are probably close enough to still be valid if changes are not expected to be drastic between messages.

CoAP over UDP normally uses port 5683 for unencrypted communication.

Efficiently distributing data

CoAP also introduces two new communication patterns: **multicast** and **Event Subscription** or **Observe** as it is called in CoAP. Since CoAP is based on UDP and UDP supports multicasting, using the **Internet Group Management Protocol**, or **IGMP**, CoAP messages can also be multicast, at least when encryption is not used. This is done by sending CoAP messages to predefined multicast addresses.

For IPv4, the CoAP multicast address is 224.0.1.187. For IPv6, it's [FF02::FD] or [FF05:FD] for the link-local or site-local scope.

Multicasting not only allows for efficient distribution, it also allows clients to find CoAP devices with multicast support by multicasting requests. Multicasting a request and monitoring responses allows you to find new devices in the local network. Typically, multicasting (IGMP) is turned off in many gateways, however.

Care must be taken when using CoAP multicasting, since encryption is not allowed using the current versions of the standards. This is expected to change in the future.

Understanding the Observe pattern

For sensors reporting data regularly and securely, the greatest optimization is the use of the **Observe** (or **Event Subscription**) pattern. Using this pattern, the requestor, or **subscriber**, is only required to send one request, called the **subscription**. Just as with a normal request, the device returns a response containing the data it wants to return. The difference lies in when the resource changes. When that happens, the device automatically sends a new response to the subscriber, without having to wait for a corresponding request.

Resources that support the Observe pattern are called **observable resources**. Observing resources is defined in RFC 7641:
`https://tools.ietf.org/html/rfc7641`

In a normal case, this reduces the number of messages sent on the network by a factor of (close to) two. From four messages, it's possible to reduce this to (close to) one, depending on the direction of communication. If data is pushed from the device to the receiver, the number of messages is reduced by a factor of (close to) four in the normal unacknowledged case. If data is polled by the client, the number of messages depends on how often the polling is done. Either a great reduction of messages is achieved (if rapid polling is used to achieve low latency), or an increase in the number of messages is achieved (if slow polling is used with long latency). But in both cases, the **latency**, or the delay it takes for the receiving party to get its mirrored value updated, is reduced.

Typically, an observable resource updates its value using a regular time interval. More sophisticated methods are possible by using parameters in the request, letting the server know how often to report a value, if interval-based reporting is desired, or when to report it, if event-based or hysteresis-based reporting is desired.

The preceding image shows the transfer of unacknowledged sensor data using the Observe pattern:

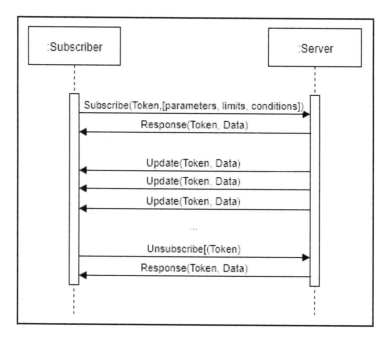

Transfer of unacknowledged sensor data using the Observe pattern

 Observed data can be transported using both the acknowledged and unacknowledged service. Typically, the server will use the same service as the subscriber did when making the original subscription, if not explicitly defined by the resource itself. Larger content sent using blocked transfer can also be observed.

Securing CoAP communication

HTTP is secured using **Transport Layer Security** (**TLS**), as presented in previous chapters. But TLS requires an underlying stream of data such as that provided by TCP connections. Since the order of UDP datagrams is not preserved, TLS cannot be used with UDP directly. For this purpose, **Datagram Transport Layer Security** (**DTLS**), was developed. DTLS is a modification of TLS; it can be used by protocols such as UDP that lose, and possibly reorder, datagrams.

CoAP normally uses port 5684 for DTLS encrypted communication.

Since DTLS is often used in resource-constrained environment, DTLS implementations are also significantly more lightweight than traditional TLS implementations. At least, if not a large security library is used that implements each corresponding technology available. Typically, the use of certificates can be avoided by using simple and efficient authenticated encryption algorithms, such as the **AES CCM** cipher suite, prescribed as one of two mandatory cipher suites for use with CoAP (the other being based on Elliptic Curve public keys). The AES CCM cipher provides AES encryption of data using keys of 128 or 256 bits. It also includes a signature and validation scheme for each datagram sent, based on the AES CCM algorithm, using either 64 or 128 bits (8 or 16 bytes). This makes injection of telegrams into the stream difficult.

Typically, **pre-shared keys (PSK)** is used together with AES CCM in CoAP. To be able to establish a DTLS session, the client and server need to validate each other using an **identity** and **key** pair, where the key is the **shared secret**. If both reach the same result using the algorithm, both are seen to be authenticated and encrypted application data (CoAP) can ensue. While certificates, or a plethora of other cipher suites, can be used together with CoAP to make it even more secure, the AES CCM PSK ciphers require only a small code footprint. They add reasonably little overhead to datagrams, while providing a reasonable level of security, making them suitable for use with CoAP, except in situations where very strong encryption is required.

 AES CCM with PSK does not enjoy the property of **forward secrecy**. This is a property where the compromise of long-term keys (such as the PSK) does not compromise past session keys.

Understanding DTLS sessions

Since UDP is not based on connections, it is easy for anybody to transmit datagrams to anyone, on any port. For this reason, DTLS needs to have a mechanism that prevents the injection of datagrams into existing sessions, or sessions being negotiated. It must also be able to reject replays of earlier conversations. It does this by introducing explicit counters into datagrams, and it adds a **client cookie**, which is typically calculated on attributes the server can retrieve from the client.

This adds a pair of messages to the handshake, compared to TLS. But if we use an AES CCM PSK cipher suite to authenticate and encrypt data, we avoid the overhead of sending certificates, which might require multiple datagrams to complete, since these can be large and need to be divided into multiple fragments.

DTLS v1.2 is defined by IETF in RFC 6347:
`https://tools.ietf.org/html/rfc6347`

The preceding image shows the flow of messages in a DTLS handshake when using PSK:

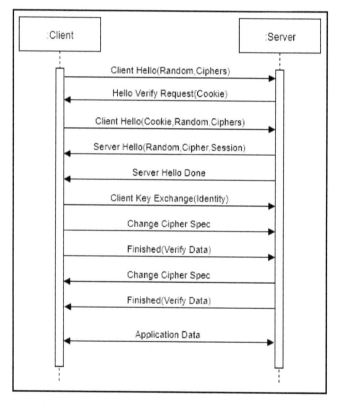

DTLS handshake when using PSK

Before communicating CoAP over DTLS, one of the endpoints needs to establish a DTLS session with the other. Let's call the first the client and the other the server in this case, even though these roles might not necessarily be correct in the CoAP sense. (The DTLS client establishing the session might be the CoAP server, and vice versa.)

The DTLS client starts by sending a hello message to the server. Since anybody can do that, the server responds with a hello verification request, and sends a cookie. The client now sends a new hello message, with the cookie and the same random number. The cookie pins the DTLS client to a given IP address and the random number provided. The client hello message also contains an array of all the cipher suites it can use, ordered by preference. The server now responds with two messages: one server hello and one server hello done message. These are typically included in the same datagram for improved performance. The server passes its random number, the cipher it selects from the list provided by the client, and the session ID. This session ID can be used to reconnect to an existing session.

When the pleasantries of salutation have been completed, the client sends its corresponding cipher keys for the cipher the server selected. In our example, it is the AES CCM PSK cipher. The key consists of the identity part of the identity-key pair. It then tells the server, using the change cipher specification message, that the next message will be encrypted using the negotiated cipher and parameters. Following this message, the client sends a finished message containing verification data. This verification data is a salted SHA-256 hash of the handshake conversation up to that point. Typically, all three messages are sent in the same UDP datagram, for performance.

The server receives the verification data and validates it with its secret key. If successful, it returns two messages. The first tells the client that the server will change to the new cipher settings. The second provides verification data to the client, allowing the client to validate the identity of the server, avoiding **man-in-the-middle** (**MITM**) attacks.

When both have validated the authenticity of the other, application data (in our case, CoAP messages) can be sent using the DTLS cipher established in the session. Since DTLS sessions are not based on connections, it is up to the client and server to decide how long the session is remembered for. If a session becomes invalid, a new session must be negotiated. To avoid the possibility of the other end forgetting a session, sessions should be closed when not used. Regular events, such as those provided by the observe pattern, also make sure a session is kept alive over time.

Encoding content

Encoding content in HTTP is relatively easy, but decoding is complicated. Since it is easy to encode and provide a content type string, the decoder needs to be very flexible to support all the content types that might be used, including all the individual variants, character encodings, and so on. You can even create proprietary and vendor-specific encodings very easily.

CoAP has reversed these relationships. In CoAP, it is more complicated to encode the content you want to transfer, but this makes it much easier for the receiving end, who need to decode the information. Only of few of all available Internet Content Types, or Media Types, are possible to encode in CoAP. Fewer options means it's easier to decode, but more difficult to encode that which you want to encode. The Content Type string is replaced with a short numeric **Content Format**, which is also much easier to encode and parse. But since plain text, XML, and JSON are available as CoAP Content Formats (as content formats 0, 41, and 50 correspondingly), they will be fine for our purposes.

 A registry of available content formats for use in CoAP is maintained by IANA at
https://www.iana.org/assignments/core-parameters/core-parameters
.xhtml.

Adding CoAP to our devices

We are now ready to implement CoAP in our projects. To do this, we create two new projects, which we will call `SensorCoap` and `ActuatorCoap`, copying the corresponding code from the `Sensor` and `Actuator` projects. If we wish to retain HTTP functionality, we can copy the code from the `SensorHttp` and `ActuatorHttp` projects instead. Our devices can support multiple protocols. We use the same hardware as we used in previous chapters. We add the `Waher.Networking.CoAP.UWP` NuGet package to both projects.

 For .NET standard, .NET Core, or traditional .NET Framework projects, you can use the **Waher.Networking.CoAP** NuGet instead. *Universal Windows Platform* apps use different libraries and runtime binaries when it comes to accessing network adaptors. For this reason, it requires a somewhat modified version of the original library.

We must also make sure to initialize the runtime inventory of classes with a reference to the CoAP library assembly, in the beginning of the application, to make sure content encoding and decoding includes the content formats defined in it:

```
Types.Initialize(
    typeof(FilesProvider).GetTypeInfo().Assembly,
    typeof(RuntimeSettings).GetTypeInfo().Assembly,
    typeof(IContentEncoder).GetTypeInfo().Assembly,
    typeof(ICoapContentFormat).GetTypeInfo().Assembly,
    typeof(IDtlsCredentials).GetTypeInfo().Assembly,
    typeof(App).GetTypeInfo().Assembly);
```

 We must not forget to add the `internetClientServer` capability to our set of capabilities in the `Package.appxmanifest` files as well:

```
<Capability Name="internetClientServer" />
```

 We must also make sure to create a **Device ID**, as we did in the HTTP chapter.

Creating a CoAP endpoint

Since directionality in CoAP is not as stringent as in HTTP, the same class is used for both clients and servers, both named **endpoints** to make things simpler. We add a `CoapEndpoint` field (defined in the `Waher.Networking.CoAP` namespace) for our endpoint:

```
private CoapEndpoint coapEndpoint = null;
```

To start using CoAP, we begin by creating an unencrypted CoAP endpoint using the default port number (5683):

```
this.coapEndpoint = new CoapEndpoint();
```

Publishing interval-based observable data

Let us begin publishing sensor data. This is done in a similar way to the HTTP case, by adding **resources** to our endpoint. There are two additions we must consider. First, we want to support **observable resources**. This means we need to store a reference to the resource we create, so that we can tell it when values change. These reference variables will be of `CoapResource` type. We also specify what messaging service to use when updating values to subscribers. For our ambient light sensor, we will choose the unacknowledged service.

We will also add some metadata about the resources we create, for interoperability. We will discuss this more in the next chapter. For now, it's sufficient to know that we give a human-readable title to our resource, as well as specify the content formats our resource supports:

```
this.lightResource = this.coapEndpoint.Register("/Light",
    (req, resp) =>
    {
        string s;

        if (this.lastLight.HasValue)
            s = ToString(this.lastLight.Value, 2) + " %";
        else
            s = "-";

        resp.Respond(CoapCode.Content, s, 64);
    }, Notifications.Unacknowledged, "Light, in %.", null, null,
    new int[] { PlainText.ContentFormatCode });
```

Classes for common content formats are available in the `Waher.Networking.CoAP.ContentFormats` namespace.

To let the resource know it should update any subscribers using a regular time interval, we call the `TriggerAll()` method on the resource, with the time interval we want to define:

```
this.lightResource?.TriggerAll(new TimeSpan(0, 0, 5));
```

In this case, subscribers will be updated every five seconds about changes to the light value. We don't have to worry more about this; the CoAP library takes care of the rest.

The `?.` operator executes the method, but only if the object reference is not null. This avoids exceptions during the initialization or termination phases of an application.

Publishing event-based observable data

Similarly, we add a resource for our motion detector. But for this resource, we will use the acknowledged service, since missing a value when expecting one might have serious consequences:

```
this.motionResource = this.coapEndpoint.Register("/Motion",
    (req, resp) =>
    {
        string s;

        if (this.lastMotion.HasValue)
            s = this.lastMotion.Value ? "true" : "false";
        else
            s = "-";

        resp.Respond(CoapCode.Content, s, 64);
    }, Notifications.Acknowledged, "Motion detector.", null, null,
    new int[] { PlainText.ContentFormatCode });
```

We will use this resource to illustrate event-based observable data. When the motion detector changes value, we don't want a delay in the sending of the new value to any subscribers, as we want the value to be sent immediately. To do this, we also call the `TriggerAll()` method on the resource, but this time, without an interval parameter, and only when we want the value to change. We update our event handler that is called when the motion detector pin changes value:

```
this.lastMotion = (value == PinState.HIGH);
this.motionResource?.TriggerAll();
```

Now the resource will be triggered immediately when the motion detector value changes. Having done that, we add a time interval-based trigger to the resource as well, but with a longer time interval. This will ensure the receiver knows the resource still works and that the subscription is alive, even when the value does not change. It also makes sure the underlying DTLS session is kept alive. We add an interval of 1 minute:

```
this.motionResource?.TriggerAll(new TimeSpan(0, 1, 0));
```

More advanced algorithms can be used to decide when an observable resource should be triggered. One could allow the client to decide when a resource is to be updated, for instance using query parameters in the subscription request.

Choosing the desired representation

As in HTTP, CoAP supports **RESTful** interfaces. This means that the same resource can be represented in different ways, based on the preferences of the client. We will create a momentary resource that returns all momentary values when called. While the previous resources only support plain text responses, the momentary resource will support XML and JSON as well. The actual representation will be chosen based on the Accept header provided by the client. If no Accept header is provided, plain text will be returned by default:

```
this.momentaryResource = this.coapEndpoint.Register("/Momentary",
    (req, resp) =>
    {
        if (req.IsAcceptable(Xml.ContentFormatCode))
            this.ReturnMomentaryAsXml(req, resp);
        else if (req.IsAcceptable(Json.ContentFormatCode))
            this.ReturnMomentaryAsJson(req, resp);
        else if (req.IsAcceptable(PlainText.ContentFormatCode))
            this.ReturnMomentaryAsPlainText(req, resp);
        else if (req.Accept.HasValue)
            throw new CoapException(CoapCode.NotAcceptable);
        else
            this.ReturnMomentaryAsPlainText(req, resp);
    }, Notifications.Acknowledged, "Momentary values.",
    null, null, new int[] { Xml.ContentFormatCode,
    Json.ContentFormatCode, PlainText.ContentFormatCode });
```

Returning CoAP content

To illustrate how to return content in CoAP, let's look at the plain text example. The XML and JSON examples are analogous. Content encoding and decoding is based on the same encoding/decoding principles as defined in the Waher.Content library, which maps objects in memory to and from their corresponding Internet Content Types and binary encodings. CoAP works with Content Format codes instead, and a much-reduced set of Internet Content Types that are supported, as described earlier. So, to return plain text, we simply build a string and return it as follows. We've chosen a block size of 64 bytes. Any payload larger than this will be automatically divided into blocks, each one sent separately. The blocks are automatically reassembled at the receiving end:

```
private void ReturnMomentaryAsPlainText(CoapMessage Request,
    CoapResponse Response)
{
    StringBuilder s = new StringBuilder();
```

```
s.Append("Timestamp: ");
s.AppendLine(DateTime.Now.ToUniversalTime().ToString());

if (this.lastLight.HasValue)
{
        s.Append("Light: ");
        s.Append(ToString(this.lastLight.Value, 2));
        s.AppendLine(" %");
}

if (this.lastMotion.HasValue)
{
        s.Append("Motion detected: ");
        s.AppendLine(this.lastMotion.Value ? "true" : "false");
}

Response.Respond(CoapCode.Content, s.ToString(), 64);
}
```

To facilitate implementation, you can also override the content format selected during encoding by explicitly providing the content format you wish to use. Since both XML and JSON are text based, we can encode them as strings and override the content format with that corresponding to the actual code we want to use. This simplifies matters, since you don't need to return an XmlDocument object to get it encoded as XML. You just encode it as a string, and explicitly set the content format to its XML counterpart:

```
Response.Respond(CoapCode.Content, s.ToString(), 64,
    new CoapOptionContentFormat(Xml.ContentFormatCode));
```

The same applies to JSON:

```
Response.Respond(CoapCode.Content, s.ToString(), 64,
    new CoapOptionContentFormat(Json.ContentFormatCode));
```

 The different CoAP Option classes that you can use, in both requests and responses, are available in the Waher.Networking.CoAP.Options namespace.

The XML and JSON serializations used in the GitHub CoAP projects mimic the ones made for HTTP, except the output has been shortened to illustrate constrained bandwidth devices normally targeted by CoAP, and to minimize the number of blocks required to transport the content.

Adding a control resource to our actuator

Out actuator will have a simpler interface. We will only register one observable resource called `Output`. It will return the current state of the output. Clients can subscribe to changes to the resource to be notified whenever the output changes, for any reason. Apart from adding a `GET` method handler, we will also add a `POST` method handler, allowing clients to change the output from the network. We begin by adding the `GET` method handler:

```
this.outputResource = this.coapEndpoint.Register("/Output",
    (req, resp) =>
    {
        string s;

        if (this.output.HasValue)
            s = this.output.Value ? "true" : "false";
        else
            s = "-";

        resp.Respond(CoapCode.Content, s, 64);
```

The resource returns a simple Boolean value (`true` or `false`), depending on the state of the output. If the state is unknown, – is returned. The response will be encoded as plain text in both cases.

Responding to change requests

We follow up by adding the `POST` method. We implement this as an asynchronous method. The library supports both synchronous responses and asynchronous responses. The main difference is that you must trap any exceptions in asynchronous methods, unless you want the application to terminate unexpectedly if one is thrown.

The first thing we do is try to decode the payload in the request. The library does this for you if the request comes with a content format specified. If one is missing, we decode the payload as if it were plain text. We also use the `CommonTypes.TryParse` method, which is forgiving. It recognizes 1, `true`, `yes`, and `on` as true values, and 0, `false`, `no`, and `off` as false values, using case-insensitive comparisons. If we're unable to understand the request, we return an error using an `RST` message. Otherwise, we simply state that the operation has been successful, and that the state has been `Changed`:

```
}, async (req, resp) =>
{
    try
    {
```

```
        string s = req.Decode() as string;
        if (s == null && req.Payload != null)
            s = Encoding.UTF8.GetString(req.Payload);

        if (s == null || !CommonTypes.TryParse(s,
            out bool Output))
            resp.RST(CoapCode.BadRequest);
        else
        {
            resp.Respond(CoapCode.Changed);
            await this.SetOutput(Output, req.From.ToString());
        }
    }
}
catch (Exception ex)
{
        Log.Critical(ex);
}
```

There are four message types in CoAP: Acknowledged messages called **Confirmable** messages (CON), Unacknowledged messages called **Non-confirmable** messages (NON), **Acknowledgement** messages (ACK), and Error messages called **Reset** messages (RST).

Typically, requests are made using CON, and asynchronous messages are sent using CON or NON. Error responses are returned using RST. You can also stop observing resources using an RST message. Responses can be sent back either **piggy-backed** on an ACK or in a separate CON or NON message. In a synchronous resource, the response is probably piggy-backed on the ACK, to avoid having to send two messages. Asynchronous resources can respond immediately using an ACK message, if one is required, and then send the response in a separate CON or NON message when the response is ready.

We also tell the resource to send event notifications using the Acknowledged messaging service, to avoid important state changes getting lost:

```
}, Notifications.Acknowledged, "Digital Output.", null, null,
    new int[] { PlainText.ContentFormatCode });
```

Adding output triggers

As we did for the other observable resources we added to the sensor, we need to specify when the output resource is to be triggered. We mimic the motion detector setup in that we first add a longer interval of 1 minute to let the subscriber know the subscription is active:

```
this.outputResource?.TriggerAll(new TimeSpan(0, 1, 0));
```

We then update the `SetOutput` method to trigger the resource whenever the resource is changed, whether internally or from an incoming request:

```
internal async Task SetOutput(bool On, string Actor)
{
    ...

    this.outputResource?.TriggerAll();
}
```

Testing your devices

You are now ready to test your new CoAP-enabled devices. The easiest way to do this is to use a publicly available CoAP test tool. In this book, we will use the *Copper (Cu)* plugin from Firefox, which adds the `coap` URI scheme to the browser and allows you to explore CoAP resources easily. In the next chapter, we will show how you can create CoAP clients communicating with CoAP servers using the `CoapEndpoint` class.

 The Copper (Cu) plugin can be found at `https://addons.mozilla.org/sv-se/firefox/addon/copper-270430/`. If your CoAP server device is made available online, you can also use `http://coap.me/` to test it. Check `http://coap.technology/tools.html` for a list of the different tools available.

Discovering the contents of your device

Now, open Firefox and install the *Copper (Cu)* plugin. Then navigate to your sensor device by simply entering `coap://IP_ADDRESS/` into the address field of the browser; you replace `IP_ADDRESS` with the actual IP address of your device. Once you press *Enter, Copper (Cu)* is shown.

In UWP, you cannot connect to your device using the loopback interface. To connect to a UWP app running locally, do so from another machine in the network.

Now press the **Discover** button. By doing that, a CoAP GET request is made to the /.well-known/core resource. This is a resource that is built automatically by the CoAP endpoint class. It describes registered resources according to a link format specified in CoRE. We will learn more about CoRE in the next chapter. The resources appear in the browser window. Notice that observable resources are displayed differently to non-observable resources:

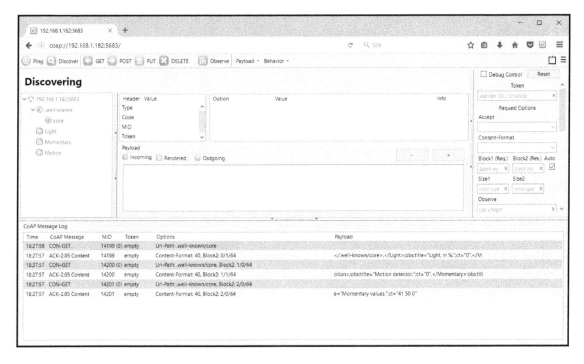

Discovery of the sensor CoAP interface

You can now select any of the resources you see and press the **GET** button. Doing that will perform a GET on the resource. You can see the actual CoAP communication taking place in the bottom part of the browser window. The **Incoming** tab in the center portion of the window will display the result. Pressing the **Observe** button will make a subscription to the corresponding resource. You can then see the value update in the window every time the device sends a notification message. Press the **Cancel** button to cancel the subscription.

Make sure you notice the difference between acknowledged messages and unacknowledged messages by subscribing to the Light and Motion resources. Also notice the difference between interval updates and updates triggered by events.

 If your client supports CoAP over DTLS, you can also use the URI scheme coaps to interact with your device securely.

Controlling your device

In the same way, you can navigate to your activator device and press the **Discover** button. You should see your Output resource. As with the resources on the sensor, you can read the resource and subscribe to it by pressing the **GET** and **Observe** buttons respectively. But you can also control it. You do that by writing the value you want to send to the device in the **Outgoing** tab in the central portion of the browser window. Try writing 1 here, and then press the **POST** button. Then write 0 and press **POST**. You should see how the output toggles. You can also see the status code of the action in the status area, as well as the round-trip time (**RTT**) just below the buttons. If you're observing the resource at the same time, you'll get notified of the changes as well. You can also check the corresponding checkbox in the app window, and see how that generates notifications as well:

Controlling the actuator

Securing your devices

Up to this point, we've only used unsecured and unencrypted CoAP. This should only be done while developing, and in closed networks. On the internet, and if the data is personal, CoAP should always be *encrypted,* and access to the device should always be *authenticated* and *authorized.* All these things can be managed directly by the DTLS layer.

To enable DTLS, we create our CoAP endpoint in a different manner:

```
this.coapEndpoint = new CoapEndpoint(
    CoapEndpoint.DefaultCoapsPort, this.users);
```

Here, we utilize the `IUserSource` source of `users` defined in the previous chapters. Remember that it defined one user, with the username `MIoT` and the password `rox`. The password was hashed, however, and it is this hash that will be used as a *pre-shared key*. The username acts as the *identity* used by DTLS to identify the *pre-shared key*. So, to access the device using these settings, a session needs to be established by the device using DTLS and the PSK identity of `MIoT` and the binary pre-shared key of:

```
SHA-256(UTF-8-Encode("rox" + ":" + DEVICE_ID))
```

The DEVICE_ID is the ID of the device. You can find it in the log. Unfortunately, you cannot use the Copper (Cu) add-on to test DTLS, but the next chapter will provide you with examples of how to test this.

You can enable both unencrypted and encrypted CoAP communications on the endpoint by creating the endpoint in the following manner:

The string after the user source, if not empty, limits access to the endpoint to users with the corresponding privileges only. The two last Boolean parameters determine if loopback interfaces can be used for reception or transmission. But since loopback is not enabled in UWP apps, we set these to `false`.

```
this.coapEndpoint = new CoapEndpoint(
        new int[] { CoapEndpoint.DefaultCoapPort },
        new int[] { CoapEndpoint.DefaultCoapsPort },
        this.users, string.Empty, false, false);
```

If unencrypted CoAP is enabled on the device, make sure the unencrypted port is not published on the internet. Only encrypted ports should be available on the internet.

Limitations of CoAP

As with HTTP, CoAP suffers from a topology problem. You need to choose in which direction communication is to be performed. If a firewall exists between two endpoints, the client needs to be the one residing inside the firewall, and the server needs to reside outside. The alternative is to open a hole in the firewall to allow external entities to access your device. Since management of such security privileges is difficult to manage in a dynamic network, vulnerabilities are easy to create unknowingly.

The next chapter will discuss a setup where we switch roles, and devices become clients instead of servers as in this example. In such cases, sensors report data to a central server, which can act as a **broker**. Brokers can be used to circumvent the topology problem by making sure devices behind different firewalls can still talk to each other through the broker.

Other limitations discussed in this chapter are consciously-made decisions that meet the needs of resource-constrained devices. Devices can be resource constrained in terms of memory, processing power, and network bandwidth. For this reason, CoAP is lightweight, with small telegrams. Large payloads are time-consuming to transfer, since they are divided into many blocks. Content encoding is also limited to a small set of recognized formats. If richer content is to be transferred, it must be transferred in a binary manner, using proprietary encoding or other protocols.

> For clients that are unable to communicate over UDP, or use DTLS, RFC 8323 defines a mechanism for communicating CoAP over TCP, TLS and WebSockets: `https://tools.ietf.org/html/rfc8323`
>
> Even though this removes many of the advantages of using CoAP, it might be necessary to support this in certain cases. Another method that can be used by clients that can only communicate using HTTP, such as web clients, is to use a HTTP<->CoAP proxy. This is defined in section 10 of RFC 7252: `https://tools.ietf.org/html/rfc7252#section-10`

Summary

In this chapter, you've been shown how you can use CoAP to publish RESTful interfaces for your devices. You've learned the basic principles behind CoAP and DTLS, its strengths and limitations, as well as the basics for the new observe or event subscription pattern. You've encoded content in CoAP, published sensor data and created observable resources and triggered events. You've also published control parameters and learned how to discover resources on a device. You know how to test your resources, and how to secure them using encryption, authentication, and authorization. In the next chapter, you will learn how the **Lightweight Machine-to-Machine**, or **LWM2M**, protocol can be used to provide your CoAP devices with an interoperability layer, making it easier to interact with CoAP devices from different manufacturers.

8
Interoperability

Up to this point, we have been satisfied with making our devices communicate using IP-based protocols. We've created our own communication interfaces. Doing so might be simple and a quick way to get started, but it has serious disadvantages: nobody else will be able to communicate without great effort, and we will not be able to use standardized software to help us with our tasks.

In this chapter, we will introduce the concept of application-level **interoperability**, how standardized technologies can help us in our work. You'll be introduced to **Constrained RESTful Environments (CoRE)**, the **Light-weight Machine-to-Machine enabler (LWM2M)**, a standardized object model for the management of devices based on CoAP and CoRE. **IPSO Smart Objects**, a set of standardized object interfaces for sensors and actuators, will also be presented. Standardized technologies will allow you to utilize existing software to interact and manage your devices, which in turn will allow you to spend more time on more productive tasks.

The chapter covers:

- An introduction to application-layer interoperability
- The difference between tight and loose coupling
- An introduction to CoRE
- An introduction to the LWM2M object model
- An introduction to IPSO Smart Objects
- An introduction to open software for LWM2M device management
- Publishing sensor data using LWM2M
- Reacting to actuator commands using LWM2M

Understanding the benefits of interoperability

While designing proprietary technologies might be exciting, fun, and a quick way to start experimenting and learning, it might not always be the best option. Often, there are alternatives. Others have often solved similar problems and created solutions that you might explore. Some of these might even include technologies that have been standardized by recognized standardization bodies. While these technologies might restrict you at first glance, they provide several positive advantages as well. One of these is peer review. Often, simple and obvious mistakes are caught and corrected during peer review. Experience gained during experimentation is fed back into the process, resulting in better design. Standards are more stable, and do not change quickly over time. Changes are also made in a way which avoid breaking compatibility. This makes your solutions based on them resilient and more future-proof. The technology is also more battle tested. The pros and cons are often well known.

Another big advantage of using standardized technologies is that you can use existing software to solve parts of your tasks. When building IoT applications, you must make sure your things are backed by the corresponding infrastructure. Building backend servers and services is time-consuming and often non-productive from a commercial point of view, as customers do not pay for infrastructure, only added value, most often in terms of functionality. When using standardized technologies, you often get access to open software you can use, to help you build your infrastructure and backend services. This allows you to focus more of your time on commercially productive tasks, making you more productive.

The benefits of application-layer standards

Although we have used standards in earlier chapters, these have been Transport-layer (TCP, UDP), Session-layer (MQTT), and Presentation-layer (HTTP, CoAP) standards, as displayed in Figure 1. Here, we've used the **Open Systems Interconnection** (**OSI**) model, as a good way to illustrate communication between applications in a network. The standards on different levels facilitate development and deployment. But we have had to add the remaining application-layer to our code, in a proprietary fashion. If we manage to use standardized technologies in the application layer as well, we can say that our application becomes **interoperable**. Devices from different manufacturers can interact, in a standardized manner, without having to resort to customized development. Products become replaceable. This opens systems up to competition, but also to opportunities.

The competition will provide for better devices and systems. Manufacturers using application-layer standards will be able to reach a market they would otherwise not have access to. You can use devices from others, while others can use your devices. You can use software from others, while others can use your software:

 Application-layer standards provide the basis for true **interoperability**.

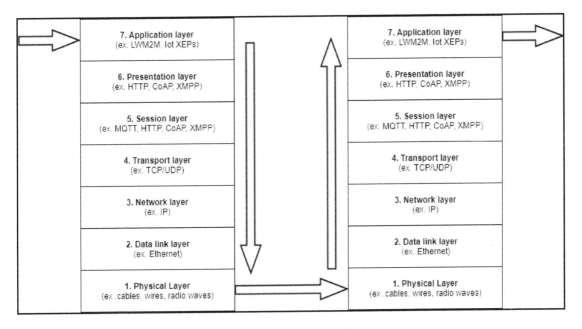

Information flow through the OSI model

Understanding coupling

Application-layer interfaces can be either **tightly coupled** or **loosely coupled**. Applications using tightly coupled interfaces require previous knowledge about the detailed functionality of each other. This makes them deterministic and simple to implement and test, but also difficult to extend outside of the intended use cases.

Applications using loosely coupled interfaces on the other hand, avoid making assumptions about the capabilities of the other party. Instead, metadata is used to describe the capabilities, allowing each participant to discover the capabilities of the other. Implementing loosely coupled architectures is more demanding, but the results become more flexible. It's easier to extend and to maintain backwards compatibility in loosely coupled architectures. Testing, on the other hand, becomes more difficult, since variations and complexity increases.

We will begin our journey into the realm of interoperability, by introducing some tightly coupled interfaces, based on CoAP. Since applications using CoAP strive to work well in resource constrained networks, tightly coupled interfaces provide a good option. These allow for more compact messages since a minimum of metadata is required to be transmitted. In the following sections, we will contrast these by presenting some loosely coupled alternatives and examine the differences.

Achieving interoperability using CoAP

Application-layer interoperability using CoAP can be achieved by the introduction of three technologies: CoRE, LWM2M, and IPSO Smart Objects.

Discovering resources using CoRE

We've already mentioned CoRE in the previous chapter. The CoAP protocol is an artefact published by the IETF CoRE Working Group. Another artefact is the **CoRE Link Format**, which we've used to find what resources are available on a device. By performing a GET method call on the /.well-known/core resource, the caller will receive a Link Format document, briefly describing what resources are available on the device, and some minimal set of corresponding information, such as if the resource is observable or not.

The following is an example Link Format document, generated by our SensorCoap application developed in the previous chapter. New lines have been added for readability. Resources are separated by commas (,), and parameters for each resource are separated by semicolons (;). The obs parameter tells the receiver the resource is observable. The title parameter provides a human-readable title. Content formatting is provided by the ct parameter. If multiple formats are supported, these are separated by spaces, and the entire set of values is encased by quotes ("). It's not much, but it is a start:

```
</.well-known/core>,
</Light>;obs;title="Light, in %.";ct="0",
```

```
</Motion>;obs;title="Motion detector.";ct="0",
</Momentary>;obs;title="Momentary values.";ct="41 50 0"
```

The CoRE Link Format is defined in RFC 6690:
https://tools.ietf.org/html/rfc6690

Understanding the LWM2M object model

LWM2M adds standardized application-layer functionality to your device. It does this by first dividing the device into **objects**. Each object can be instantiated into one or more **object instances**. Each object instance has a set of **resources**, which in turn can optionally contain a set of **resource instances**. The preceding image illustrates this relationship:

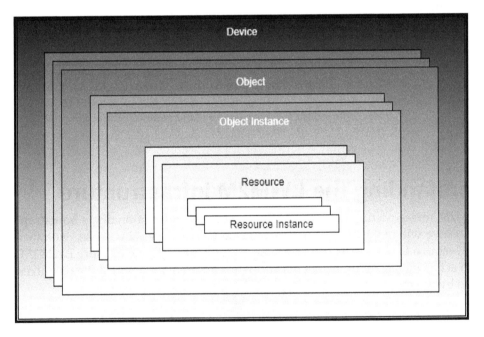

The LWM2M object model

Each object, object instance, resource, and resource instance are identified by non-negative integers. Each participant must know beforehand what these integers mean, what resources relate to such objects, and their corresponding functionality. LWM2M defines a set of objects that are used for managing the device. Later in this chapter, we will introduce IPSO Smart Objects, which define a set of objects that can be used by common types of sensors and actuators. The following table lists some of the common objects defined by LWM2M:

Index	Meaning
0	Security object: Defines the URL of a server and credentials for establishing a session with the server.
1	Server object: Defines which of the security objects are bootstrap servers and which are normal LWM2M servers.
2	Access control object: Defines access control lists, for who can access what resources.
3	Device object: Provides general information, such as make, model, and serial number of the device.

 LWM2M is standardized by **Open Mobile Alliance (OMA)**. You can read the specification at:
http://www.openmobilealliance.org/release/LightweightM2M/V1_0-20
170208-A/OMA-TS-LightweightM2M-V1_0-20170208-A.pdf

Understanding the LWM2M infrastructure

The LWM2M infrastructure consists of **clients**, **servers** and, optionally, a **bootstrap server**. The devices we will make in this book are all clients in an LWM2M sense, even though they act as servers in a CoAP sense. LWM2M clients **register** with one or more LWM2M servers, who then act as managers of the clients and who can read and control the resources published by the clients.

Bootstrapping is a method whereby the clients are configured in the network. This part is optional, and clients can be preconfigured with what servers to connect and register with. If such a configuration is not available, the client first establishes a session with a bootstrap server. The bootstrap server then provides information about what servers to register with, and any credentials required to establish secure sessions. When the bootstrap procedure is finished, the client connects to the set of servers provided and registers with those.

Registrations are made for a given amount of time. Before that time elapses, the client needs to update the registration, to keep it alive. This registration update procedure allows the servers to remove references to devices that are no longer alive.

Understanding LWM2M server operations

When the servers are aware of the clients, they can begin to interact with them. First, they discover what objects, instances, and resources are available. This is done using CoAP GET method calls on the device, object, or object instance levels. The LWM2M returns CoRE Link Format Documents, describing available child CoAP resources.

Servers can then begin to **read** LWM2M resource values, by executing CoAP GET calls on the resources or resource instances. Typically, resources must support a simple binary content format that is relatively compact, called the **Type-Length-Value**, or **TLV**, format. Optionally, the device can also support JSON, based on **SenML**, and a plain text format. Since resources are RESTful, the LWM2M server can choose what format the LWM2M client should respond with. If the resource is observable, the LWM2M server can also choose to **subscribe** to event notifications from the resource, using the CoAP observe pattern.

Some resources are writable and others are executable. Resources are **written** by the LWM2M server, by sending a PUT or POST request to the client, on the given resource, providing the new content as content payload, encoded using TLV. Some resources are content-less and can be used to model actions. When sending a PUT or POST request to such a resource, no content payload is required. Instead, the request results in the corresponding action being **executed**.

All objects, object instances, resources, and resource instances are published over CoAP as CoAP resources. The path of the corresponding resource consists of the integer identifiers of each corresponding step. The following are some examples:

Resource	Meaning
/3	Object 3, the device object.
/3/0	Instance 0, on Object 3-the default device object instance.
/3/0/11	Resource 11, on Object 3, object instance 0-Error code.
/3/0/11/1	Resource instance 1, or the Error code resource on the default device object instance.

Using IPSO Smart Objects

While the LWM2M interface provides an application-layer standard for device management over CoAP, it lacks by itself object definitions for sensors and actuators. These are, however, provided by the IPSO Alliance. Some IPSO Smart Objects that we will use are presented in the following table. Notice that there is a slight overlap:

Object	IPSO Smart Object definition
3200	IPSO Digital Input
3201	IPSO Digital Output
3202	IPSO Analogue Input
3203	IPSO Analogue Output
3300	IPSO Generic Sensor
3301	IPSO Illuminance Sensor
3302	IPSO Presence Sensor
3306	IPSO Actuation
3320	IPSO Percentage

For a list of defined object types available for LWM2M, see:
`http://www.openmobilealliance.org/wp/OMNA/LwM2M/LwM2MRegistry.html`

IPSO Smart Object descriptions can be downloaded from: `https://www.ipso-alliance.org/ipso-community/resources/smart-objects-interoperability/`

You can participate in the development of existing and new IPSO Smart Objects through this GitHub
repository: `https://github.com/IPSO-Alliance/pub`

Adding LWM2M to our devices

We are now ready to implement LWM2M in our projects. To do this, we create two new projects which we will call `SensorLwm2m` and `ActuatorLwm2m`, copying the corresponding code from the `SensorCoap` and `ActuatorCoap` projects. This allows us to immediately inherit what we've done to enable CoAP in our devices. We use the same hardware we've used in previous chapters. We add the `Waher.Networking.LWM2M.UWP` NuGet package to both projects.

 For .NET standard, .NET Core, or traditional .NET Framework projects, you can use the `Waher.Networking.LWM2M` NuGet instead. Universal Windows Platform apps use different libraries and runtime binaries when it comes to accessing network adaptors. For this reason, it requires a somewhat modified version of the original library.

We must also make sure to initialize the runtime inventory of classes with a reference to the `LWM2M` library assembly, at the beginning of the application, to make sure content encoding and decoding includes the content formats defined in it:

```
Types.Initialize(
    typeof(FilesProvider).GetTypeInfo().Assembly,
    typeof(RuntimeSettings).GetTypeInfo().Assembly,
    typeof(IContentEncoder).GetTypeInfo().Assembly,
 typeof(ICoapContentFormat).GetTypeInfo().Assembly,
    typeof(IDtlsCredentials).GetTypeInfo().Assembly,
    typeof(Lwm2mClient).GetTypeInfo().Assembly,
    typeof(App).GetTypeInfo().Assembly);
```

 We must not forget to add the `internetClientServer` capability to our set of capabilities in the `Package.appxmanifest` files as well:

```
<Capability Name="internetClientServer" />
```

Creating an LWM2M client

We begin by declaring a new field member of type `Lwm2mClient` (defined in the namespace `Waher.Networking.Lwm2m`):

```
private Lwm2mClient lwm2mClient = null;
```

The `Lwm2mClient` class provides the basic LWM2M functionality described previously. When we instantiate it, we need to provide it with a client name, a reference to the CoAP endpoint that will be used for communication, and some basic LWM2M objects. We begin by providing it with the security object (0), the server object (1), the access control object (2), and the device object (3). We don't have to provide any details for the first three. We will let the bootstrap process take care of filling these with values. The device object, however, requires some parameters for us to fill in, including manufacturer, serial number, and version numbers. These values will be presented to the server and can be used to identify the type of device the client represents. Make sure to update these values so they correspond to what you're doing:

```
this.lwm2mClient = new Lwm2mClient("MIoT:Sensor:" + this.deviceId,
   this.coapEndpoint,
   new Lwm2mSecurityObject(),
   new Lwm2mServerObject(),
   new Lwm2mAccessControlObject(),
   new Lwm2mDeviceObject("Waher Data AB", "SensorLwm2m",
      this.deviceId, "1.0", "Sensor", "1.0", "1.0"));
```

For the actuator, all mentions of `Sensor` should be replaced by `Actuator`.

Performing the bootstrap procedure

We will use a bootstrap server in our example. When the application starts, we want it to connect to the previous bootstrap server to see if there's any new information for it. If there's no configured bootstrap server available, we provide a reference to one. Data provided by the bootstrap server will be persisted in the persistence layer. This data will include what LWM2M servers to register with, and what credentials to use. So, to begin, we first need to load any previous data, if such is available. Directly after creating our client, we call the `LoadBootstrapInfo` method:

```
await this.lwm2mClient.LoadBootstrapInfo();
```

We then initiate the bootstrap procedure. If no bootstrap information was found, we ask it to connect to a default bootstrap server provided by eclipse.org, situated at leshan.eclipse.org, port number `5783` (not `5683`, the default CoAP port, which goes to the LWM2M server, not the bootstrap server):

```
if (!await this.lwm2mClient.RequestBootstrap())
  await this.lwm2mClient.RequestBootstrap(
  new Lwm2mServerReference("leshan.eclipse.org", 5783));
```

The bootstrap procedure might take some time to complete, depending on whether the client is required to respect a hold-off time or not. Such a **client hold-off time** is used to avoid spamming the bootstrap server if many clients awake simultaneously, for instance, after a power outage.

Leshan is an open source LWM2M server implementation available on GitHub. It provides simple web interfaces that you can use to interact with your LWM2M clients. It also contains a bootstrap server. Using its APIs, you can interact with LWM2M clients registered with it. You can choose to use the public sandboxes available online, hosted by eclipse.org, or download and host your own servers. Some links of interest are:

GitHub: `https://github.com/eclipse/leshan`

Public server sandbox: `http://leshan.eclipse.org/`

Public Bootstrap server sandbox: `http://leshan.eclipse.org/bs/`

Registering with the LWM2M servers

As soon as the bootstrap procedure completes, the LWM2M client will automatically register itself with the LWM2M servers configured to it by the bootstrap server. But if you do not want to use a bootstrap server to configure your device, you need to perform this registration yourself:

```
this.lwm2mClient.Register(60,
  new Lwm2mServerReference("leshan.eclipse.org", 5683));
```

The first parameter provides the lifetime, in seconds, of the registration. You should perform a registration update before that time elapses for instance, after half that time. You do that by just making the following call:

```
this.lwm2mClient.RegisterUpdate();
```

Deregistration is performed automatically by disposing the client object. If you want to deregister, without disposing the object, you can simply call the `Deregister()` method.

Following the progress

You can keep track of LWM2M state changes by registering event handlers on any of a series of events published on the `Lwm2mClient` object:

Event	Raised when
`OnStateChanged`	The internal state of the LWM2M client changes.
`OnBootstrapCompleted`	The bootstrap procedure completes.
`OnBootstrapFailed`	The bootstrap procedure fails. Use this event handler to schedule a retry at a suitable time.
`OnRegistrationSuccessful`	The registration procedure completes on one server.
`OnRegistrationFailed`	The registration procedure fails on one server. There's no need to schedule a retry when this happens, since this is automatically performed by the LWM2M client object.
`OnDeregistrationSuccessful`	The deregistration procedure completes on one server.
`OnDeregistrationFailed`	The deregistration procedure fails on one server.
`OnRebootRequest`	A server requests the client to perform a reboot.

Two events require special mention. The `OnBootstrapFailed` event is raised if the bootstrap procedure failed for some reason. This probably means that the LWM2M client lacks the information it requires to register itself with the LWM2M servers. When this happens, we should reschedule an attempt to perform the bootstrap procedure. We can use the `ScheduleEvent()` method on the `CoapEndpoint` object for this purpose.

A server can also request the client to reboot, for management purposes. When this happens, the `OnRebootRequest` event is raised. UWP apps cannot ask the application or system to reboot programmatically, however. So, when this event is raised, we can choose to simply reinitiate the bootstrap procedure instead.

Defining Smart Objects

We are now ready to add our first IPSO Smart Object. The *IPSO Smart Object Guidelines*, from the *Smart Objects Starter Pack*, contains the object definitions we need. If you haven't downloaded these already, do so now. The **Digital Input** smart object is defined as follows:

Name	Res.	R/W/E	M/O	Type	Description
Digital Input State	5500	R	M	Boolean	The current state of a digital input.
Digital Input Counter	5501	R	O	Integer	The cumulative value of the active state detected
Digital Input Polarity	5502	RW	O	Boolean	The polarity of the digital input as a Boolean (0 = Normal, 1= Reversed)
Digital Input Debounce Period	5503	RW	O	Integer	The debounce period in milliseconds.
Digital Input Edge Selection	5504	RW	O	Integer	The edge selection as an integer (1 = Falling edge, 2 = Rising edge, 3 = Both Rising and Falling edge)
Digital Input Counter Reset	5505	E	O		Reset the Counter value
Application Type	5750	RW	O	String	The application type of the sensor or actuator as a string, for instance, "Air Pressure".
Sensor Type	5751	R	O	String	The type of the sensor, for instance, PIR type.

We notice that the object only has one mandatory resource, the current state. In our implementation, we will also provide support for the counter and counter reset resources, as well as the two string resources describing the sensor. There is one command resource, the counter reset command. It can be **executed** (**E**). Four resources can be **written** to (**W**), and all, except the command, can be **read** (**R**).

Creating the digital input object class

To begin our implementation, we create a subfolder to our project called IPSO. In it, we will put all IPSO-related classes. We begin by defining a class for the Digital Input object. It's quite small: all it does is provide a placeholder for an array of Digital Input object instances, and define the object ID:

```
public class DigitalInput : Lwm2mObject
{
  public DigitalInput(params DigitalInputInstance[] Inputs)
    : base(3200, Inputs)
  {
  }
}
```

Creating the digital input object instance class

Similarly, we create a class for the Digital Input Object Instance. In it, we define member fields for each resource our object instances will have:

```
public class DigitalInputInstance : Lwm2mObjectInstance
{
  private Lwm2mResourceBoolean state;
  private Lwm2mResourceInteger counter;
  private Lwm2mResourceCommand counterReset;
  private Lwm2mResourceString applicationType;
  private Lwm2mResourceString sensorType;
```

In the constructor, we create the corresponding resource objects, using their types, and providing them with the corresponding resource identities, names, and initial values. We also define whether we want the resource to be writable or not, and whether writable, if we want the resource to persist the value:

```
public DigitalInputInstance(ushort InstanceId, bool? CurrentState,
  string ApplicationType, string SensorType)
  : base(3200, InstanceId)
{
  this.state = new Lwm2mResourceBoolean("Digital Input State",
    3200, InstanceId, 5500, false, false, CurrentState);
  this.counter = new Lwm2mResourceInteger(
    "Digital Input Counter", 3200, InstanceId, 5501,
    false, false, 0, false);
  this.counterReset = new Lwm2mResourceCommand(
    "Digital Input Counter Reset", 3200, InstanceId, 5505);
  this.applicationType = new Lwm2mResourceString(
```

```
    "Application Type", 3200, InstanceId, 5750,
      true, true, ApplicationType);
  this.sensorType = new Lwm2mResourceString("Sensor Type", 3200,
    InstanceId, 5751, false, false, SensorType);
```

For our command, we provide a simple event handler that will be called when the command is executed. We reset the value, and trigger all corresponding resources, to make sure subscribers get alerted about the event:

```
this.counterReset.OnExecute += (sender, e) =>
{
  this.counter.IntegerValue = 0;
  this.counter.TriggerAll();
  this.TriggerAll();
};
```

Finally, we need to register the resources just created so that the object instance can publish them correctly:

```
this.Add(this.state);
this.Add(this.counter);
this.Add(this.counterReset);
this.Add(this.applicationType);
this.Add(this.sensorType);
}
```

To create a resource with dynamically calculated values, add an event handler for the OnBeforeGet event on the resource object. It allows you to calculate and set a new value before the value is sent to the server.

Defining trigger intervals for observable resources

Object instances and their readable resources are, by default observable, in LWM2M. All we need to do is tell the framework when event notifications should be triggered. As in the previous chapter, we will first define a long interval with which the resources are triggered by default. This will allow subscribers to keep track of what subscriptions are still alive. Defining trigger intervals must be done after the resources have been registered with the CoapEndpoint class. For this reason, it cannot be done in the constructor. We therefore override the AfterRegister() method to define trigger intervals:

```
public override void AfterRegister(Lwm2mClient Client)
{
  base.AfterRegister(Client);
```

```
    this.TriggerAll(new TimeSpan(0, 1, 0));
    this.state.TriggerAll(new TimeSpan(0, 1, 0));
    this.counter.TriggerAll(new TimeSpan(0, 1, 0));
}
```

Notifying subscribers manually

We also need to be able to manually trigger our observable notifications. For digital input objects, this is easy. We do this every time the digital input changes state:

```
public void Set(bool Value)
{
    if (!this.state.BooleanValue.HasValue ||
        this.state.BooleanValue.Value != Value)
    {
        this.state.BooleanValue = Value;
        this.state.TriggerAll();

        if (Value)
        {
            this.counter.IntegerValue++;
            this.counter.TriggerAll();
        }

        this.TriggerAll();
    }
}
```

Instantiating the digital input object

We are now almost done with our digital input smart object. In our application class, we create a field member `digitalInput0` to hold a reference to our digital input object instance. We instantiate it, by adding it to the list of LWM2M objects supported by our LWM2M client:

```
this.lwm2mClient = new Lwm2mClient("MIoT:Sensor:" + this.deviceId,
    this.coapEndpoint,
    new Lwm2mSecurityObject(),
    new Lwm2mServerObject(),
    new Lwm2mAccessControlObject(),
    new Lwm2mDeviceObject("Waher Data AB", "SensorLwm2m",
        this.deviceId, "1.0", "Sensor", "1.0", "1.0"),
    new DigitalInput(
        this.digitalInput0 = new DigitalInputInstance(0,
```

```
        this.lastMotion, "Motion Detector", "PIR")));
```

The last thing we need to do, to get our digital input object to work, is to report new values to it. We update our pin update event, to report new values to our digital input object:

```
bool Input = (value == PinState.HIGH);
this.lastMotion = Input;
this.digitalInput0?.Set(Input);
this.motionResource?.TriggerAll();
this.momentaryResource?.TriggerAll();
```

 Now that you know how to publish one LWM2M sensor object, the procedure for publishing more sensor objects and object instances is straightforward. The `SensorLwm2m` project in the GitHub repository adds objects and object instances representing an analog input, two generic sensors, one illuminance sensor, one presence sensor, and one percentage sensor to the application. They will present the motion detector and light sensor values through different IPSO Smart Object interfaces, allowing for increased interoperability.

Creating the digital output object instance class

We now proceed with the actuator. We prepare the `ActuatorLwm2m` project in the same way as the `SensorLwm2m` project. The main difference is the types of objects and object instances we choose to add to the `Lwm2mClient` object.

Just as there's an IPSO Digital Input object, there's an IPSO Digital Output smart object. It is quite similar with one main difference: the main parameter is writable, and we need to connect the value of that parameter to our output. Following the steps outlined previously, for the creation of the `DigitalInput` and `DigitalInputInstance` classes, we create similar `DigitalOutput` and `DigitalOutputInstance` classes. When it is time to create the main resource, the digital output state, we make sure to trap the `OnRemoteUpdate` event on the resource. We make sure to forward this event, as follows:

```
this.state = new Lwm2mResourceBoolean("Digital Output State",
    ObjectInstanceId, InstanceId, 5550, true, false,
    CurrentState);

this.state.OnRemoteUpdate += (sender, e) =>
{
    this.state.TriggerAll();
    this.TriggerAll();
```

```
  try
  {
    this.OnRemoteUpdate?.Invoke(this, e);
  }
  catch (Exception ex)
  {
    Log.Critical(ex);
  }
};
```

Where the OnRemoteUpdate event is defined as follows:

```
public event CoapRequestEventHandler OnRemoteUpdate = null;
```

Setting remotely updated output values

We then only need to trap these events from our main application. We instantiate the IPSO Digital Output smart object as follows:

```
this.lwm2mClient = new Lwm2mClient("MIoT:Actuator:" +
  this.deviceId, this.coapEndpoint,
  new Lwm2mSecurityObject(),
  new Lwm2mServerObject(),
  new Lwm2mAccessControlObject(),
  new Lwm2mDeviceObject("Waher Data AB", "ActuatorLwm2m",
    this.deviceId, "1.0", "Actuator", "1.0", "1.0"),
  new DigitalOutput(
    this.digitalOutput0 = new DigitalOutputInstance(0,
    this.output.HasValue && this.output.Value, "Relay")));
```

It's then easy to forward incoming changes to the rest of the application by attaching an event handler on the OnRemoteUpdate event we just created:

```
this.digitalOutput0.OnRemoteUpdate += async (sender, e) =>
{
  try
  {
    await this.SetOutput(this.digitalOutput0.Value,
      e.Request.From.ToString());
  }
  catch (Exception ex)
  {
    Log.Critical(ex);
  }
};
```

Testing your LWM2M device

We are now ready to test our LWM2M devices. You can use any LWM2M-enabled server, either publicly available on the internet or hosted by yourself. This is one of the benefits of using standards. The examples in this chapter assume we use the publicly available Leshan server sandbox hosted by eclipse.org. The following table summarizes some of the communication parameters:

LWM2M Server Web portal:	`http://leshan.eclipse.org/`
LWM2M CoAP/UDP port:	`5683`
LWM2M CoAP/DTLS/UDP port:	`5684`
Bootstrap portal:	`http://leshan.eclipse.org/bs/`
Bootstrap CoAP/UDP port:	`5783`
Bootstrap CoAP/DTLS/UDP port:	`5784`
Home page:	`https://eclipse.org/leshan/`
GitHub:	`https://github.com/eclipse/leshan`

Configuring the bootstrap server

The first step is to configure the bootstrap server. Go to the bootstrap portal and click **Add new client bootstrap configuration**. The web portal will allow you to create a bootstrap configuration, where the client connects to the bootstrap server using unencrypted CoAP, and then gets redirected to one LWM2M server using either unencrypted or encrypted CoAP. The interface supports configuring credentials using pre-shared keys, as shown in Figure 3. Add the name of the LWM2M client under **Client endpoint** and leave the **LWM2M Server URL** as it is. The default URL will work. We can reutilize the client name in the Identity field if we want, as long as we make sure to use the same identity when we configure the LWM2M server.

As a key, enter a random hexadecimal string. Also, add a similar configuration for the actuator:

Configuring the bootstrap server

 If you host a Leshan server locally, you will have more options on how to configure the bootstrap and LWM2M servers.

Configuring the LWM2M server

When the bootstrap server has been configured, we do a similar configuration in the LWM2M server. Go to the server portal, click the **Security** tab, and then click the **Add new client security configuration** button. Fill in the same information that you provided for the bootstrap server, as shown in following image:

New security configuration   ×

Client endpoint   MIoT:Sensor:c8c6797201f2406689c9698aeec75837

Security mode   Pre-Shared Key   ⌄

Identity   MIoT:Sensor:c8c6797201f2406689c9698aeec75837

Key   DB7329139E18443BA8B772AD37DDEA57

                                                      Close   Create

Configuring the LWM2M server

Interacting with your devices

After adding two client security configurations, you can now run your applications. If you click the **Clients** tab in the web portal, you will see them appear as they register. Click on any of the connected devices, to view their objects, object instances, and resources. You can also interact with them. Each object instance, or individual resource can be read, observed, or written to, and commands can be executed. Just press the **Read**, **Observe**, **Write**, and **Exec** buttons.

If the web interface does not update itself automatically, when something changes, try another browser. At the time of writing, Firefox could display the dynamic content and react to events.

Use the sensor to test the **Read** and **Observe** parameters. See how the different resource parameters work. Use the actuator to try the `write` command and see how you can use it to control the relay. Since there are multiple object interfaces showing similar things, try to observe all resource parameters, and see how they update on all objects, when you write to only one.

Summary

In this chapter, you've been shown how application-layer standards can help you in your development by providing third-party infrastructure software you can use, as well as enabling them to interact with others without having to customize your code.

As you've seen, tightly-coupled interfaces are straightforward to implement. However, if you want to do something that goes beyond the interfaces that have already been established, it all becomes a bit tricky. All of the software interacting with your devices needs to be updated to take into consideration the new interfaces you create. If you want your interfaces standardized, it becomes even harder.

In this chapter, you've learned also learned the basics of CoRE, the LWM2M object model and IPSO Smart Objects. You've been introduced to the Leshan project and used it to publish sensor data and actuator control parameters using LWM2M. In the coming chapters, you will learn more about **XMPP** and how its **loosely coupled** IoT interfaces can be used to perform similar tasks, but without locking you into predefined object templates.

9
Social Interaction with Your Devices Using XMPP

In the previous chapters of this book, we discussed different relatively simple protocols and communication patterns to illustrate how communication can be done with devices, in different ways. In the second part of this book, we will introduce a more advanced paradigm of communication that allows us to do much more interesting things with our devices, in a more secure and interoperable, yet flexible, manner. The following chapters will be dedicated to the **Extensible Messaging and Presence Protocol** (**XMPP**). Since it provides such a rich set of tools that Internet of things (IoT) developers can use, the scope of the XMPP protocol will be presented throughout several of the following chapters.

This chapter will focus on social interaction with things. It covers:

- An introduction to XMPP
- The basics of XMPP Extension Protocols (XEPs)
- Trust-based communication
- Request/response pattern using XMPP
- Event subscription pattern using XMPP
- Publish/subscribe pattern using XMPP
- Controlling devices
- Human-to-machine chat interfaces

Introducing XMPP

The **XMPP** was developed within the **Jabber** project in the late 1990s as a means to provide the necessary communication infrastructure for **instant messaging** (or chat) applications. These kinds of applications required an open, flexible, and extensible protocol that allowed peers to communicate with each other, even if they were residing behind separate firewalls.

The protocol has since grown and covers a lot of different use cases requiring instant messaging (that is, asynchronous messaging between peers) that are not related to chat. The protocol is also maintained by a separate organization, called the **XMPP Standards Foundation** (**XSF**). The core of the XMPP protocol is also standardized by the Internet Engineering Task Force (IETF). **XMPP Extension Protocols** (**XEPs**) are maintained and published by the XSF.

Using XML

The XMPP protocol is based on the **Extensible Markup Language**, or **XML**. It is XML that makes the protocol **extensible**, in a well-defined manner. Since XML elements are defined by **namespaces**, it is easy to mix content from different parties, without mixing meaning or semantics. Namespaces also provide a mechanism to control versioning and maintaining backward compatibility as interfaces are developed. As long as you control a namespace, for instance, by using your own domain, you can freely extend the protocol with anything you like, without negatively affecting other entities in the network.

Understanding the value of brokers

By default, XMPP uses **brokers**, or **XMPP servers**, to relay communication between entities in the network. XMPP can work in a server-less mode as well, but the default mode of operation is for entities to connect to a broker. As we have seen in earlier chapters, a broker provides a lot of features to the network that are very valuable, especially for the IoT.

One such feature makes the network **topology independent**, or more topology independent. Since clients in the network connect to brokers, they can all reside behind separate firewalls and still communicate with each other. This is also a security feature since connections are outbound. Firewalls can block incoming connections without preventing clients inside the firewalls from communicating with each other.

Providing global scalability

Each broker operates on a **domain**, and each domain is protected by a domain certificate. Clients connect to the domain using Transmission Control Protocol (TCP) and Transport Layer Security (TLS) and validate the certificate. Connections can be normal **binary socket connections, EXI compressed connections, Bidirectional-streams Over Synchronous HTTP**, or **BOSH connections**. The latter is typically used by web clients. These connections are typically named **client-to-server**, or **c2s** connections.

 Encryption using TLS is optional. It is typically negotiated over the same connection. With the policy of **ubiquitous encryption**, more and more brokers require the use of TLS.

Brokers on different domains can interchange information through the process of **federation**. This requires that both brokers be accessible to each other. They can interconnect, and authenticate each other by validating the certificate of the other party. Through the process of **dial-back**, servers typically perform a dual connection to make sure the original caller is from the domain it claims to be. Once both parties have successfully identified the other, they can interchange communication between each other, and of each other's clients. These connections are named **server-to-server** or **s2s** connections.

 The default port for c2s connections is 5222, and for s2s connections, it is 5269.

It is the feature of the federation that makes the XMPP network **globally scalable**. Anyone can set up its own XMPP server or XMPP servers on domains it controls. As long as the brokers are reachable by other brokers, it can potentially communicate with any client on any of these brokers. As we will see, this communication can also be made in a secure manner.

Extending server functionality

The third type of connections are component connections. **Component connections** can be used by external software, typically running on the same machine as the broker, or in the same local area network, to extend the functionality of the server. Components are identified using **sub-domains** to the server domain. Clients can browse the server for available components and interact with them as if they were parts of the actual server.

Authenticating clients

Each broker is responsible for authenticating its clients. This is done using the extensible **Simple Authentication and Security Layer** (**SASL**). The broker references the authentication methods available, in order of preference, and the client chooses the first method it recognizes. Communication between entities in the network cannot begin before the clients have been successfully authenticated and activated by the corresponding broker.

Once a client has been authenticated, its authenticated identity will always be forwarded in any communication it performs. It is this federated mechanism of authenticated users and forwarding their authenticated identities that will have huge data protection implications, It simplifies security decisions a great deal for clients connected to the network, since clients do not have to identify each other, but are still able to make security decisions based on the identities of each other.

The principles of authentication, federation, and routing are defined in IETF RFC 6120: `https://tools.ietf.org/html/rfc6120`.

Understanding XMPP addresses

Typically, but not necessarily, brokers authenticate clients to accounts. Each account typically has an account name or username. When forming an **XMPP address**, this account name or username is called the **local part**. The XMPP address can have one to three parts. Apart from the local part, there is the **domain part**, which is simply the domain of the broker or a sub-domain. Finally, the address can also have a **resource part**. Since multiple connections can be made to the same account using the same account or username, the connections are distinguished by the use of a resource part, which is typically a random string, for security reasons. These three parts can be combined in different ways, to address different entities in the network:

Address format	Meaning
Domain	Addresses a broker, or one of its components if the domain represents a sub-domain.
Local@Domain	Addresses a user account on the broker identified by the domain part. Addresses of this kind are often referred to as Bare JIDs, or Bare Jabber IDs.
Local@Domain/Resource	Addresses a client connection made by a client to the account identified by the local part on the broker identified by the domain part. Addresses using this format are often referred to as Full JIDs.

The XMPP Address format is standardized in IETF RFC 6122:
`https://tools.ietf.org/html/rfc6122`.

XMPP clients in the network are often referred to as **peers**. Being a peer means being equal to those with whom you communicate. When referring to XMPP clients as clients, we typically refer to their role in the TCP network layer (OSI level 3), since they connect to the broker or server. On the network layer, the client and the server have two different roles. But once the XMPP session is established, and the XMPP client becomes active, it can communicate with any other XMPP client, as if it was a peer, or equal. Here, we refer to its role in the application layer (OSI level 7).

Using trust-based communication to secure the network

Instant messaging, such as that permitted by XMPP, and social networking, build on **trust**. Using the trust negotiated in your network, you can secure your Internet of Things applications in an efficient manner. Since all participants in the network are identified, and their identities are propagated in your network, it is easy for each thing to build a list of authenticated identities (in XMPP, it is called a **roster**), which should have access to its information. Since the identities, and their corresponding broker domains, are already authenticated, the things do not need to perform the authentication themselves.

In XMPP, trust between entities in the network is implemented using **presence subscriptions**. To be able to communicate effectively with another client, you need to have the Full JID of that client. Normally, only the Bare JID is available. The resource part of the corresponding client is normally random. The reason for this is to make sure the resource part cannot easily be guessed. Only entities with an approved presence subscription to that resource part will receive it when it is made available.

A client who wants to receive the resource part of another, therefore, sends a presence subscription request to the other. The other can choose to accept or reject this request. Once the presence subscription is accepted, the first will become aware of the presence of the second. The second can also choose to send a presence subscription to the first, in turn. If the first accepts this request, the presence subscription is mutual, and both will be informed about the presence of each other. Any presence subscription accepted can be canceled at a later time.

The option to block further requests and report the requestor for spam is also possible, as defined in XMPP extensions XEP-0191 and XEP-0377.

There are various ways in which presence subscriptions can be managed. The device itself can manage it or it can also be managed by another client. All clients connected to the same Bare JID will receive the requests. All clients will also become aware of the decisions made by any other clients connected to the same Bare JID. In the examples in this chapter, we will simply accept all requests. In later chapters, we will introduce a method of delegation of trust, where a provisioning server helps our things to make the correct decisions.

The principles of managing presence subscription and the roster are defined in IETF RFC 6121 at `https://tools.ietf.org/html/rfc6121`.

Understanding XMPP communication patterns

What makes XMPP so versatile, apart from its extensibility and scalability, is its **flexibility**. While many of the other protocols we've discussed only support one basic communication pattern, and some two, XMPP supports three of the most important communication patterns, from which most other communication patterns can be easily derived. Apart from the ability to send asynchronous messages, performing request/response and publish/subscribe, XMPP is also federated (globally scalable), uses brokers to avoid network topology limits, and allows for peer-to-peer communication (from the application layer, OSI level 7). Among the protocols presented in this book, XMPP is the only protocol with these capabilities:

	Async. Msg.	Req/Resp	Pub/Sub	Federation	Broker	P2P$_7$
MQTT			✓		✓	✓
HTTP		✓		✓		
CoAP	✓	✓		✓		
XMPP	✓	✓	✓	✓	✓	✓

Understanding stanzas

An XMPP client sends XML fragments on its XMPP connection. The root elements of these fragments are called **stanzas**. There are three basic types of stanzas, each one corresponding to one of the three basic communication patterns available: asynchronous message (`message`), request/respond (`iq`, short for Information Query), and Publish/Subscribe (`presence`).

XMPP has a second Publish/Subscribe mechanism as well, which is defined in XEP-0060.

There are five common attributes each stanza can have, most of which are optional at one stage or another:

Attribute	Meaning
id	It's possible to assign an identity to the stanza. This identity can be used in references. Typical use is in the request/response pattern. But it can be used elsewhere as well.
to	To whom a stanza is addressed. The server might provide this value, especially in the publish/subscribe case.
from	From whom a stanza is sent. The server provides or overwrites this value. It doesn't have to be provided by the sending client.
type	Provides further types of information about the stanza. Depends on which stanza is being used.
xml:lang	Optional way to identify the language used, as defined in IETF RFC: https://tools.ietf.org/html/rfc5646.

The address provided in the to attribute might work differently depending on the stanza being used. If a Full JID is provided, the stanza is delivered to the client connection that corresponds to that Full JID.

If a Bare JID is provided, the corresponding account is referenced. If a message stanza is sent to a Bare JID, the corresponding server might, or might not, forward the message to one or more of the corresponding clients. If an iq stanza is sent to a Bare JID, it is never forwarded to a client. Instead, it is processed by the server managing the corresponding account.

For presence stanzas, it is not necessary to provide a to attribute for clients. Instead, the stanza is forwarded to all clients in the roster, which have a presence subscription approved by the sender.

In all cases, the server sets the `from` attribute of the stanza to the Full JID of the sender. This allows the recipient to know from where the stanza came. It is also this feature that lets presence subscribers become aware of the resource part of the Full JID of the sender. Through this Full JID, the receiver will be able to send `iq` request/response stanzas to the original sender.

Extending XMPP

The first word in the acronym XMPP, the Extensible Messaging and Presence Protocol, highlights the **extensible** nature of XMPP. It is extensible in a well-defined, well-behaved and deterministic sense.

We have already mentioned that XMPP is based on XML. During the negotiation, the XML root element (level 1) is sent by both parties. It is this element that indicates to both parties that XMPP will be used. During the course of communication, XML fragments are sent. The root element of each such fragment (level 2 XML element) is called a stanza. The contents of the stanza, however, are defined by fully qualified XML elements (level 3 XML elements) in an extensible manner. Being fully qualified in XML means the elements have both a **local name** and a **namespace**. If you control the namespace, you can embed any valid XML content you like there, as long as you maintain your fragment within the maximum allowed stanza size defined by the server. Recipients of the stanza will only process it, if it recognizes the fully qualified name, and knows how to process it.

The maximum stanza size is server-specific. But RFC 6120 states that it must not be smaller than 10,000 bytes.

The XMPP Standards Foundation maintains a set of XMPP extensions, defining different such extensions and their corresponding semantics, for interoperability purposes. Most XMPP clients support a set of these extensions already, while other extensions are available as plugins to the clients. Yet other extensions must be implemented by the developer using the client.

A list of extensions maintained by the XMPP Standards Foundation can be seen at `https://xmpp.org/extensions/`.

Selecting a client library

In order to use XMPP in your projects, the easiest way is to use a predefined client library. Such a library will help you with the basics of connecting and maintaining an XMPP connection, allow you to define and add extensions, send and receive stanzas, and so on. It will also provide you with a basic set of extensions already implemented, and a mechanism to add plugins.

There are many libraries on the internet to choose from, too many to list here. The XSF publishes a shortened list of client libraries at https://xmpp.org/software/libraries.html.

In this book, we will use the Waher.Networking.XMPP client library, written in C#. It's available on GitHub and as NuGets (in two versions: one .NET Standard and one for the first generation Universal Windows Platform, UWP). There are also plugins available for the Internet of Things that we will use.

The operating principle of this library is simple. In the constructor, you define sufficient information to connect. You then connect calling the Connect method. The reception of standard stanzas triggers events on the client. Extensions are added by registering message, iq, and presence handlers on the client. During initialization, you simply provide the fully qualified names of the elements you extend the client with, and the corresponding callback methods the client will call when the corresponding extensions are referenced.

Selecting a broker

To use XMPP, you also need to select an XMPP broker. You have to choose if you want to host your own XMPP server under your own domain name or use a publicly available XMPP broker. There are many to choose from.

For a short list of XMPP server software, you can use to set up your own domain, visit https://xmpp.org/software/servers.html. To find a publicly available XMPP server, visit https://www.google.se/search?source=hp&q=public+xmpp+server.

In this book, we will use the XMPP broker available at waher.se. While not necessary for this chapter, it will help us in later chapters when we introduce provisioning.

Readers of this book can request an account at
`https://waher.se/Broker.md` and
`https://waher.se/RequestAccount.md`. Don't forget to mention this book
in the registration. Classes and organizations can request API keys at
`https://waher.se/RequestApiKey.md`. This will allow them to
automatically generate a given number of accounts securely. Please allow
some time for the application to be processed.

Adding XMPP to our devices

We now have sufficient information to begin using XMPP in our projects. To do this, we
create two new projects, which we will call `SensorXmpp` and `ActuatorXmpp`, copying the
corresponding code from the `Sensor` and `Actuator` projects as we have done earlier. As
with the previous chapters, we use the same hardware.

For reference, the projects are available on GitHub
at `https://github.com/PeterWaher/MIoT`.

We also add a series of NuGet packages to our projects:

NuGet	Description
`Waher.Networking.XMPP.UWP`	XMPP client library.
`Waher.Networking.XMPP.Sensor.UWP`	XMPP IoT sensor data plugin. Added to both projects.
`Waher.Networking.XMPP.Chat.UWP`	XMPP IoT chat plugin.
`Waher.Networking.XMPP.Control.UWP`	XMPP IoT control plugin. Only added to the `ActuatorXmpp` project.
`Waher.Networking.XMPP.Provisioning.UWP`	Added to both projects. We will discuss this module in a later chapter.

For .NET Standard, .NET Core, second-generation UWP, or traditional .NET Framework projects, you can use the package versions without UWP instead. First-generation *UWP* apps use different libraries and runtime binaries when it comes to accessing network adaptors. For this reason, they require a somewhat modified version of the original library.

When we initialize our runtime environment, we must make sure to include the assemblies defining relevant classes, at the beginning of the application. We will include the capability of using a rich chat environment using the formatted syntax (based on markdown) and graphs (based on the script engine), so we include these assemblies as well:

```
Types.Initialize(
typeof(FilesProvider).GetTypeInfo().Assembly,
typeof(RuntimeSettings).GetTypeInfo().Assembly,
typeof(IContentEncoder).GetTypeInfo().Assembly,
typeof(XmppClient).GetTypeInfo().Assembly,
typeof(Waher.Content.Markdown.MarkdownDocument).
GetTypeInfo().Assembly,
typeof(Waher.Content.Xml.XML).GetTypeInfo().Assembly,
typeof(Waher.Script.Expression).GetTypeInfo().Assembly,
typeof(Waher.Script.Graphs.Graph).GetTypeInfo().Assembly,
typeof(App).GetTypeInfo().Assembly);
```

We must not forget to add the `internetClientServer` capability to our set of capabilities in the `Package.appxmanifest` files as well:

```
<Capability Name="internetClientServer" />
```

Connecting to our broker

The first thing we will need to do is to connect to the XMPP broker we've chosen. We need the name of the host (preferably a domain name), the port number to use, and the client credentials.

XMPP allows us to work with password hashes, depending on the SASL mechanism used to authenticate the client. This is a great data protection mechanism not available in the other protocols discussed. It allows us to persist the hash instead of the actual password. Since the hash value will vary depending on the domain connecting to it, it cannot be reused in other settings, which is often the case when passwords are reused between services.

Getting persisted credentials

We will use the persistent settings library we presented earlier to check if we've got persisted credentials from earlier sessions:

```
string Host = await RuntimeSettings.GetAsync(
"XmppHost","waher.se");
int Port = (int)await RuntimeSettings.GetAsync("XmppPort", 5222);
string UserName = await RuntimeSettings.GetAsync(
"XmppUserName",string.Empty);
string PasswordHash = await RuntimeSettings.GetAsync(
"XmppPasswordHash", string.Empty);
string PasswordHashMethod = await RuntimeSettings.GetAsync(
"XmppPasswordHashMethod", string.Empty);
```

Preparing the connection for first-time use

The first time the application is run, there will be no credentials available. There are various ways in which credentials can be obtained:

- We can ask the user for credentials
- We can preprogram or configure credentials
- We can generate new credentials

The projects in GitHub will ask the user for account information using a simple dialog. Here the user will be prompted with a dialog the first time the application is run. The dialog will be displayed until valid credentials are provided. These will later be persisted using the static `RuntimeSettings` class, and will be available to the application the next time it is executed.

 The problem of presenting a dialog to the user is that things normally don't have a display where the dialog can be viewed. For laboratory experiments, it might be sufficient, however. If you choose to present dialogs in your app, you can download and run the **Windows IoT Remote Client** on your development machine. You also need to enable the **Windows IoT Remote Server** under the **Remote** tab in the **Device Portal** of the device. The Remote Client software will allow you not only to view the display of the device remotely, but it also allows you to interact with it using the mouse and keyboard. While some latency in the input is present, it works perfectly for entering credentials in the connection dialog.

Remember: don't forget to disable the Remote Server once you're done!

Connecting to the server

Once we have our credentials, or if we've chosen to automatically create new credentials, we are ready to connect to the server. We first need to create a variable to hold our XMPP client:

```
private XmppClient xmppClient = null;
```

We then create the client using the connection details we've procured. We also provide the default language code that we will use, as well as a reference to the assembly that represents the current application. This assembly will be used to extract some basic information about the application, such as the application name and version. This information can be requested by other participants in the network:

```
this.xmppClient = new XmppClient(Host, Port,
UserName, PasswordHash, PasswordHashMethod, "en",
typeof(App).GetTypeInfo().Assembly)
{
AllowCramMD5 = false,
AllowDigestMD5 = false,
AllowPlain = false,
AllowScramSHA1 = true
};
this.xmppClient.OnStateChanged += this.StateChanged;
this.xmppClient.OnConnectionError += this.ConnectionError;
this.AttachFeatures();

Log.Informational("Connecting to " + this.xmppClient.Host + ":" +
this.xmppClient.Port.ToString());
this.xmppClient.Connect();
```

When authenticating itself with the server, the client will use one authentication mechanism from a list of mechanisms presented to it by the server. Some of these mechanisms are more secure than others. While the client will validate the server certificate and check that it corresponds to the domain name, there's still a risk of losing user credentials if somebody manages to perform a **downgrade attack** while presenting a valid certificate anyway — especially if valid domain names are not used. To prevent credentials from leaking, you can explicitly turn off unsecure authentication mechanisms, such as PLAIN, CRAM-MD5, and DIGEST-MD5, and only allow SCRAM-SHA-1. This requires, however, that the server you connect to supports the SCRAM-SHA-1 mechanism.

Following the connection process

By using the OnStateChanged and OnConnectionError events, we have a simple mechanism with which we can follow the connection process. We also become aware of the Full JID of the connection, once the connection has become active and you're fully connected to the XMPP network:

```
private void StateChanged(object Sender, XmppState State)
{
Log.Informational("Changing state: " + State.ToString());

if (State == XmppState.Connected)
Log.Informational("Connected as " +
this.xmppClient.FullJID);
}

private void ConnectionError(object Sender, Exception ex)
{
Log.Error(ex.Message);
}
```

Registering a new account

In XMPP, clients can register for a new account, using the XMPP connection itself. This is called **In-Band Registration** and is defined in XEP-0077. To enable this feature, you have to call the AllowRegistration() method, before connecting to the network:

```
this.xmppClient.AllowRegistration();
```

You must also make sure to create the `XmppClient` using a proper password, not a password hash:

```
this.xmppClient = new XmppClient(Host, Port, UserName, Password,
"en", typeof(App).GetTypeInfo().Assembly)
```

Once the server gets to the part of authenticating the client and learns that such an account does not exist, it will attempt to register the account, using the credentials provided. If successful, the proper password hash and password hash method will be available, once the connection has been fully established. Make sure to persist them!

Allowing In-Band Registration on a server makes the server vulnerable to malicious bots or users that swamp the server with account generation requests. To mitigate this effect, some servers have added different protection measures. Some servers include a CAPTCHA image containing text that the user will have to be able to read and enter in the registration form (which the client processes). This method is not well suited to the Internet of Things, which typically lacks human interfaces.

Another method, more suited to the IoT, is to force the sender of the registration form to sign it using a shared secret. This is the principle used by the XMPP server at waher.se, for instance. Using an API **key** and a shared **secret**, the form is signed. Only valid signatures will be accepted, and accounts will be created only to the extent permitted by the corresponding key. This process of signing registration forms is defined in XEP-0348. To activate this feature, you call `AllowRegistration` with the corresponding key and secret, as follows:

```
this.xmppClient.AllowRegistration(Key, Secret);
```

Maintaining the connection

The `XmppClient` object will try to maintain the connection live. This includes pinging the server and trying to reconnect if something happens. But connectivity can get lost for many reasons. The application should therefore regularly check the connection, and force a reconnection attempt if it finds it offline or in an error state. In our sensor project, we can check the connection every minute, and force it to reconnect if necessary. We can take the opportunity to use our sampling timer to achieve this:

```
if (Timestamp.Second == 0 && this.xmppClient != null &&
(this.xmppClient.State == XmppState.Error ||
this.xmppClient.State == XmppState.Offline))
```

```
{
this.xmppClient.Reconnect();
}
```

In the actuator, as we don't have a sampling timer, we need to create a separate timer for this task:

```
this.minuteTimer = new Timer((State) =>
{
if (this.xmppClient != null &&
(this.xmppClient.State == XmppState.Error ||
this.xmppClient.State == XmppState.Offline))
{
this.xmppClient.Reconnect();
}
}, null, 60000, 60000);
```

Managing the roster

Apart from connecting to the XMPP network, we need a way to manage our roster, or who our friends are. In this chapter, we will use the simplest, but not safest, approach, by accepting all presence subscription requests:

```
private void AttachFeatures()
{
this.xmppClient.OnPresenceSubscribe += (Sender, e) =>
{
Log.Informational("Accepting friendship request.",
this.xmppClient.BareJID, e.From);
e.Accept();
};

this.xmppClient.OnPresenceUnsubscribe += (Sender, e) =>
{
Log.Informational("Friendship removed.",
this.xmppClient.BareJID, e.From);
e.Accept();
};

this.xmppClient.OnPresenceSubscribed += (Sender, e) =>
Log.Informational("Friendship request accepted.",
this.xmppClient.BareJID, e.From);
this.xmppClient.OnPresenceUnsubscribed += (Sender, e) =>
Log.Informational("Friendship removal accepted.",
this.xmppClient.BareJID, e.From);
```

We also take the opportunity to log events of interest:

```
this.xmppClient.OnError += (Sender, ex) => Log.Error(ex);
this.xmppClient.OnPasswordChanged += (Sender, e) =>
Log.Informational("Password changed.",
this.xmppClient.BareJID);
}
```

 Note that anyone with an active subscription to your device's presence will be able to request sensor data from it, and be able to request control actions to be performed on it. In a later chapter, we will discuss how to secure this.

Making sensor data available over XMPP

The NuGet `Waher.Networking.XMPP.Sensor[.UWP]` provides a `SensorServer` class that helps a sensor to publish its sensor data on the XMPP network. It also contains a `SensorClient` class, which can be used to request sensor data from other entities on the XMPP network. These classes use interoperability interfaces defined in the **IEEE IoT Harmonization** working group, which we will discuss more deeply in a later chapter. (These sensor data interfaces are in turn based on legacy interfaces defined in XEP-0323.) They support a wide array of features that are important in the IoT, some of which we will cover in later chapters:

- They allow for small quick sensors returning simple result sets
- They allow for slow asynchronous processes with progress updates for immediate (near real-time) feedback
- They allow for large result sets that are reported in segments
- They allow for queueing and scheduling of requests
- Request/response, event subscription and publish/subscribe patterns are supported
- Representation is loosely coupled and does not require interface changes for new types of devices
- Interfaces allow for sufficient metadata to be included in result sets for it to be possible to use in both **machine-to-machine** (M2M) and **human-to-machine** (H2M) interfaces
- Interfaces support localization
- Secure distributed transactions are supported
- Limitation of requests (provisioning) is supported

The IEEE IoT Harmonization working group interfaces are published at `https://gitlab.com/IEEE-SA/XMPPI/IoT`.

The URL will be updated before publication of the book.

Understanding the conceptual model

The sensor data model in XMPP is similar to how we treated sensor data in previous chapters. Each **device** maintains a collection of **timestamps**; each one is comprised of a set of **fields**, as shown in *Figure 1*. The model also allows for measurement or communication errors to be reported. Apart from a value, each field also has a name, optional localization information, field type information, quality of service information, and custom annotations. In a later chapter, we will build on this model by introducing the concept of nodes, where a device can be said to host a set of **nodes**, or virtual devices:

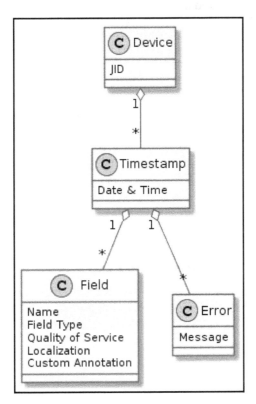

Figure 1. Conceptual model of sensor data in XMPP

There are different kinds of fields that can be represented in this model. They all share the aforementioned common properties, but represent the corresponding value differently:

Representation	Description
Physical Quantity	Represents a floating-point numerical value (`xsd:double`) together with a string (`xsd:string`) unit value. The number of decimals used in the representation corresponds to the precision of the value.
String	Value encoded as `xsd:string`.
Boolean	Value encoded as `xsd:boolean`.
Date	Value encoded as `xsd:date`.
DateTime	Value encoded as `xsd:dateTime`.
Duration	Value encoded as `xsd:duration`.
Enumeration	Represents a string value (`xsd:string`) from a discrete enumeration. The enumeration is defined using a type attribute (`xsd:string`).
Int32	Value encoded as `xsd:int`.
Int64	Value encoded as `xsd:long`.
Time	Value encoded as `xsd:time`.

 XML datatypes are defined in the W3C XML Schema Definition Language (XSD) at `http://www.w3.org/TR/xmlschema11-2/`.

Creating an XMPP sensor server

To make our data available on the network, we create a `SensorServer` object in both of our projects. We need a variable to reference our server:

```
private SensorServer sensorServer = null;
```

In our `AttachFeatures` method, we create an instance of this object, and provide an event handler for the principle event: `OnExecuteReadoutRequest`. This event is triggered each time a sensor data request is received. It is also triggered when a subscription event is triggered, and an event message is being created. The `SensorServer` object takes care of registering required handlers on our XMPP client:

```
this.sensorServer = new SensorServer(this.xmppClient, true);
this.sensorServer.OnExecuteReadoutRequest += async (sender, e) =>
{
try
{
Log.Informational("Performing readout.",
this.xmppClient.BareJID, e.Actor);

List<Field> Fields = new List<Field>();
DateTime Now = DateTime.Now;
```

Field classes for the different fields are defined in the `Waher.Things.SensorData` namespace.

Returning momentary values

We can use the event arguments provided in the handler to learn things about the original request, such as who made the request (the `Actor`) and which types of data are desired. The interface is loosely coupled, so we just return a set of fields. We don't have to be exact unless it saves processing time. Interfaces will filter the contents not desired or permitted anyway, to avoid information leaks because checks were omitted:

```
if (e.IsIncluded(FieldType.Identity))
Fields.Add(new StringField(ThingReference.Empty, Now,
"Device ID", this.deviceId, FieldType.Identity,
FieldQoS.AutomaticReadout));

if (this.lastLight.HasValue)
Fields.Add(new QuantityField(ThingReference.Empty, Now,
"Light", this.lastLight.Value, 2, "%",
FieldType.Momentary, FieldQoS.AutomaticReadout));

if (this.lastMotion.HasValue)
Fields.Add(new BooleanField(ThingReference.Empty, Now,
"Motion", this.lastMotion.Value,
FieldType.Momentary, FieldQoS.AutomaticReadout));
```

Returning historical values

If historical values are desired, we can send our partial results immediately, to allow the client to provide some immediate feedback. Loading historical data can take a little time, depending on the underlying storage medium and amount of data stored:

```
if (e.IsIncluded(FieldType.Historical))
{
e.ReportFields(false, Fields);
Fields.Clear();
```

To avoid too large stanzas and allow the client to follow the progress, we can choose to return historical elements, 50 at a time:

```
foreach (LastMinute Rec in
await Database.Find<LastMinute>(new FilterAnd(
new FilterFieldGreaterOrEqualTo("Timestamp", e.From),
new FilterFieldLesserOrEqualTo("Timestamp", e.To)),
"Timestamp"))
{
if (Fields.Count > 50)
{
e.ReportFields(false, Fields);
Fields.Clear();
}

if (Rec.AvgLight.HasValue)
{
Fields.Add(new QuantityField(ThingReference.Empty,
Rec.Timestamp, "Light, Minute, Average",
Rec.AvgLight.Value, 2, "%", FieldType.Computed |
FieldType.Historical, FieldQoS.AutomaticReadout));
}

...
}
```

The population of the field list with all elements in each record is straightforward and is also repeated for the hourly values in the same way.

Returning writable values

In the general case, some momentary values might correspond to control parameters in an actuator. To highlight this, an overload exists for the field constructors, allowing the application to signal which one of the fields is "writable", or which ones correspond to control parameters with the same name. In our actuator, we report our output value as a writable parameter, by appending a Boolean argument to the value `true`:

```
if (this.output.HasValue)
{
Fields.Add(new BooleanField(ThingReference.Empty, Now,
"Output", this.output.Value,
FieldType.Momentary, FieldQoS.AutomaticReadout, true));
}
```

Triggering events

As mentioned earlier, the sensor data interfaces support event subscription as well as the readout on request. When subscribing to events, you provide minimum and maximum time intervals for events. You can also provide information about individual fields, and describe threshold values for how much a value is allowed to change until an event is triggered. To enable this feature properly, the application needs to report new momentary values to the `Sensor Server` object. The object, in turn, keeps track of all active subscriptions and makes sure events are triggered as they should be. When they are triggered, the `OnExecuteReadoutRequest` event is triggered as if a request would have been received. The event arguments point to the original subscription request when processing the readout.

Reporting new momentary values is easy. You only call the `NewMomentaryValues()` method whenever you calculate a new momentary value. For example:

```
this.sensorServer?.NewMomentaryValues(new QuantityField(
ThingReference.Empty,Timestamp, "Light", Light, 2, "%",
FieldType.Momentary, FieldQoS.AutomaticReadout));
```

And we do the same for our motion:

```
this.sensorServer?.NewMomentaryValues(
new BooleanField(ThingReference.Empty, this.lastPublished,
"Motion", Motion, FieldType.Momentary,
FieldQoS.AutomaticReadout));
```

Similarly, we should also report each change of the output value in our actuator. This would allow others to subscribe to events relating to the change of the switch:

```
this.sensorServer?.NewMomentaryValues(
new BooleanField(ThingReference.Empty, DateTime.Now, "Output",
On, FieldType.Momentary, FieldQoS.AutomaticReadout));
```

Publishing control parameters

The NuGets `Waher.Networking.XMPP.Control[.UWP]` provides a `ControlServer` class that helps an actuator to publish its control parameters on the XMPP network. It also contains a `Control Client` class that can be used to set control parameter values on other entities on the XMPP network. As with the sensor interfaces, the control classes use interoperability interfaces defined in the **IEEE IoT Harmonization** working group. (These sensor data interfaces are in turn based on the legacy interfaces defined in XEP-0325.) The control interfaces support:

- Simple atomic set operations
- Complex group set operations
- The representation that is loosely coupled and does not require interface changes for new types of devices
- Interfaces that allow for sufficient metadata to be included in result sets for it to be possible to use in both M2M and H2M interfaces
- Interfaces that support localization
- Secure distributed transactions
- The limitation of requests (provisioning)

Understanding the conceptual model

The control data model in XMPP is very simple. Each device just consists of a set of **control parameters**. When we introduce nodes in later chapters and allow our devices to be divided into nodes, we can allow each controllable node to have its own set of control parameters:

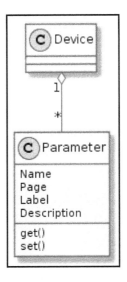

Figure 2. Conceptual model of control parameters in XMPP

As with sensor data, there are different kinds of control parameters that can be represented in this model. They all share the common parameters presented in *Figure 2*, but represent the corresponding control value differently:

Representation	Description
String	Value encoded as `xsd:string`.
Boolean	Value encoded as `xsd:boolean`.
Color	Value encoded as a six- or eight-character hexadecimal string in the format RRGGBB or RRGGBBAA.
Date	Value encoded as `xsd:date`.
DateTime	Value encoded as `xsd:dateTime`.
Double	Value encoded as `xsd:double`.
Duration	Value encoded as `xsd:duration`.
Int32	Value encoded as `xsd:int`.
Int64	Value encoded as `xsd:long`.
Time	Value encoded as `xsd:time`.

Parameter classes for the different control parameters are defined in the `Waher.Things.ControlParameters` namespace.

Creating an XMPP control server

To make our parameters available, we create a `ControlServer` object in our actuator project. We need a variable to reference our server:

```
private ControlServer controlServer = null;
```

In our `AttachFeatures` method, we create our instance of the control server. We can either choose to provide a set of control parameters in the constructor of the control server, or override the `OnGetControlParameters` event and provide a dynamic set each time a set is requested. The first method is simplest, if we're building a simple actuator, as we do in our example. If we want to provide different control parameter sets for different nodes in the device, we must choose the second option.

The control server object does not have an event that is raised when control parameters are set. Instead, such callback methods are provided individually, for each control parameter. Apart from providing a name for each parameter, we also have to provide (in order) a page (think "tabbed dialog"), a label for the parameter, and a description (a tool-tip), as well as a *get* and a *set* callback method. These two methods are used whenever the control server needs to know the current value of the parameter, and when it wants the value to be updated. For our actuator, we define the control server as follows:

```
this.controlServer = new ControlServer(this.xmppClient,
new BooleanControlParameter("Output",
"Actuator", "Output:","Digital output.",
(Node) => this.output,
async (Node, Value) =>
{
try
{
await this.SetOutput(Value, "XMPP");
}
catch (Exception ex)
{
Log.Critical(ex);
}
}));
```

If you're implementing asynchronous callback methods, make sure you trap all exceptions. Exceptions in asynchronous methods with a `void` return types that, if not caught, will cause the application to shut down unexpectedly.

Adding a chat interface

At this point, both our projects have machine interfaces for sensor data readout event subscriptions, and control parameter operations. What we lack is a human interface. As XMPP was built for chat, it would be nice if we could add a chat interface to our devices.

To send a chat message, we can call the `SendChatMethod()` on our `XmppClient` object. Messages sent to the client can be received through the `OnChatMessage` event. All you need to do to provide a custom chat interface is work with these two. There are some interoperability issues you might need to consider, however, relating to sending formatted messages, images, and so on. If you want, you can start with the `Waher.Networking.XMPP.Chat[.UWP]` NuGet, which integrates both the `SensorServer` and `ControlServer` objects, to provide a simple chat interface. When reading the sensor, it will detect longer time series, and present these values in graph form, instead of tabular form. It will also include multiple compatible series into one, if it detects series with names ending with "Average," "Minimum," and "Maximum," respectively.

Source code for the chat interface is available in the **IoT Gateway** project, at
`https://github.com/PeterWaher/IoTGateway/tree/master/Networking/Waher.Networking.XMPP.Chat`.

Creating an XMPP chat server

As with the other server objects, we first need a variable to hold the reference to our chat server. We also need a **Bits of Binary** client. Bits of Binary is a mechanism to transfer small chunks of binary information from one client to another and is defined in XEP-0231. It is one of several methods the chat server can use to transfer images:

```
private BobClient bobClient = null;
private ChatServer chatServer = null;
```

In our `AttachFeatures` method, we create the instance as follows. We ask our Bits of Binary-client to temporarily use the TEMP folder to store binary information, if necessary. In the constructor of our chat server, we also provide a reference to our sensor server:

```
this.bobClient = new BobClient(this.xmppClient,
Path.Combine(Path.GetTempPath(), "BitsOfBinary"));
this.chatServer = new ChatServer(this.xmppClient, this.bobClient,
this.sensorServer);
```

In the actuator case, we need to provide a reference to the control server as well:

```
this.chatServer = new ChatServer(this.xmppClient, this.bobClient,
this.sensorServer, this.controlServer);
```

Images will be transferred using one of the following methods, depending on the capabilities of the receiver or your broker:

- Embedding an image using the data URI scheme
- Uploading the image to your broker and sending an image tag referencing the uploaded image, or providing a simple URL to the uploaded image
- Using Bits of Binary as a transport mechanism, embedding an as an image tag with a reference to the Bits of Binary content

Testing your devices

You are now ready to test your applications. In the next chapter, we will see how we can interact with our devices from code. In this chapter, however, we have to test our devices using external software.

Testing the human interface

As we have added chat interfaces, we can begin by testing our devices using any instant messaging client supporting XMPP. If you don't already have one, download one, create an account using an appropriate broker, and connect to your newly created devices, by adding them to your roster in your chat client. The devices should automatically accept your requests. Then start chatting with them. *Figure 3* shows an example chat with the sensor. You can also chat with the actuator, and control its output using the chat interface. Check the menu to see how to do that:

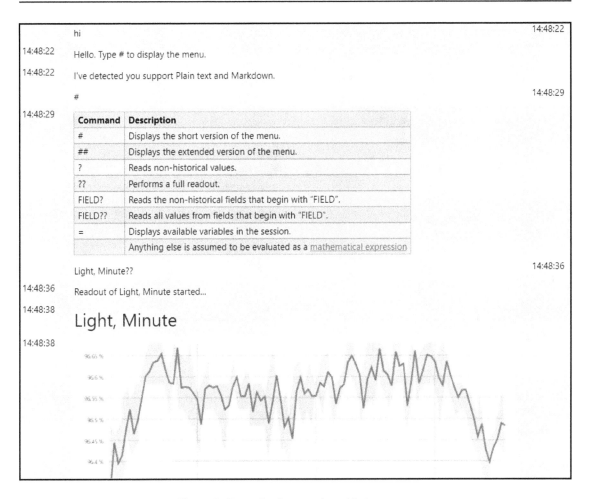

Figure 3. Example chat session with the sensor

Testing the machine interface

To test the machine interface, we need a tool we can use. The **IoT Gateway** project on GitHub contains such a tool written in .NET, called simply `Waher.Client.WPF`. An executable version can be downloaded as well. You can use this to test both the machine and chat interfaces of your devices. You can create one or more XMPP connections and add contacts. If they are sensors or actuators, you can read them, control their parameters, and subscribe to events from them. You can also listen on the XMPP communication to learn what is being communicated. *Figure 4* shows the main interface of this simple XMPP IoT client:

The IoT Gateway project is available at
https://github.com/PeterWaher/IoTGateway.

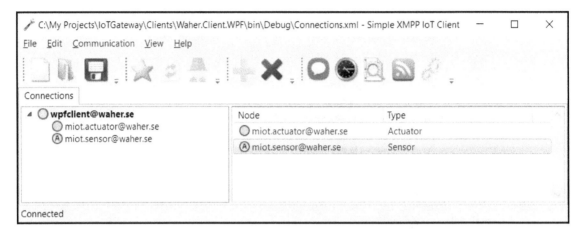

Figure 4. Simple XMPP IoT Client (Waher.Client.WPF)

The first group of buttons in the main window allows you to create a new connection file, load an existing file, or save your current connections to a file. The second group allows you to add a new connection to your window. This represents an XMPP connection, or a connection to an XMPP broker. You can recycle a connection and spy (listen to) a connection. The third group allows you to add and remove items to the tree in the left pane. If you select a connection and press the addition symbol, you add a contact to your connection. The last group lets you interact with your contacts: you can chat with them, read momentary values, read all values, subscribe to events, and configure them. Buttons are enabled if the corresponding action is available for the current selection.

For further study

The `SensorXmpp` and `ActuatorXmpp` projects in the MIoT repository on GitHub provide the support for XEP-0054 to publish contact information using vCards. If you're interested in learning how to implement your own extensions, search for `0054` in the code to see how to register handlers and send stanzas.

The `SensorXmpp` project also includes a method of publishing current momentary values using the publish/subscribe pattern provided by the `presence` stanza. This behavior is commented out in the default version, to avoid spamming the broker. If you want to play with this pattern, check the `PublishMomentaryValues()` method.

 The Mastering Internet of Things, or MIoT project on GitHub can be found at `https://github.com/PeterWaher/MIoT`.

Summary

In this chapter, you've been shown the basic principles of how XMPP works, and how XMPP can be used to provide a flexible, extensible, and scalable infrastructure for devices. You've learned how brokers help devices cross topology barriers such as firewalls, and how stanzas are related to important communication patterns. You've also learned the basics of trust-based communication and loosely coupled interfaces for the IoT. You know how to publish sensor data and control parameters over XMPP and how to test your sensors and actuators using XMPP. In the following chapters, you will learn how to interact with your devices with code.

10
The Controller

Up to this point, we have mostly focused on creating things, either sensors or actuators that publish data in one form or another and allow other actors to perform control operations on them. In this chapter, we will focus on how to find such devices, consume their data, and how to issue control operations on them. The chapter covers:

- Discovery of devices on the Internet of Things
- An introduction to Thing Registry
- How to register a device in a registry
- How to discover devices in a registry
- How to subscribe to sensor data events
- How to issue control operations

Discovering things on the internet

When creating a controller that will use devices connected to the internet, you must solve the problem of finding the devices you want to use. You can choose to preconfigure the identities of the devices in a production environment, or to manually configure the identities after installation. These methods require additional effort on the part of the manufacturer, operator, or installer. It would be nice if the things could discover themselves somehow.

In local area networks, discovery is easier. You can use a multi-cast based protocol, such as the **Simple Service Discovery Protocol (SSDP)**, part of **Universal Plug and Play (UPnP)**, to let your devices multi-cast their existence and capabilities in the network. Controllers can listen to these messages, and connect to suitable devices they find. But on the internet, such a method is not feasible for many reasons, and it is difficult to secure.

Introducing Thing Registry

On the internet, you cannot multi-cast information freely, for scalability and security reasons. While the IPv6 protocol allows for multi-casting on many layers, the feature is often restricted in routers. But you can achieve a similar feature by the introduction of a neutral third party: a **Thing Registry**. Thing Registries act as bulletin boards for things. When things are installed and get their network identity, they can register their existence, network identity, and **conceptual identity** on the registry. The network identity would typically be the communication address (and protocol) used to communicate with the thing. The conceptual identity would include meta-information about the thing, such as class, type, manufacturer, location, serial number, and so on. The conceptual identity can be used to *indirectly* identify the thing, while the network identity can be used to *directly* identify it.

Propagating information

Consumers that want to discover things register with the same thing registry. Depending on the type of registry used, consumers can find their corresponding things in different ways. There are two principal types of methods available, for the propagation of information about things registered with the registry: event-based methods and search-based methods.

Event-based methods are typically based on the Publish/Subscribe communication pattern. Things register their existence by publishing information about themselves on a topic. Consumers of devices subscribe to relevant topics and get informed about the existence of devices through events on the corresponding topics. The topic tree becomes tightly coupled with the types of devices registering with the registry. To interconnect things using an event-based approach, publishers and subscribers typically need to be connected simultaneously, or consumers need to be able to traverse the history of each topic to find the corresponding things among all those available for the respective topic. Publishers also need to repeatedly publish their existence during their lifetime.

Search-based methods, on the other hand, allow consumers to search more freely on the metadata things registered in the registry. It is requirement-based instead of event-based. Consumers search when they need to find entities, not when things register and become available. Search-based methods are more scalable and allow for finding things using a multi-dimensional set of tags, rather a restricted topic tree. They are also more loosely coupled to the types of devices available. Things only need to register and unregister and update their registration when their information changes. This method, however, does not include a way to inform consumers of changes in registrations, or when new devices are registered.

Claiming ownership of things

One of the major drawbacks of an event-based approach is that it is very difficult to protect devices. The device, or its owner, cannot control who can have access to it. It publishes its identity and anybody with access to the registry can find it. There's no method for the owner of the thing to claim it for itself. And there's no method for the owner to control who can access the thing and what is done with it.

Search-based methods, however, can be adapted to allow for ownership claims. The basic principle is as follows, and is outlined in the following diagram:

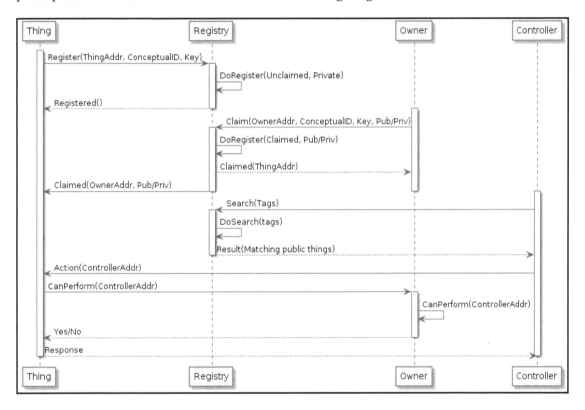

Discovery of things using a Thing Registry

1. A thing registers its network identity and conceptual identity, together with a **key**.
2. The thing is registered as a **private unclaimed** thing. Private things are never published in search results.

3. The owner makes an **ownership claim**. An ownership claim is a special kind of search, where the owner needs to present the same conceptual identity (all tags) of the thing, including the key, to the registry. The first one to do this is considered the owner of the thing.

4. A claimed thing is presented with the network identity of its owner, and the owner the network identity of the thing. They now both *know* each other. The thing is set to **claim**. The owner can choose if the thing is made **public** or if it remains **private**. The key is removed. If public, it will be made available in matching search results.

5. Other entities may perform searches on any of the tags available in the database. Claimed public things with meta-information matching the search will be returned.

6. When somebody connects to the thing and wants to perform an action, the thing now knows who is responsible for permitting the action or not. It can ask the owner, if it hasn't done so earlier, and allow the request if the owner permits it.

 In the next chapter, you'll learn how to disown a thing, and how to transfer ownership of a thing to a new owner.

Transferring the conceptual identity to the owner

One of the tasks required to realize the previous sequence of events is to make a successful ownership claim. This requires the owner to be able to present the same conceptual identity as the thing, including the key, to the registry. Since the amount of information might make manual editing of this information impractical, an efficient approach is needed to efficiently transmit the information to the owner out of band.

One such method is defined using the **Uniform Resource Identifier** (URI) scheme `iotdisco`. This method allows the encoding of the information into a URI, which can then be presented as a presented as a Quick Response (**QR**) code, perhaps on a sticker. The owner can scan it, for instance, using a smartphone application, and send the information to the same registry to make the matching claim.

As an example, consider the following set of meta-information about a thing:

Tag	Value
CLASS	Controller
TYPE	MIoT Controller
MAN	waher.se
MODEL	MIoT ControllerXmpp
PURL	`https://github.com/PeterWaher/MIoT`
SN	ebfe45db82884676bdaf1adcb93c70d3
V	1.0
KEY	9b3c08a2a246468aaaa6dd00a258cdc5

The preceding information can be encoded into a URI as follows, which in turn is encoded into a QR-code, as shown in preceding image:

```
iotdisco:CLASS=Controller;Type=MIoT%20Controller;MAN=waher.se;MODEL=MIoT%20
ControllerXmpp;PURL=https%3A%2F%2Fgithub.com%2FPeterWaher%2FMIoT;SN=ebfe45d
b82884676bdaf1adcb93c70d3;#V=1.0;KEY=9b3c08a2a246468aaaa6dd00a258cdc5
```

QR-code containing conceptual identity of a thing.

For more information about the `iotdisco` URI scheme, visit `https://www.iana.org/assignments/uri-schemes/prov/iotdisco.pdf`.

Using thing registries in XMPP

Using XMPP for the implementation of thing registries has several benefits: it allows for ad hoc connections and real-time communication between peers, regardless of obstacles in the network topology imposed by firewalls. It automatically forwards the network identity of all actors in the network in a way that cannot be spoofed easily. It is also federated, which makes it globally scalable and avoids the creation of centralized bottlenecks. While Thing Registries imply some form of centralization, at least of the bulletin board, the federated aspect of XMPP allows anybody to create their own bulletin boards (registries).

There is also an open extension available for Thing Registries in XMPP. It is defined in XEP-0347. It also defines a mechanism for publishing thing registries: they are made available as components on the XMPP server. A thing, controller, or the owner using a custom XMPP client can automatically detect the registry by browsing available components on its broker. If participants use the same broker, they will automatically find the same registry, regardless of where they are located on the internet, and can, therefore, use it to exchange identities securely. It also allows for the use of Thing Registries to be reachable at other locations.

The XMPP broker available at waher.se has an integrated Thing Registry.

Registering our devices

Before we create a controller, we need to update our sensor and actuator projects. They need to search their brokers for available thing registries and register themselves with them. Since the process is the same for both the sensor and the actuator, only changes to the sensor project will be presented here.

A thing registry client is made available in the `Waher.Networking.Provisioning` NuGet (or the `Waher.Networking.Provisioning.UWP` NuGet). It ties into the other XMPP libraries presented so far. We begin by defining a variable for it:

```
private ThingRegistryClient registryClient = null;
```

Once the XMPP client establishes a connection, we call a new method called
`RegisterDevice`. We will define this function to be asynchronous:

```
Task.Run(this.RegisterDevice);
```

Or:

```
await this.RegisterDevice();
```

Looping through available components

The first step is to find the thing registry. We assume that it is made available as a
component of the same broker that we are connected to. To avoid searching the broker
every time the device is restarted, we first check if we already know the address of the
registry:

```
private async Task RegisterDevice()
{
    string ThingRegistryJid = await RuntimeSettings.GetAsync(
        "ThingRegistry.JID", string.Empty);

    if (!string.IsNullOrEmpty(ThingRegistryJid))
        await this.RegisterDevice(ThingRegistryJid);
    else
    {
        Log.Informational("Searching for Thing Registry.");
```

Our search begins by looping through all *items* on the broker. These *items* publish a set of
features. These items and features are accessed through **Service Discovery**:

```
this.xmppClient.SendServiceItemsDiscoveryRequest(
    this.xmppClient.Domain, (sender, e) =>
{
    foreach (Item Item in e.Items)
    {
        this.xmppClient.SendServiceDiscoveryRequest(
            Item.JID, async (sender2, e2) =>
        {
```

 Service Discovery is an extension to XMPP, and is defined in XEP-0030.
Service Discovery classes are defined in the
`Waher.Networking.XMPP.ServiceDiscovery` namespace.

Finding the thing registry

We then analyze the set of features presented by each item, or component. If any of them present the namespace defined in XEP-0347 for Thing Registries, we use the JID presented by the component as the address for the registry:

```
try
{
    Item Item2 = (Item)e2.State;

    if (e2.HasFeature(ThingRegistryClient.NamespaceDiscovery))
    {
        Log.Informational("Thing registry found.", Item2.JID);

        await RuntimeSettings.SetAsync(
            "ThingRegistry.JID", Item2.JID);
        await this.RegisterDevice(Item2.JID);
    }
}
catch (Exception ex)
{
    Log.Critical(ex);
}
```

Creating a Thing Registry client

Now that we know the address of the Thing Registry, we must create a `ThingRegistryClient` object to communicate with it:

```
private async Task RegisterDevice(string RegistryJid)
{
    if (this.registryClient == null ||
        this.registryClient.ThingRegistryAddress != RegistryJid)
    {
        if (this.registryClient != null)
        {
            this.registryClient.Dispose();
            this.registryClient = null;
        }

        this.registryClient = new ThingRegistryClient(
            this.xmppClient, RegistryJid);
    }
```

Defining the conceptual identity of the thing

The next step is to define a set of metadata tags that will constitute the *conceptual identity* of the device. You can choose any tags you like. Tags are simply key-value pairs. Keys are always strings, and values can be either strings or numeric (floating-point) values. Each key tag (or name) is case insensitive. Some keys are defined in the IANA `iotdisco` URI scheme definition, as well as XEP-0347. You should adhere to these for interoperability. They include tags for physical identity, identity of the manufacturer, make, model, and version of the device, as well as location information, and so on. We begin with some static information:

```
string s;
List<MetaDataTag> MetaInfo = new List<MetaDataTag>()
{
    new MetaDataStringTag("CLASS", "Sensor"),
    new MetaDataStringTag("TYPE", "MIoT Sensor"),
    new MetaDataStringTag("MAN", "waher.se"),
    new MetaDataStringTag("MODEL", "MIoT SensorXmpp"),
    new MetaDataStringTag("PURL",
            "https://github.com/PeterWaher/MIoT"),
    new MetaDataStringTag("SN", this.deviceId),
    new MetaDataNumericTag("V", 1.0)
};
```

For a list of pre-defined tags, see
`https://xmpp.org/extensions/xep-0347.html#tags`.

Adding existing location information

To allow a controller to find things in its vicinity, we must register the **location** of the devices it wants to find. We can do this either using numeric **longitude**, **latitude**, and **altitude** values or using geographic reference tags. The longitude, latitude, and altitude values might be valuable if you do applications that are geographically sensitive. But they are difficult to use in smart city applications since vicinity is not defined by concepts of geographical distance, but by other concepts, such as room, apartment, office, department, address, and so on.

In our examples, we will use the second approach. We first check if we have these values available. If so, we add them to our metadata information about the device, using the tags COUNTRY, REGION, CITY, AREA, STREET, STREETNR, BLD, APT, ROOM, and NAME, some of which can be empty. By the virtue of having these values, we also assume we update an existing registration:

```
if (await RuntimeSettings.GetAsync(
    "ThingRegistry.Location", false))
{
    s = await RuntimeSettings.GetAsync(
        "ThingRegistry.Country", string.Empty);
    if (!string.IsNullOrEmpty(s))
        MetaInfo.Add(new MetaDataStringTag("COUNTRY", s));

    ...

    this.UpdateRegistration(MetaInfo.ToArray());
}
```

Collecting location information

If we don't have access to this location information, we will use a simple approach of displaying a dialog to the user. There the user can provide the required information:

```
else
{
    try
    {
        await MainPage.Instance.Dispatcher.RunAsync(
            CoreDispatcherPriority.Normal, async () =>
        {
            try
            {
                RegistrationDialog Dialog = new RegistrationDialog();

                switch (await Dialog.ShowAsync())
                {
```

If the user fills in the form and presses the **Register** button, the information is persisted to be used the next time the device is restarted. If the user presses the **Cancel** button, the registration process starts again (since registration in our simple example is required). The form included in the projects looks like the one shown in the following screenshot. Note that the fields are optional. Depending on the granularity you need, different sets of fields can be used:

```
case ContentDialogResult.Primary:
    await RuntimeSettings.SetAsync("ThingRegistry.Country",
        s = Dialog.Reg_Country);
    if (!string.IsNullOrEmpty(s))
        MetaInfo.Add(new MetaDataStringTag("COUNTRY", s));

    ...

    this.RegisterDevice(MetaInfo.ToArray());
    break;

case ContentDialogResult.Secondary:
    await this.RegisterDevice();
break;
```

Collecting location information.

Registering the device

Now that we have the metadata information we require for the device, it's an easy task to register it with the Thing Registry. We simply call the `RegisterThing` method on the thing registry client and monitor the success of the operation in the result.

The first parameter in the `RegisterThing()` method call is a Boolean parameter that lets the registry know if the thing is **self-owned** or not. A device that is self-owned makes its own security decisions. For now, we will work with self-owned devices, so we set this parameter to `true`. In the next chapter, we will introduce the concept of **provisioning**, where the owner of a device can control who can access the device and do what with it:

```
private void RegisterDevice(MetaDataTag[] MetaInfo)
{
    Log.Informational("Registering device.");

    this.registryClient.RegisterThing(true, MetaInfo,
        async (sender, e) =>
        {
            try
            {
                if (e.Ok)
                {
                    Log.Informational(
                        "Registration successful.");

                    await RuntimeSettings.SetAsync(
                        "ThingRegistry.Location",
                        true);
                }
                else
                {
                    Log.Error("Registration failed.");
                    await this.RegisterDevice();
                }
            }
            catch (Exception ex)
            {
                Log.Critical(ex);
            }
        }, null);
}
```

You can call the `Unregister()` method to unregister the thing from the registry.

Updating a registration

After a thing has been registered, we can *update* the registration as many times as we want. We can only update our own registration. The difference between a registration and an update is that a registration rewrites the complete set of metadata for the device, while an update only changes, updates, or adds tags to the set, but it does not remove tags not mentioned. Updates only work if there's a previous registration, however. If the update procedure fails, we try to re-register the thing instead:

```
private void UpdateRegistration(MetaDataTag[] MetaInfo)
{
    Log.Informational("Updating registration of device.");

    this.registryClient.UpdateThing(MetaInfo, (sender, e) =>
    {
        if (e.Ok)
            Log.Informational(
                "Registration update successful.");
        else
        {
            Log.Error("Registration update failed.");
            this.RegisterDevice(MetaInfo);
        }
    }, null);
}
```

Updates are useful, especially if you have tags that change during the lifetime of the device. This may include the longitude, latitude, and altitude of a moving device, for instance. When you update a registration, only the tags being updated or added are included. If you want to remove a tag, set it to the empty string.

Creating a controller

We are now ready to create our controller application. This controller application will register itself with any available thing registry published by its broker, using the same method presented earlier. It will then use the same registry to find our sensor and actuator, by searching for the corresponding conceptual identities of both, limited to the same geographical information the controller has. In this way, we can automatically detect devices in our vicinity, regardless of how many instances of the sensor and actuator applications there are registered in the registry.

Identifying things

While we have worked with standalone things (each one identified using a single XMPP address called a **JID**), generic things on the XMPP network, as registered in a Thing Registry, can be addressed using one, two, three, or four parameters, depending on the size of the host publishing the interface to the thing:

JID	XMPP address of device.
Node ID	Address of virtual node inside device.
Source ID	Larger devices might divide their nodes into sets, called data sources. Node identities are unique within their data source, if specified.
Partition	Large data sources might be further partitioned into subsets. If this is the case, it is the triplet (node ID, data source ID, partition) that is considered unique.

Devices that publish more than one logical device (or node) are also referred to as **concentrators**, since they concentrate several, possibly virtual, devices behind a single XMPP endpoint. This can be used by composite devices, such as **Programmable Logical Controllers (PLCs)**, that encapsulate logical functions as nodes inside a single physical unit. Concentrators can also be used in protocol bridges or when interfacing larger systems. We will discuss concentrators more in the next chapter. For now, it's sufficient to recognize that a thing in the network can be identified using one to four of these parameters, where the JID parameter is the only required parameter. We define the corresponding variables for these references:

```
private string sensorJid = null;
private string actuatorJid = null;
private ThingReference sensor = null;
private ThingReference actuator = null;
```

The `ThingReference` class, defined in `Waher.Things`, contains `NodeId`, `SourceId` and `Partition` properties.

Finding friends in the roster

After a successful registration or update of an existing registration in the Thing Registry, the controller calls the `FindFriends` method with the metadata used in the registration:

```
this.FindFriends(MetaInfo);
```

The `FindFriends` method will connect the controller to the corresponding sensor and actuator in its vicinity. The first step is to check that such connections are not already defined. We will use the roster of our XMPP connection, that is, our list of "friends," as the knowledge base of our contacts. To each contact on our roster, we can assign *groups*. Groups are just string tags we annotate each contact with. We can use this array of groups to describe our contacts. These descriptions are stored on the broker, and follow our account, rather than our local storage. This means that if you change hardware, but reuse the XMPP account, it will retain the information and friendships. So, the first thing we need to do is check our roster if we already have our sensor and actuator identified:

```
private void FindFriends(MetaDataTag[] MetaInfo)
{
    this.sensorJid = null;
    this.sensor = null;
    this.actuator = null;
    this.actuatorJid = null;

    foreach (RosterItem Item in this.xmppClient.Roster)
    {
        if (Item.IsInGroup("Sensor"))
        {
            this.sensorJid = Item.BareJid;
            this.sensor = this.GetReference(Item, "Sensor");
        }

        if (Item.IsInGroup("Actuator"))
        {
            this.actuatorJid = Item.BareJid;
            this.actuator = this.GetReference(Item,
                "Actuator");
        }
    }
}
```

Here, the `GetReference()` method loops through all groups to extract any `NodeId`, `SourceId`, and `Partition` parameters made available by the presence of optional group names, such as `Sensor.nid:NODEID`, `Sensor.sid:SOURCEID`, and `Sensor.prt:PARTITION`. See the GitHub source example for the details.

Limiting the search domain

If we have already a sensor connection defined, we skip to the subscription of sensor data directly. There's no need to perform an actual search:

```
if (!string.IsNullOrEmpty(this.sensorJid))
    this.SubscribeToSensorData();
```

If, on the other hand, a sensor connection is not defined, or if an actuator connection is not defined, we need to perform a search. We want to find appropriate devices near where the controller is. We do this by preparing the search and aggregating search operators (defined in the `Waher.Networking.XMPP.Provisioning.SearchOperators` namespace) corresponding to the location-based metadata tags we are using in our registration:

```
if (string.IsNullOrEmpty(this.sensorJid) ||
    string.IsNullOrEmpty(this.actuatorJid))
{
    List<SearchOperator> Search = new List<SearchOperator>();

    foreach (MetaDataTag Tag in MetaInfo)
    {
        if (Tag is MetaDataStringTag StringTag)
        {
            switch (StringTag.Name)
            {
                case "COUNTRY":
                case "REGION":
                case "CITY":
                case "AREA":
                case "STREET":
                case "STREETNR":
                case "BLD":
                case "APT":
                case "ROOM":
                case "NAME":
                    Search.Add(new StringTagEqualTo(
                        StringTag.Name,
                        StringTag.StringValue));
```

```
                              break;
                    }
            }
    }
```

We top off the search by limiting it to the types of devices that we are interested in:

```
Search.Add(new StringTagGreaterThan("TYPE", "MIoT "));
```

Performing the search

Now that we have the scope of the search defined, performing the search is easy. We call the `Search` method on the registry client, submitting an offset, the maximum number of nodes to return in the search result, and a `callback` method to call when the result is returned:

```
Log.Informational("Searching for MIoT devices in my vicinity.");

this.registryClient.Search(0, 100, Search.ToArray(),
    (sender, e) =>
    {
            Log.Informational(e.Things.Length.ToString() +
                    (e.More ? "+" : string.Empty) + " things found.");
```

Picking suitable devices

Each thing in the search result, apart from being `public`, is also returned with the complete set of metadata tags it has registered with the registry. We loop through the things found, and analyze the TYPE tag to identify which things correspond to our sensor and actuator:

```
foreach (SearchResultThing Thing in e.Things)
{
    foreach (MetaDataTag Tag in Thing.Tags)
    {
        if (Tag.Name == "TYPE" &&
                Tag is MetaDataStringTag StringTag)
        {
            switch (Tag.StringValue)
            {
                case "MIoT Sensor":
                    if (string.IsNullOrEmpty(
                            this.sensorJid))
                    {
```

```
this.sensorJid = Thing.Jid;
this.sensor = Thing.Node;
```

 Only the sensor case will be demonstrated. The actuator case is completely analogous.

Making new friends

When we have identified a device we need access to, we need to update our roster accordingly by annotating the contact with the corresponding groups. If a roster item already exists, we update it. If one does not exist, we add one. We also need to send a presence subscription to the corresponding device, if one is not already available, to be able to communicate with it:

```
RosterItem Item = this.xmppClient[this.sensorJid];
if (Item != null)
{
        this.xmppClient.UpdateRosterItem(this.sensorJid,
                Item.Name, this.AddReference(Item.Groups,
                "Sensor", Thing.Node));

        if (Item.State != SubscriptionState.Both &&
                Item.State != SubscriptionState.To)
        {
                this.xmppClient.RequestPresenceSubscription(
                        this.sensorJid);
        }
}
else
{
        this.xmppClient.AddRosterItem(
                new RosterItem(this.sensorJid, string.Empty,
                this.AddReference(null, "Sensor", Thing.Node)));

        this.xmppClient.RequestPresenceSubscription(
                this.sensorJid);
}
}
break;
```

Here, the `AddReference()` method does the opposite of what the `GetReference()` method does: it adds group names encoding the identity of the device. See the GitHub repository for details.

Reacting to roster events

Changes to the roster may occur for different reasons. You might change the roster yourself. Another application, logged in to the same account as you, may change the roster. And those that you have presence subscriptions to may change the state of the subscription. Your application therefore needs to respond to changes in the roster, to maintain its state of operation. There are three events you need to listen to: when roster items are added, updated, or deleted:

```
this.xmppClient.OnRosterItemAdded +=
    XmppClient_OnRosterItemAdded;
this.xmppClient.OnRosterItemUpdated +=
    XmppClient_OnRosterItemUpdated;
this.xmppClient.OnRosterItemRemoved +=
    XmppClient_OnRosterItemRemoved;
```

Adding a friend

When a new roster item has been added, you need to make sure you subscribe to its presence if it's a sensor or actuator. Otherwise, you will not be able to communicate with it properly:

```
private void XmppClient_OnRosterItemAdded(object Sender,
    RosterItem Item)
{
    Log.Informational("Roster item added.", Item.BareJid);

    if (Item.IsInGroup("Sensor") || Item.IsInGroup("Actuator"))
    {
        Log.Informational("Requesting presence subscription.",
            Item.BareJid);

        this.xmppClient.RequestPresenceSubscription(
            Item.BareJid);
    }
}
```

Losing a friend

When you lose a connection, or a friend, you might need to update your state or find new devices, if the connection that was lost was your sensor or actuator. Since this may happen for various reasons, we create a function for this event:

```
private void XmppClient_OnRosterItemRemoved(object Sender,
    RosterItem Item)
{
    Log.Informational("Roster item removed.", Item.BareJid);
    this.FriendshipLost(Item);
}
```

When this happens, we restart the registration procedure, which in turn triggers the search procedure. This will allow the controller to eventually find new devices in its vicinity to which it can connect, to continue its operation:

```
private void FriendshipLost(RosterItem Item)
{
    bool UpdateRegistration = false;

    if (string.Compare(Item.BareJid, this.sensorJid, true) == 0)
    {
        this.sensorJid = null;
        this.sensor = null;
        UpdateRegistration = true;
    }

    if (string.Compare(Item.BareJid, this.actuatorJid, true) == 0)
    {
        this.actuatorJid = null;
        this.actuator = null;
        UpdateRegistration = true;
    }

    if (UpdateRegistration)
        Task.Run(this.RegisterDevice);
}
```

Reacting to revoked presence subscriptions

If one of your contacts cancels your presence subscription, you need to reorganize yourself as well, since you will no longer be able to communicate properly with that device. You should treat this case in the same way as if the roster item was removed. Any other changes might be caused by changes in the remote device. So, to make sure, you should re-subscribe to its sensor data, if it's a sensor, to make sure you continue to get information from it:

```
private void XmppClient_OnRosterItemUpdated(object Sender,
    RosterItem Item)
{
    bool IsSensor;

    Log.Informational("Roster item updated.", Item.BareJid);

    if (((IsSensor = (this.sensorJid != null &&
            string.Compare(Item.BareJid,this.sensorJid,true)==0)) ||
            (this.actuatorJid != null &&
            string.Compare(Item.BareJid,
                this.actuatorJid,true)==0)) &&
            (Item.State == SubscriptionState.None ||
            Item.State == SubscriptionState.From) &&
            Item.PendingSubscription!=PendingSubscription.Subscribe)
    {
        this.FriendshipLost(Item);
    }
    else if (IsSensor)
        this.SubscribeToSensorData();
}
```

Reacting to presence changes

Now that you have presence subscriptions active for your contacts, you need to react to changes in presence. They may indicate that the corresponding device has restarted, for instance. So, you need to register an event handler that is called when presence changes for one of your contacts in the roster:

```
this.xmppClient.OnPresence += XmppClient_OnPresence;
```

Whenever your sensor signals an online presence, you should re-subscribe to it, to make sure events are delivered in a timely fashion:

```
private void XmppClient_OnPresence(object Sender, PresenceEventArgs e)
{
    Log.Informational("Presence received.",
        e.Availability.ToString(), e.From);

    if (this.sensorJid != null &&
        string.Compare(e.FromBareJID,this.sensorJid,true)==0 &&
        e.IsOnline)
    {
        this.SubscribeToSensorData();
    }
}
```

Interacting with devices

We now have what we need to start interacting with our devices. In the previous chapter, we demonstrated how to create a sensor server and an actuator server. The controller, however, will be a sensor client and actuator client. We prepare the controller with variables for this purpose. The classes are available in the same NuGets and namespaces as the server counterparts:

```
private SensorClient sensorClient = null;
private ControlClient controlClient = null;
```

When we instantiate them, we provide them with a reference to our XMPP client:

```
this.sensorClient = new SensorClient(this.xmppClient);
this.controlClient = new ControlClient(this.xmppClient);
```

We will also maintain the current state, from the controller point of view, of the current values of the sensor and actuator, as well as the timestamps of when the values were last assigned:

```
private double? light = null;
private bool? motion = null;
private bool? output = null;
private DateTime lastEventFields = DateTime.Now;
private DateTime lastEventErrors = DateTime.Now;
private DateTime lastOutput = DateTime.Now;
```

As a sensor client, we have two options to retrieve data. Either we poll it, using the Request/Response pattern, or we use the event subscription pattern to get informed of changes as they occur. As hinted at in previous sections, the latter is the best option for our controller. We will maintain our current subscription in a separate variable:

```
private SensorDataSubscriptionRequest subscription = null;
```

Subscribing to sensor data events

From several sections of the code, we've made references to a `SubscribeToSensorData()` method that will be called when we're ready to subscribe to the sensor data from the sensor. We are now ready to focus on how this is done. The first thing to note is that we can only perform a subscription if we know a sensor, and if it is online:

```
private void SubscribeToSensorData()
{
    RosterItem SensorItem;

    if (!string.IsNullOrEmpty(this.sensorJid) &&
            (SensorItem=this.xmppClient[this.sensorJid]) != null &&
            SensorItem.HasLastPresence &&
            SensorItem.LastPresence.IsOnline)
    {
```

If a previous subscription exists, we make sure to unsubscribe to it. This has the effect that if stray messages are received on this subscription, they are thrown away, and the sender informed the subscription is no longer active:

```
if (this.subscription != null)
{
    this.subscription.Unsubscribe();
    this.subscription = null;
}
```

Performing the subscription is done by calling the `Subscribe()` method on the `SensorClient` object. You need to consider if the subscription is made to a node in a *concentrator* or to a standalone device. You also need to provide which types of fields you are interested in, any subscription rules, and minimum and maximum time intervals for events. In our case, we are only interested in momentary values, and the Light and Motion fields. We're interested in Light as soon as it changes by one unit of a percent. The motion should be sent when it changes by 1, which is the same to say, as when it changes value since it is a Boolean value. We don't want events more often than once a second, and no less often than once a minute. These two parameters are important since they make sure we don't get spammed, while at the same time they give us a means to measure if the subscription is active or not. If we don't get an event in a little more than a minute, we can be certain the subscription has been forgotten for one reason or another:

```
ThingReference[] Nodes;

if (this.sensor.IsEmpty)
    Nodes = null;
else
    Nodes = new ThingReference[] { this.sensor };

Log.Informational("Subscribing to events.",
SensorItem.LastPresenceFullJid);

this.subscription =
this.sensorClient.Subscribe(SensorItem.LastPresenceFullJid,
    Nodes, FieldType.Momentary, new FieldSubscriptionRule[]
    {
        new FieldSubscriptionRule("Light", this.light, 1),
        new FieldSubscriptionRule("Motion",
            this.motion.HasValue ?
            (double?)(this.motion.Value ? 1 : 0) : null, 1),
    },
    new Waher.Content.Duration(false, 0, 0, 0, 0, 0, 1),
    new Waher.Content.Duration(false, 0, 0, 0, 0, 1, 0), true);
```

Reacting to sensor data events

Any incoming events related to our subscription can be accessed through event handlers on the subscription object that is returned from the subscription request. To follow these events, we define three event handlers:

```
this.subscription.OnStateChanged +=
    Subscription_OnStateChanged;
this.subscription.OnFieldsReceived +=
```

```
              Subscription_OnFieldsReceived;
        this.subscription.OnErrorsReceived +=
              Subscription_OnErrorsReceived;
    }
}
```

For two of these events, we will simply output their state to the event log, so we can follow the process:

```
private void Subscription_OnStateChanged(object Sender,
    SensorDataReadoutState NewState)
{
    Log.Informational("Sensor subscription state changed.",
         NewState.ToString());
}

private void Subscription_OnErrorsReceived(object Sender,
    IEnumerable<ThingError> NewErrors)
{
    this.lastEventErrors = DateTime.Now;

    foreach (ThingError Error in NewErrors)
         Log.Error(Error.ErrorMessage);
}
```

Collecting relevant sensor data

The field event handler is called when sensor data is received from the subscription. It will contain an enumeration of fields. All we need to do is loop through them and see if we can find the fields we are looking for. If we do, we update our internal state, and make sure we update the controller output. We also make sure to update our main window, so that we get visual feedback:

```
private void Subscription_OnFieldsReceived(object Sender,
    IEnumerable<Field> NewFields)
{
    bool RecalcOutput = false;

    this.lastEventFields = DateTime.Now;

    foreach (Field Field in NewFields)
    {
         switch (Field.Name)
         {
              case "Light":
```

```
                if (Field is QuantityField Q)
                {
                        MainPage.Instance.LightUpdated(
                                Q.Value, Q.NrDecimals, Q.Unit);
                        if (Q.Unit == "%")
                        {
                                this.light = Q.Value;
                                RecalcOutput = true;
                        }
                }
                break;

        case "Motion":
                if (Field is BooleanField B)
                {
                        MainPage.Instance.MotionUpdated(
                                B.Value);
                        this.motion = B.Value;
                        RecalcOutput = true;
                }
                break;
        }
    }
```

Calculating control output

For this example, we will use a very simple formula to compute the expected control output: we will turn the relay on, if motion is detected when it's dark, which we interpret as when the (ambient) light sensor reports a light of less than 25%. The relay is turned off when there's no motion, or when it's not dark anymore:

```
if (RecalcOutput && this.motion.HasValue && this.light.HasValue)
{
    bool Output = this.motion.Value && this.light.Value < 25;
```

 Care must be taken when installing the light sensor, so that it is not affected by, say, a lamp, connected to the relay. The expected output should also have a time component, to avoid intermittent blinking states.

Performing control action

We are now ready to perform the control action. First, we need to get the full JID of the actuator. This is done by checking the last presence sent by the actuator. This is stored in the corresponding roster item. Note that we can only perform the control action if the actuator is online:

```
if (!string.IsNullOrEmpty(this.actuatorJid) &&
    (!this.output.HasValue || this.output.Value != Output))
{
    RosterItem Actuator = this.xmppClient[this.actuatorJid];

    if (Actuator != null &&
            Actuator.HasLastPresence &&
            Actuator.LastPresence.IsOnline)
    {
```

Performing a control operation on an actuator is done by calling the Set() method on the ControlClient object instance. As when subscribing to events, we must differentiate between an actuator that runs standalone and an actuator that operates as a node inside a concentrator:

```
ThingReference[] Nodes;

if (this.actuator.IsEmpty)
        Nodes = null;
else
        Nodes = new ThingReference[]
                { this.actuator };

this.controlClient.Set(
        Actuator.LastPresenceFullJid,
        "Output", Output, Nodes);
this.output = Output;
this.lastOutput = DateTime.Now;

MainPage.Instance.RelayUpdated(Output);
                }
            }
        }
    }
```

Recovering from stale states

The final thing we need to do before our controller is ready, is to add a mechanism to recover from stale states. There are many reasons why a controller might end up in a stale state. A **stale state** is defined as a state that does not correspond to reality. There might be network problems for the controller, or any of the devices it depends on. The devices might be broken, replaced, or simply restarted. To build in some form of resilience into our controller, we need to monitor that we get sensor data in a timely fashion and that we can perform control actions properly.

There are basically three things we need to monitor:

- That we receive subscription events properly
- That the device connections are still valid
- That we have a proper configuration at all

To monitor these, we set up a timer that is executed regularly every second. We define a variable for it:

```
private Timer secondTimer = null;
```

And initiate it during initialization of the controller:

```
this.secondTimer = new Timer(SecondTimerCallback, null,
    1000, 1000);
```

Re-subscribing to sensor data

Our first test is to compute the number of seconds since we got some information from our subscription. If it's more than 70 seconds (remember that we configured a maximum interval of 60 seconds), we draw the conclusion that the subscription is no longer active. So we make a new subscription request:

```
private void SecondTimerCallback(object State)
{
    DateTime Now = DateTime.Now;
    double SecondsSinceLastEvent = Math.Min(
            (Now - this.lastEventFields).TotalSeconds,
            (Now - this.lastEventErrors).TotalSeconds);
    double SecondsSinceLastOutput =
            (Now - this.lastOutput).TotalSeconds;
    RosterItem Item;
    bool Search = false;
```

```
if (this.subscription != null && SecondsSinceLastEvent > 70)
    this.SubscribeToSensorData();
```

Invalidating existing friendships

If more than a day has passed, and we still do not get data from the sensor, we invalidate the connection, and remove the annotations we have stored for the corresponding roster item:

```
else if (SecondsSinceLastEvent > 60 * 60 * 24)
{
    if (!string.IsNullOrEmpty(this.sensorJid))
    {
        Item = this.xmppClient[this.sensorJid];

        this.sensor = null;
        this.sensorJid = null;

        if (Item != null)
        {
            this.xmppClient.UpdateRosterItem(this.sensorJid,
                Item.Name, this.RemoveReference(Item.Groups,
                "Sensor"));
        }
    }

    Search = true;
}
```

 Here, the `RemoveReference()` method removes the groups used for annotating the roster item, and that is used by the `AddReference()` and `GetReference()` methods. See the GitHub repository for details.

Reconfiguring the controller

We do an identical test for the actuator. If we haven't been able to configure the actuator for a day, we assume the connection is no longer valid, so we invalidate it. The local `Search` variable is used to signal if we need a reconfiguration. If that is the case, we just re-register the controller with the thing registry again. That process will, in turn, trigger a new search, and find new devices:

```
    if (Search)
        Task.Run(this.RegisterDevice);
}
```

Decommissioning of devices

We are now done with our controller. The controller will now work and control the actuator based on input from the sensor, if both have been registered in the same registry, using the same location tags.

There are two issues we have not covered in this chapter, but need considering in a real-life scenario:

- **Provisioning**: The next chapter will introduce this concept. It will allow the owner of a device to control who can do what with it. Provisioning also handles a transfer of ownership of devices.
- **Decommissioning**: When a device is no longer to be used on the internet, it should be unregistered from the Thing Registry, so that others cannot find it and try to interact with it. A device unregisters itself by calling the `Unregister()` method on the `ThingRegistryClient` object instance. A controller may also need to test multiple devices in the search result, assuming some of them might not be valid anymore.

Summary

In this chapter, you've been shown the basic principles of how to create a controller that dynamically finds, connects to, and interacts with devices in its vicinity on the internet. You've been introduced to the fundamentals of discovery on the internet, as well as the basic principles of Thing Registries and how these can be used to interconnect entities on the internet. You have learned the difference between conceptual and network identities, and how these can be paired using an ownership claim procedure. You've also learned how XMPP helps realize discovery and interaction between devices, how to register self-owner devices, update metadata about the device, and search for devices in a Thing Registry. You also know how to maintain a sensor data subscription alive with a sensor and how to perform control operations on an actuator. In the next chapter, we will delve deeper into the concepts of security and interoperability between things on the internet and see how standardization efforts can help you solve some of these issues.

11
Product Life Cycle

Managing devices in an IoT infrastructure is more complicated than just installing devices, finding them, and starting to communicate with them, as we did in the previous chapter. You need to manage the devices over their entire life cycle. Furthermore, if you're planning to host an open network of IoT devices, you need to make sure the owners of each device can manage their own devices. Otherwise, the operator of the network will quickly become overloaded with work managing other people's devices. Lastly, interaction between devices and other entities must also be done in a secure manner. This chapter presents a method for how to accomplish all these things. It covers:

- A definition of ownership of data
- Claiming things as your own
- Determining who is allowed to befriend your things
- Determining who can read your things
- Determining who can control your things
- Automatic decision support for things
- Transfer of ownership
- Decommissioning of things

Defining ownership of data

In recent years, the predatory exploitation of information on the internet has highlighted the problem that there's no clear definition of **ownership** of data on the internet. Huge corporations are pushing the **big data** paradigm to hoard as much information as they possibly can, in the hope that it can be mined in the future to create additional value. This value will obviously fall into the hands of the companies doing the hoarding themselves, not the original creators of the information being hoarded. While big data and data mining have their obvious valuable use cases, their drawbacks must be clearly understood to be effectively addressed.

While certain types of information are protected by different types of legislation, there's no generic legislation that can be used to define ownership of data, and control its use, as well as profit from its usage. There is intellectual property and copyright legislation to protect ideas and created content. Trade secrets, legislation can be used to protect sensitive information. Privacy legislation can be used to protect personally identifiable information. While certain types of sensor data could be personal information, and thus protected by privacy legislation, it is far from the case in general. And the possibility of automatically hoarding sensor data from the internet makes any policing of such laws very difficult. In short, generally, there are no laws that can be used to protect sensor data on the internet. The responsibility to protect your data therefore lies with the owner.

Choosing who should own the data

Before we can try to define ownership of data, we must understand who should be the owner of the data. There are different candidates:

- Should the owner be the person or entity generating or inventing the data? For IoT, that would best correspond to the owner of the device generating the data.
- Or should the owner be the person or entity processing or controlling the data? In that case, it could be the big data corporation hoarding information from the internet that becomes the owner of the information it has hoarded.
- Another possibility is that the owner of the information could be the person whom the data relates to.

Owners of devices would prefer the first option to be true. They invested in the devices, and want to own any information those devices generate. Big data enterprises in turn prefer the second option. They want to benefit from mining any information they can get access to, and benefit from being able to decide with or to whom to share or sell this information. The disadvantages of such an approach for the owners of the devices and private persons should be obvious. Privacy activists in turn would opt for the third option. A fanatic interpretation of this is also problematic, since it would prohibit legitimate uses of certain personal information by others as well. The approach chosen in this book is the first option, empowering the owner of a device to control the information that device produces.

Understanding ownership of physical objects

Before we define ownership of information, let's first look at how ownership of physical objects is defined and enforced, to see if we can mimic it for information as well.

If you own something, how do you enforce your ownership of this thing in the general case? Certain types of items, such as vehicles or real estate, have **central registries** where ownership is defined, and where third parties can go to verify ownership claims. Valuable things can also be registered in a similar manner, by sending information and photographic evidence of the things to an insurance company, for instance. In that way, claims of ownership can be verified.

But how do you enforce ownership of less valuable things? If you place them openly in the street, can you still successfully claim the things are yours if somebody chooses to take them? Obviously not. You need to protect the things behind **lock and key**. Insurance companies will not respond to claims of lost things that have not been appropriately protected. But more is required. If you carelessly allow anybody access to the thing, including people that are not trustworthy, can you complain if the thing is lost or destroyed? Of course not. You also need to **limit access** to the thing, based on **trust**.

If you haven't seen your thing in long a while, can you still claim that you are in possession of it? If you haven't seen a thing in decades, are you sure it is still there? Claiming ownership of a thing also requires knowledge of presence, or **monitoring**.

You **demonstrate** your ownership of a thing if you comply with all of the aforementioned factors.

Defining ownership of information

We are now ready to define ownership of information, in a congruent manner. The cornerstone of defining ownership of information is using **decentralization** of storage and processing of the information as the **principal method**. This is in stark contrast to centralized storage and processing, as defined in big data.

 Note that decentralization as a principal means of processing is not opposed to centralized processing of (parts of) the information. It just means that centralized processing is secondary, and always with approval from the primary source.

Decentralization of processing permits you to **demonstrate your ownership** of the decentralized information, as follows:

- If the data is only available in your device, it can be protected behind **lock and key**
- If the communication infrastructure properly authenticates identities of participants, authorization can be used to **limit access** based on **trust**
- Propagation of presence of all participants to approved subscribers in the network allows you to easily **monitor** your devices
- Registration of ownership claims of devices in a **Thing Registry** allows for verification of ownership

 Note that limiting access to the data is key to controlling ownership. As soon as the data leaves your control, the other party can technically do whatever they desire with it. You should therefore only allow access to your data to those that you intimately trust, or have a **contract** with, or an other arrangement, that specifies what can be done with the data. If you don't do this, you cannot enforce your ownership of the data, and for all practical reasons, you've *lost your data*.

All the requirements for being able to control ownership of data is possible if an infrastructure based on **XMPP** is used. XMPP furthermore has the benefit of being standardized, and therefore interoperable. Of the protocols presented in this book, it is the only protocol with these properties. Ownership is enforced in XMPP by the following:

- Protection under lock and key are solved in XMPP using **authentication** and **encryption**.
- Trust is modeled using **presence subscriptions**.

- Limiting access can be done manually, or automatically, using a method called **provisioning**. We will discuss provisioning in more depth in this chapter.
- Monitoring of your devices is done using **presence**.
- Registration and discovery is performed in **Thing Registries**, as described in the previous chapter.

> Limiting access to your information has an added advantage: it provides a means to establish the **value** of your information, by controlling who has access to it. Only limited resources have value. And the value is established on the principles of supply and demand. Limiting access to information will form the basis for creating an **open market** of information in the smart society.

Understanding provisioning

The major item still left to discuss, before we have an infrastructure where we can control ownership of the information it generates, is provisioning. Provisioning is the means to control who can access your devices, and do what with them.

The **IEEE IoT Harmonization** working group, which we presented in previous chapters, provides an extension to XMPP for provisioning. (This interface is based on legacy interfaces defined in XEP-0324.) The provisioning extension provides things with decision support in answering three main questions:

- Am I allowed to accept a presence subscription request from an entity?
- Am I allowed to be read by an entity, and if so, which data?
- Am I allowed to be controlled by an entity, and if so, which parameters?

The provisioning extension defines the concept of a **provisioning server** to which all things can ask the aforementioned questions when necessary. The provisioning server in turn makes sure to ask the owner, when the owner is available, if a question arises it cannot find an answer to, based on previous responses from the owner. Before the owner can respond, the principle of **data protection by default** is used, and the request is automatically denied. But as soon as the owner has responded, successive questions will get the updated response.

Things are encouraged to cache responses to questions they pose. When rules are updated, the provisioning server simply asks the corresponding devices to clear their caches. This will make sure the devices ask the corresponding questions again, thus making sure the answers reflect the new rules. In production, the load on the provisioning server is proportional to the change of rules in the network, and not the size of the network.

Using a Thing Registry to register ownership

Figure 1 provides a schematic overview of the entire life cycle of a thing. In the previous chapter, we illustrated how a **Thing Registry** can be used as a bulletin board to discover things according to some parameters. We used **self-owned** things to illustrate the concept without complicating matters unduly. But a Thing Registry can also be used to match things and owners, and interchange their network identities with each other. This matching of ownership is basically the registry of ownership for things that we need. The initial steps are as follows:

- During **production**, only *meta-information* about each produced thing is known. This *meta-information*, or *conceptual identity*, is stored in each thing.
- During **installation**, the thing is physically installed and connected.
- During **configuration**, a *network identity* is generated. This includes IP addresses and other types of network addresses. In XMPP, this includes the creation of an XMPP address. This address is not known to anybody else other than the thing, and the broker with which the thing has registered.
- The thing then generates a random **key**. This key will be used to make sure guessing the meta-information of a thing is practically impossible.
- The thing then **registers** itself with the Thing Registry. This time, it does not register itself as self-owned. Instead, it has no owner from the beginning. In this registration process, the metadata made available from production, as well as the key, is registered with the Thing Registry.
- Somehow, the metadata is transferred from the thing to the owner. It can be done using an `iotdisco` URI, and a QR code, as described in the previous chapter.
- With the information provided, the owner can now **claim** the device as his or hers, by sending the same information to the same Thing Registry in a claim request. If there's an unclaimed thing with exactly the same information available, including the key, the thing is registered as owned, and the network identities of each are sent to the other.

Note: if QR codes on stickers, prepared in production, are to be used to transfer the meta-information to the owner, the key needs to be generated already in the production environment. If so, a decision has to be made if the same key is to be reused, or a new one generated, when transferring the ownership at a later stage.

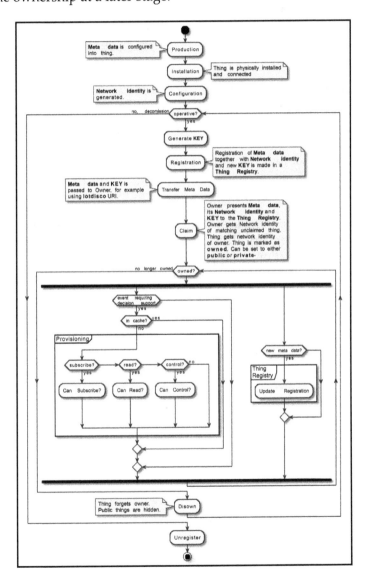

Figure 1. Life cycle of a thing

Provisioning of a claimed thing

When we created self-owned things in the previous chapter, they had to take decisions by themselves. In this chapter, as we introduce provisioning and the concept of ownership, we have an alternative. As soon as something happens in the network that the thing does not know how to respond to, it can ask the **provisioning server**, who will help the thing answer the question. The provisioning server, in turn, will ask the corresponding owner, if it does not know the answer. An example sequence is illustrated in *Figure 2*. The questions we will focus on are:

- Can an entity subscribe to presence?
- Can an entity read the device, and how much?
- Can an entity control the device, and which parameters?

The provisioning server is found in the same way as the Thing Registry was found: by examining the components made available by the XMPP broker. Typically, it can even be the same component as the Thing Registry, even though it does not have to be.

During the claimed phase, the thing is also free to update and amend the *meta-information* it has registered in the Thing Registry. This is useful, as the thing is now able to update the registry with variable information, such as position. Such information cannot be part of the original registration, since claiming ownership requires the information to be static:

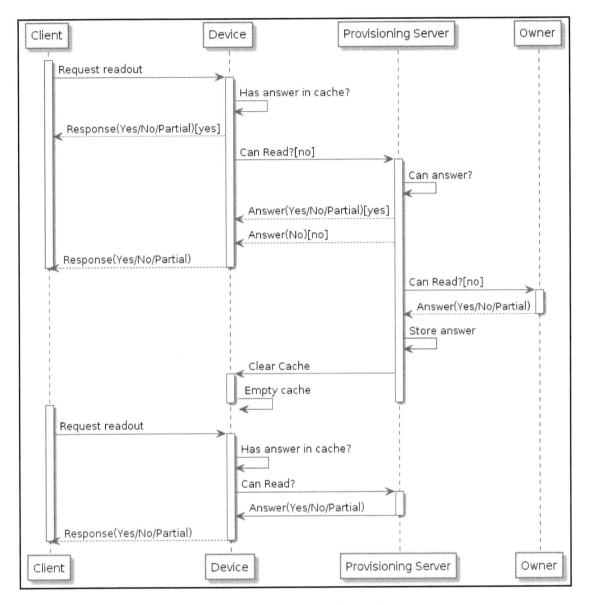

Figure 2. Interaction between device, provisioning server, and owner

Ending ownership

All ownership comes to an end, either if the thing changes owner, or the thing is thrown away or destroyed. To support these events, two operations are available: **disowning** a thing and **unregistering** a thing. Disowning a thing removes the ownership registration, but leaves the thing in the Thing Registry. The thing then re-registers itself, allowing it to be claimed by a new owner. In this way, a transfer of ownership can take place. Unregistering a thing, means the thing is removed from the Thing Registry altogether. It is the *graceful* thing to do, at the end of the life of a thing.

When the ownership of a thing gets transferred to a new owner, it is vitally important to transfer it in the provisioning server as well. Without this transfer of ownership, the old owner will be able to control the device without the knowledge of the new owner.

Adding provisioning support to our devices

We are now ready to implement support for provisioning in our devices. We create two new projects, a `SensorXmpp2` and an `ActuatorXmpp2`. We base these on the `SensorXmpp` and `ActuatorXmpp` projects, developed in the previous chapters. The `Waher.Networking.XMPP.Provisioning` namespace, already made available in these projects, contains a `ProvisioningClient` class which will do most of the work. It supports both the device and owner interfaces of provisioning.

Provisioning interfaces are published by the IEEE IoT Harmonization working group, introduced in `Chapter 9`, *Social Interaction with Your Devices Using XMPP*.

Searching for a provisioning server

For our purposes, we start with the device set of interfaces for provisioning. We add a member variable that will hold our provisioning client to both our `SensorXmpp2` and `ActuatorXmpp2` projects:

```
private ProvisioningClient provisioningClient = null;
```

When we search the components made available by the server to find a Thing Registry, we make sure to check for provisioning support as well:

```
if (e2.HasFeature(ProvisioningClient.NamespaceProvisioningDevice))
{
    Log.Informational("Provisioning server found.", Item2.JID);
    this.UseProvisioningServer(Item2.JID, OwnerJid);
    await RuntimeSettings.SetAsync("ProvisioningServer.JID",
        Item2.JID);
}
```

Here, the `OwnerJid` contains the JID to the device's owner, if known. If not, it is simply empty.

Creating a provisioning client

When we've found a component providing provisioning support, we instantiate a provisioning client, pointing to that component:

```
private void UseProvisioningServer(string JID, string OwnerJid)
{
    if (this.provisioningClient == null ||
            this.provisioningClient.ProvisioningServerAddress!=JID||
            this.provisioningClient.OwnerJid != OwnerJid)
    {
        if (this.provisioningClient != null)
        {
            this.provisioningClient.Dispose();
            this.provisioningClient = null;
        }

        this.provisioningClient = new ProvisioningClient(
            this.xmppClient, JID, OwnerJid);
        this.AttachFeatures();
    }
}
```

Now that we have created a provisioning client referencing our XMPP client, we must remove the `OnPresenceSubscribe` and `OnPresenceUnsubscribe` event handlers defined earlier. These are now managed by the provisioning client, who will forward new requests to the provisioning server, who in turn will forward any new requests to the owner.

Adding provisioning support

In the `AttachFeatures` method that we defined in previous chapters, we create the corresponding sensor, actuator, and chat servers. All we need to do to add provisioning support to these is to add a reference to the provisioning client, to each constructor. For a sensor server, we simply write:

```
this.sensorServer = new SensorServer(this.xmppClient,
    this.provisioningClient, true);
```

The control server in an actuator is instantiated in a similar manner (here, the ellipsis represents the control parameters we give the control server by default):

```
this.controlServer = new ControlServer(this.xmppClient,
    this.provisioningClient, ...);
```

Similarly, instantiation of the chat server also accepts a provisioning client as an argument:

```
this.chatServer = new ChatServer(this.xmppClient, this.bobClient,
    this.sensorServer, this.provisioningClient);
```

As soon as a readout event or control operation is received, these three server objects will now check with the provisioning client if the operation is allowed or not, or if only parts of the request are permitted. Only permitted operations will be allowed to be executed.

Registration of device

We must also modify our registration procedure with the Thing Registry. In the previous chapter, we registered *self-owned* things. These are their own owners and manage security decisions by themselves. Now we must point out that the devices are not *self-owned*:

```
this.registryClient.RegisterThing(false, MetaInfo,
    async (sender, e) =>
    {
        try
        {
```

In the response, we can learn if the thing has already been claimed. If so, we make sure to update our internal state to reflect this ownership:

```
if (e.Ok)
{
    await RuntimeSettings.SetAsync("ThingRegistry.Location",
        true);
    await RuntimeSettings.SetAsync("ThingRegistry.Owner",
```

```
                    e.OwnerJid);
```

Transmitting the conceptual identity

If our device does not have an owner, we must make it possible for the owner to claim the device. This is done by presenting *the same* meta-information as the device just registered. We do this by creating an `iotdisco` URI that we store to a file:

```
if (string.IsNullOrEmpty(e.OwnerJid))
{
    string ClaimUrl = registryClient.EncodeAsIoTDiscoURI( MetaInfo);
    string FilePath = ApplicationData.Current.LocalFolder.Path +
        Path.DirectorySeparatorChar + "Sensor.iotdisco";

    Log.Informational("Registration successful.");
    Log.Informational(ClaimUrl, new KeyValuePair<string, object>(
        "Path", FilePath));

    File.WriteAllText(FilePath, ClaimUrl);
}
```

 Instead of storing the `iotdisco` URI as a file, a more efficient way to transmit the URI is by encoding it using QR codes.

Reacting to claims

Device claims can occur either when the device is online, or when it is offline. We need to handle both cases. If the claim occurred while the device was offline, we get notified of this fact in the response to the registration call:

```
else
{
    await RuntimeSettings.SetAsync(      "ThingRegistry.Key",
        string.Empty);
    Log.Informational("Registration updated. Device has "+
        "an owner.", new KeyValuePair<string, object>(
        "Owner", e.OwnerJid));
}
```

By adding an event handler for the `Claimed` event on the `ThingRegistry` instance, we can react immediately to the event, if the device is online. We store the network address of the owner, as well as clear the key:

```
this.registryClient.Claimed += async (sender, e) =>
{
    try
    {
        await RuntimeSettings.SetAsync("ThingRegistry.Owner",
            e.JID);
        await RuntimeSettings.SetAsync("ThingRegistry.Key",
            string.Empty);
    }
    catch (Exception ex)
    {
        Log.Critical(ex);
    }
};
```

Updating the registration of our device

In the same way, we need to react to the thing being disowned. This can also happen either when the device is online or offline. If it happens offline, we detect it when we update our registration in the Thing Registry, by checking the response arguments. When the device has been disowned, we make sure to forget the identity of the previous owner, and re-register the device as a claimable device again:

```
this.registryClient.UpdateThing(MetaInfo, async (sender, e) =>
{
    try
    {
        if (e.Disowned)
        {
            await RuntimeSettings.SetAsync(
                "ThingRegistry.Owner", string.Empty);
            await this.RegisterDevice(MetaInfo);
        }
        else if (e.Ok)
            Log.Informational(
                "Registration update successful.");
        else
        {
            Log.Error("Registration update failed.");
            await this.RegisterDevice(MetaInfo);
        }
```

```
    }
    catch (Exception ex)
    {
            Log.Critical(ex);
    }
}, null);
```

Reacting to being disowned

Similarly, we must detect if the device becomes disowned while it is online. This is done by listening to the Disowned event on the ThingRegistry instance:

```
this.registryClient.Disowned += async (sender, e) =>
{
    try
    {
            await RuntimeSettings.SetAsync("ThingRegistry.Owner",
                string.Empty);
            await this.RegisterDevice();
    }
    catch (Exception ex)
    {
            Log.Critical(ex);
    }
};
```

There are some other minor changes made in the code between SensorXmpp2 and ActuatorXmpp2 compared to SensorXmpp and ActuatorXmpp that reflect the asynchronous nature of initializing the devices with provisioning. You can view the changes in the GitHub project source code, by comparing the App.xaml.cs files of the corresponding projects.

Managing the owner side

The `ProvisioningClient` instance allows you to create a GUI for the owner-side application that can be used to configure your network. When the device-side interface has requests, the owner side has corresponding events. The following events can be subscribed to, so as to listen for incoming questions from the provisioning server:

Event	Description
`IsFriendQuestion`	This event is raised when the owner needs to decide if a third party is allowed to subscribe to the device's presence or not.
`CanReadQuestion`	When the provisioning server needs to ask the owner if a third party is allowed to read one of its devices, this event is raised.
`CanControlQuestion`	When a new control operation is attempted, this event is raised to allow the owner to decide if it's allowed or not.

 Note that the owner does not need to be online when the device asks the provisioning server a question. The provisioning server keeps the message and sends it to the owner when the owner gets online.

Deciding what to do

Somehow, the owner needs to decide how to respond to the questions posed by the provisioning server. This can either be done manually, by the owner, or through some advanced method using machine learning. Regardless of the method, the owner sends back rule increments to the provisioning server. The provisioning server in turn persists these increments, helping it to respond to similar requests in the future.

The friendship question can only be responded to in the **affirmative** or **negative**. Either the third party can connect, or it cannot. The read and control responses have more flexibility. Apart from an affirmative or a negative option, it is also possible to grant **partial** permissions. Here, either the allowed categories of sensor data fields, or the actual field or parameter names, can be specified in the rule increment. If the third party tries to read or control more, only the approved fields or parameters will be allowed.

The rule increments can also be based on the **origin** of the request. For friendship questions, the origin can be limited to the **caller** XMPP address (or JID) of the third party, its **domain**, or it can be ignored, handling **all** future requests according to the rule increment. For the read and control options, the choice can also be based on the presence of a **service**, **device**, or **user** token. The methods available for answering questions are:

Event	Response methods
IsFriendQuestion	IsFriendResponse
CanReadQuestion	CanReadResponseCaller CanReadResponseDomain CanReadResponseService CanReadResponseDevice CanReadResponseUser CanReadResponseAll
CanControlQuestion	CanControlResponseCaller CanControlResponseDomain CanControlResponseService CanControlResponseDevice CanControlResponseUser CanControlResponseAll

Managing owned devices

The owner interface also has methods that allow you to manage your devices. You can use these methods if you don't persist the devices you own, or if you want to experiment with devices you're currently developing. Some of the more important methods are:

Method	Description
GetDevices	Gets a list of the devices you own.
ClearDeviceCache	Asks the provisioning server to request a particular device to clear its rule cache.
ClearDeviceCaches	Asks the provisioning server to request all owned devices to clear their rule caches.
DeleteDeviceRules	There are two overloads of this method. One requests the provisioning server to delete all rules pertaining to a particular owned device. The other allows the owner to delete all rules for all its devices.

Using tokens for identification

Devices, owners, or third-party services can use tokens to identify either a service, a device, or a user. These tokens are small and easy to distribute in distributed transactions. They can also be **challenged**: a process used to verify that a sender is allowed to use a given token.

To get a token, the corresponding entity registers a **certificate** with a **public key** with the provisioning server, and gets a token as a response. Anyone receiving a token can ask the provisioning server for the corresponding public certificate. But only the original sender of the certificate retains the **private key**. To challenge a token, a challenge message is sent to the sender of the token. If the token is resent from another source, the receiver of the challenge needs to forward the challenge to the original sender. The original sender can use the private key to respond to the challenge. Only the holder of the private key can do that. But anyone with the public key can verify that the response is correct.

 The challenge/response mechanism for tokens is managed by the provisioning client and the provisioning server. This process is invisible to users of the `ProvisioningClient` class.

Both readout requests and control requests can be annotated using a variable number of tokens, of three different categories (service, device, and user). By doing that, it is possible to create rules based on the use of certificates, regardless from where the corresponding request comes. This might simplify matters greatly for owners, since they can approve access based on the corresponding service, device, or user, instead of having to check who controls a given network identity.

Available methods for managing tokens include:

Method	Description
GetToken	Sends the public part of a certificate to the provisioning server. A corresponding token is returned. The token can then be distributed. Only the holder of the private part of the certificate can successfully respond to challenges.
GetCertificate	Gets the public part of a certificate corresponding to a given token. This method can be used to verify the identity of the holder of the token, by performing an X.509 certificate validation.

Testing provisioning

To test the provisioning capabilities of your devices, you can either develop your own GUI, or use the simple **IoT Client** available in the **IoT Gateway** GitHub repository. Setup files are available.

The simple IoT Client can be downloaded from:
`https://github.com/PeterWaher/IoTGateway#clients`

For source code examples of how the owner interface is implemented, see `https://github.com/PeterWaher/IoTGateway/blob/master/Clients/Waher.Client.WPF/Model/Provisioning/ThingRegistry.cs`.

Provisioning your devices

When you open your IoT Client for the first time, you need to create a connection to an XMPP broker. This is done using the **Connect to...** command (the star icon). That allows you to create an account or connect to an existing account on an XMPP broker. Connect to the same broker your devices use, so that you can automatically use the same Thing Registry and provisioning server.

Once you're connected, you will see the Thing Registry and provisioning server component or components. Right-click this component to access context-sensitive commands. You can also right-click any of your devices to get context-sensitive commands relating to provisioning and the registry. Press the **Add...** button (the plus sign). In the context of a Thing Registry command, this means you want to add a device to the list of your devices, or claim one as your own:

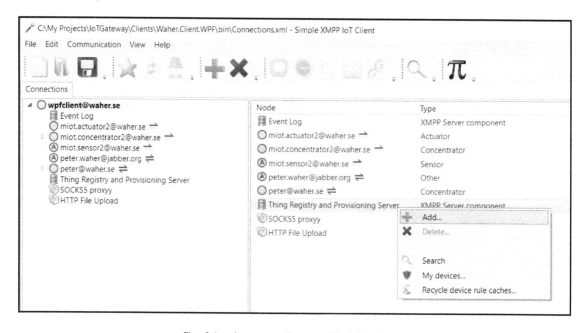

Figure 3. Accessing context-sensitive commands for the Thing Registry

Claiming a device

Now, fetch the `iotdisco` URI generated for the device you want to claim. Paste it into the dialog that appears. You will be able to see all the metadata encoded in the URI, as is shown in *Figure 4*:

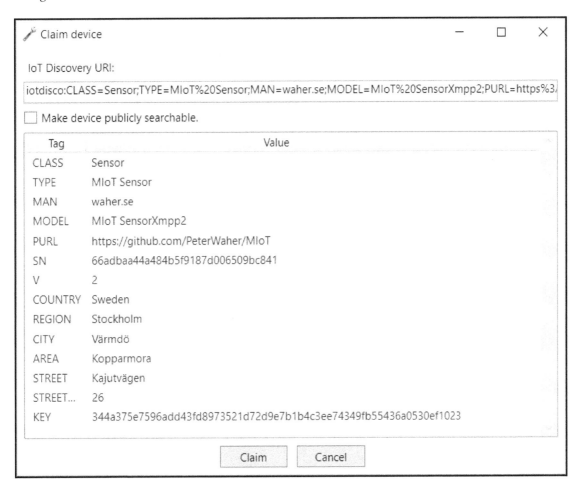

Figure 4. Claiming a device

Click the **Claim** button, and the device is yours (unless it has already been claimed by somebody else), as shown in *Figure 5*. As it is yours, you can now do anything with it:

Figure 5. Claim successful

Adding rules

If somebody else tries to connect to your device, a tab will appear called **Questions**. In this tab anything you need to decide will be shown. *Figure 6* shows an example of when a third party tries to read the device. Note that you can choose how much you will allow the third party to be able to read:

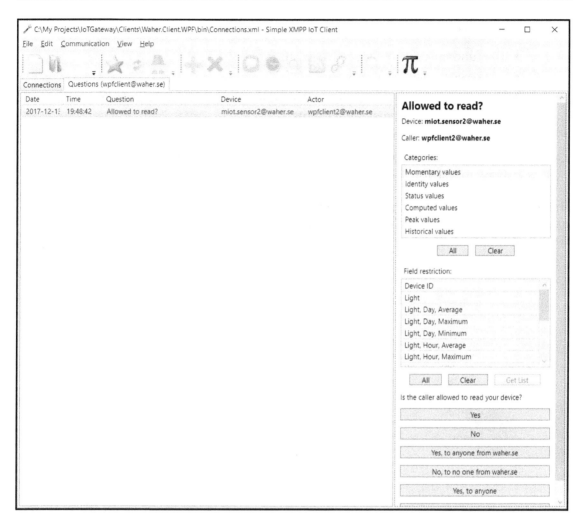

Figure 6. Answering questions from the provisioning server

Summary

In this chapter, you've been shown the basic principles of how to add provisioning support to your devices, and how to control who can do what with your things.

In this chapter, you've learned:

- The fundamentals of ownership of information
- The basic principles of provisioning
- How to add provisioning support to your devices
- How to react to provisioning events
- How to manage your devices
- How certificates and tokens can be used for identification
- How to test your devices

In the next chapter, we will analyze how we can build even more powerful things, by analyzing the concept of concentrators, and how to manage multiple virtual devices inside a single physical entity.

12
Concentrators and Bridges

Real-world devices are sometimes complex. They often host multiple logical entities or logical devices providing different functionalities inside themselves. This encapsulation of virtual devices inside one communicating entity is called a **concentrator**. A concentrator concentrates multiple virtual or logical devices into one physical device. A method is presented that allows you to work with virtual devices seamlessly, as if they were standalone devices on the network. The same technique can be used to bridge between protocol islands, either using the same or different types of communication protocols, or to integrate backend systems into the network. This chapter covers:

- An introduction to the concept of concentrators
- How concentrators can be used to model embedded devices
- How concentrators can be used to bridge between protocols
- How concentrators can be used to integrate backend systems
- How embedded nodes are referenced
- How concentrators are managed
- How to create a concentrator that hosts both our sensor and actuator
- How to provision embedded devices in a concentrator

Introducing concentrators

Up to this point, we've studied relatively simple devices, each fitting neatly into a physical device. But often, you can add value to your physical device, if you divide it into multiple logical devices. A simple example may be our sensor. It senses two different things: ambient light and motion. These two things are independent of each other and could be modeled as individual sensors logically. But running them on different Raspberry Pi would be more expensive and would only make sense if the actual sensors were separated by some distance. For that reason, it is more cost efficient to implement them into one single unit. They share the same Raspberry Pi, operating system, and network connection.

Dividing a device into multiple logical devices permits you to do things you normally would not do with a single device: you can manage and operate them separately on the network. You can also provision them differently and assign different owners to the different logical devices. Sometimes, this makes a lot of sense, as we will soon see.

Understanding concentrators in XMPP

Since a concentrator is a single physical device with a single connection to the network, another form of internal addressing is required to identify which internal device is referenced in a request. In XMPP, the physical device, or the concentrator, has a single XMPP Address, or **Jabber ID (JID)**.

Embedded devices, or logical devices, are called **nodes**, and they are identified with node identities. Optionally, these nodes can be collected into data sources, if there are many nodes with different functions. For very large concentrators, data sources can optionally be divided into partitions as well. A node identity is unique within the given partition and data source in which it resides. If there are no partitions or data sources, these can be considered blank strings.

In all IoT-related interactions except presence subscription, you can address a logical node instead of the physical device, by adding an `id` attribute (node identity), and optionally a `src` (data source) and a `pt` (partition) attribute as well. Since presence is managed on an XMPP address basis, you must manage those on a concentrator level. How these identities can be used to model different types of concentrators will be explored in the following sections.

Attribute	Meaning	Description
id	**Node identity**	Identifies the node. The identity is unique within the data source and partition in which the node resides.
src	**Data Source**	Optional data source identity. Nodes can be divided into collections called data sources. If not provided, the empty string is assumed.
pt	**Partition**	Optional partition. Data sources can be further partitioned.

Modeling a Programmable Logic Controller

A **Programmable Logic Controller**, or **PLC**, is a device with some generic functionality that can be configured (or programmed) in certain ways to interact with its surroundings. Typically, it contains a series of input or output modules, either analog, digital, and/or serial. More advanced PLCs contain other types of objects as well. If the PLC is to be connected to the network, it makes no sense to create an individual connection for each input/output module. Instead, the PLC gets a single connection.

Some PLCs can be modeled as a single sensor or actuator with a sequence of input fields (for example, Input 1, Input 2, ...) or output fields (Output 1, Output 2, and so on). But it would make more sense to model the PLC as a concentrator, where each input or output module becomes a logical device embedded in the PLC. This has several advantages:

- Each module of a similar kind gets the same type of interface, such as field names, parameters, and so on (Input or Output, for example).
- They can be registered separately and claimed by different owners.
- Interfaces for embedded devices are typically simpler.
- Service interfaces become more loosely coupled, and do not have to consider changes in the capabilities of different PLCs, such as the quantity and types of embedded devices. It is sufficient to recognize the interfaces of the embedded devices that are used.

The following diagram illustrates a PLC modeled as a concentrator. Data sources and partitions are not used in this example. Only the node identity is used to identify the corresponding embedded device:

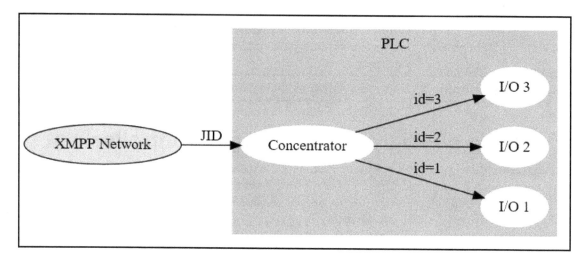

PLC modeled as a concentrator

Bridging protocols

The concentrator abstraction is versatile and can be used in many different use cases. Another common task that suits the model well is the implementation of **Protocol Bridges**. There are many advantages of building a protocol bridge that bridges devices and services from one protocol to and from XMPP using concentrators. The implementation would be seamless. Actors on the different sides would not have to know anything about the protocol on the other side. They would not even know that they are communicating with entities that use another protocol. The reason for this flexibility, is the versatility of the XMPP protocol in supporting the different communication patterns typically used in IoT-based protocols.

The following diagram illustrates a simple bridge between the XMPP network and a Modbus network. Modbus is a common protocol used in industrial automation applications. In this example, the logical devices inside the concentrators are not embedded devices, but external standalone devices, and they are communicating using Modbus, instead of XMPP. Here, devices are divided into data sources, representing different Modbus networks. Each data source is identified with the IP address of the corresponding TCP/IP Modbus gateway that is being used:

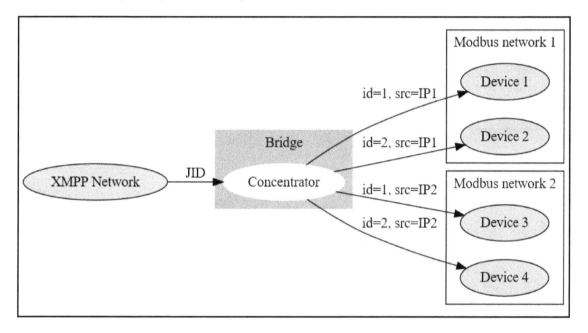

Protocol bridge modeled as a concentrator

I've prepared an MQTT to XMPP bridge, reachable at the XMPP address `iot.eclipse.org@waher.se`. It is a concentrator app that runs on a Raspberry Pi, which bridges data published on the MQTT broker, available at `iot.eclipse.org`. The topic tree is modeled as nodes in the concentrator. You can read and subscribe to data on the nodes. You can publish data to the broker by sending control operations to the corresponding topics.

Note: The bridge is provisioned to add an extra level of security on top of the MQTT. This means that the first time you try to access the bridge, it will reject your presence subscription. Send me a mail beforehand, and I will make sure you get access to the bridge.

Integrating backend systems

Another great use case for the concentrator pattern is to integrate backend systems into the network. By using a concentrator as a point of integration, data in the backend system will appear as devices in the XMPP network. This will allow services and other devices to interact with the backend system, just as if it was any other type of device in the network. This has great benefits, since it removes the need to support the backend system directly in all devices and services that need data from the backend system.

The following diagram contains a simple example of backend system integration using concentrators. Note how the partitioning of data sources allows for identities do be reused in different partitions, without the creating ambiguity. This is useful in larger systems and it can be used to solve many problems. One such problem can be the desire to reutilize object identities available in country-specific datasets, as illustrated in the following diagram:

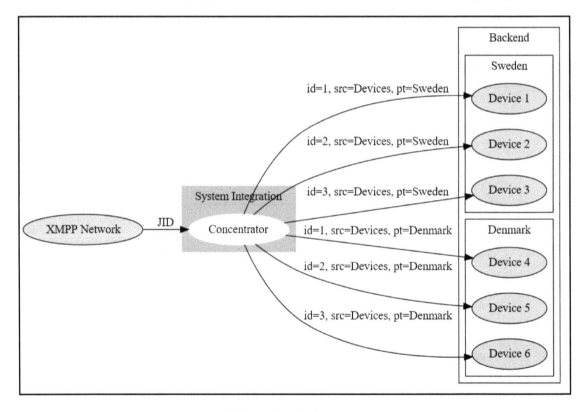

Backend system integration using concentrators

Referencing embedded nodes

In the previous chapters, we've used different classes from different NuGet packages to perform different tasks on the XMPP network. Depending on whether we've implemented a sensor, an actuator, a controller, or a combination of these, different classes have been used. The following table gives an overview of the different classes that we have used, together with their most important methods and events:

Class	Methods	Events
SensorClient	RequestReadout() Subscribe()	
SensorServer		OnExecuteReadoutRequest
ControlClient	Set() GetForm() CancelForm()	
ControlServer		OnGetControlParameters
ThingRegistryClient	RegisterThing() UpdateThing() Mine() Remove() Unregister() Disown() Search()	Claimed Removed Disowned
ProvisioningClient	GetToken() GetCertificate() IsFriend() CanRead() CanControl() IsFriendResponse() CanReadResponse*() CanControlResponse*() ClearDeviceCaches() ClearDeviceCache() GetDevices() DeleteDeviceRules()	IsFriendQuestion CanReadQuestion CanControlQuestion

Referencing embedded sensor nodes

Referencing embedded nodes is done through overloading of the methods we are already familiar with. The SensorClient class has two main methods for obtaining sensor data: the RequestReadout and Subscribe methods. The first returns data immediately, the second when new data is made available. Both methods have overloaded versions that enable you to provide a reference to one or more ThingReference objects. Each ThingReference object (class defined in Waher.Things) contains a NodeId, SourceId, and a Partition property. By adding such references to the request, you direct the request to the corresponding embedded node instead of to the concentrator itself.

 You can explicitly reference the concentrator itself, by adding a reference to the static ThingReference.Empty property. It has the three properties set to the empty string.

Sensor data is asynchronously returned to the client and provided through events on the request object. This data consists of collections of Field and ThingError objects. Each Field object has a Thing property that lets you know from which node the data comes. If the reference is empty, it comes from the device maintaining the XMPP connection itself. Each ThingError object also contains a reference to the originating node, if any.

Supporting embedded sensor nodes

Sensors instantiate the SensorServer class to publish sensor data. There is no need to instantiate one such class for each embedded sensor node. Instead, only the concentrator needs to instantiate it. Incoming requests raise the OnExecuteReadoutRequest event. The event argument class contains a Nodes property that contains the nodes referenced in the request. The event handler must then either redirect the request to the corresponding embedded sensor node, or handle the embedded nodes internally in the event handler.

During readout, a collection of Field or ThingError objects is generated. Each one contains a reference to the node from where the data originated. If the device is not a concentrator, a reference to ThingReference.Empty is used.

Referencing embedded actuator nodes

Interaction with actuators is done using the `ControlClient` class. The two main methods are `Set` and `GetForm`. The first is used to perform control actions, the second to get available control actions. Both methods have overloads accepting one or more `ThingReference` objects, referencing the embedded actuator nodes in question.

Supporting embedded actuator nodes

For simple actuators, we instantiate the `ControlServer` class with a set of control parameters that the actuator publishes. For concentrators we cannot always do this since the embedded actuators typically have different sets of control parameters.

If all embedded actuators have the same set of control parameters, we can still instantiate the `ControlServer` class with the set of control parameters to publish. The get and set event handlers contain a reference to the embedded node in question. If, on the other hand, the embedded actuators do not have the same set of control parameters, we instantiate the `ControlServer` class without parameters. Instead, we provide an event handler for the `OnGetControlParameters` event. The event handler gets a reference to the node in question from the `Node` property in the event arguments and returns a set of control parameters for the referenced node.

Using embedded nodes in Thing Registries

All devices in Thing Registries are referenced using their XMPP address, their optional node identity, source identity, and partition. If the last three are not provided, they are assumed to be blank. The `ThingRegistryClient` that we use to interact with a Thing Registry has overloaded versions of all methods accepting embedded node references. This includes the `RegisterThing`, `UpdateThing`, `Remove`, `Unregister`, and `Disown` methods.

When we claim a device, we send only metadata to the registry. But the response contains a `Node` property that together with the `JID` property identifies the corresponding node. In the same way, the `Claimed`, `Removed`, and `Disowned` events contain a `Node` reference that points to the corresponding embedded node, if not empty. When searching for things using the `Search` method, each `SearchResultThing` found also contains a `Node` reference.

The concentrator can choose to either only register itself, leaving the node identity, source identity, and partition blank or omitted, or to register relevant embedded nodes as well. The first option is useful, if provisioning of embedded nodes is not of relevance. The second option allows each embedded node to be administered by a separate owner. Each embedded node will get its own stack of rules in the provisioning server. Presence subscription will be managed by the concentrator only, however.

Consider the following example: in a building there might be a PLC installed with many input/output modules. These modules might be shared by many of the apartments in the building. If the property manager wants to allow the residents to control their input/output modules, it makes sense to provision each embedded node by itself. This would allow each resident to be able to control their modules, without letting them control the modules of their neighbors, except with their explicit permission.

Using embedded nodes in provisioning

From a device perspective, all provisioning tasks are taken care of by the `ProvisioningClient` class, together with the `SensorServer` and `ControlServer` classes. All you need to do is instantiate the `ProvisioningClient` class and provide a reference to it to the `SensorServer` and `ControlServer` object instances. These will then interact, including the management of any information related to embedded nodes.

Presence subscription can only be handled on an XMPP account basis. So, the `IsFriend` method does not take any reference to embedded nodes. However, the `CanRead` and `CanControl` methods both have overloads that accept one or more `ThingReference` objects.

From an owner perspective, the provisioning client raises events when questions are received from the provisioning server. The `IsFriendQuestion` event does not provide information about embedded nodes, nor does the `IsFriendResponse` method, as detailed earlier. But the `CanReadQuestion` and `CanControlQuestion` events both provide the node identity, source identity, and partition in the event arguments to the corresponding event handler. Likewise, the `CanReadResponse*()` and `CanControlResponse*()` methods all accept a node reference argument, for specifying any embedded node reference.

The provisioning rule caches are assumed to be managed on a concentrator level. For this reason, the `ClearDeviceCaches` and `ClearDeviceCache` methods do not take embedded node information. However, the `DeleteDeviceRules` method does accept node reference information in an overload, allowing owners to delete rules pertaining to specific embedded nodes.

Managing a concentrator

Referencing embedded nodes is only one part of managing a concentrator. While the preceding interfaces might be sufficient for interacting with small devices with a fixed number of embedded nodes, there are many cases where management of embedded devices is required.

The `Waher.Networking.XMPP.Concentrator` and `.UWP` NuGet packages define a `ConcentratorClient` and `ConcentratorServer` class that will help you with these tasks. They will help with:

- Management and discovery of data sources
- Management of nodes in data sources, including browsing, searching, updating, adding, and removing embedded nodes, including large sets of nodes
- Access management
- Execution of commands and queries
- Management of sensor data databases

All concentrator functions are optional, and the concentrator can choose which features to support. This allows the interface to support very simple concentrators (such as PLCs), medium-sized concentrators (such as bridges), and large concentrators (such as backend systems). At the same time, clients accessing concentrators will have the possibility to adapt to the features supported by the concentrator.

 The work on the concentrator interfaces is an ongoing effort within the IEEE IoT Harmonization working group. It was formerly managed in the XMPP Standards Foundation, under the name XEP-0326.

Interfacing a concentrator

The basic class for interfacing a concentrator is the `ConcentratorClient` class. You can use the `GetCapabilities` method to check which methods are supported by a specific concentrator. You can explore the data sources provided by the concentrator, by calling the `GetAllDataSources`, `GetRootDataSources`, and `GetChildDataSources` methods. If there are many data sources in a concentrator, they can be ordered in a tree structure. Similarly, nodes in data sources can also be ordered in a tree structure. Given a data source, you can access available nodes and their properties by calling the `GetNode`, `GetNodes`, `GetAllNodes`, `GetRootNodes`, and `GetChildNodes` methods.

Other methods are available. Check the corresponding classes and their code documentation for more information.

Building a concentrator

For small static concentrators, where embedded devices should be individually provisioned, there's strictly speaking not much more to do other than to manage embedded node references in your code when you interact with the Thing Registry, and when you manage sensor data and control requests from clients. The Thing Registry manages the discovery process and provisioning is transparent to the device. Your `SensorServer` and `ControlServer` instances manage requests for embedded nodes.

But this method does not allow clients, such as the owner of a concentrator, to browse available nodes on the device, and certainly not if the embedded nodes are not individually provisioned, or if more administrative tasks are required. The `ConcentratorServer` class can help you to build a more dynamic concentrator that allows clients with sufficient access privileges to administer the concentrator. It also creates an object model, which makes it easier for developers to define data sources and node structures.

Defining data sources

All concentrators created using the ControlServer class publish at least one data source. All embedded nodes reside in one of those data sources. While the concept of a data source is optional in the sensor data, control, registry, and provisioning interfaces, it is a required component when building concentrators using the ControlServer class. It gives the ControlClient class a means to browse nodes in a logical sense. It also gives the developer a logical model for publishing nodes.

All data sources implement the IDataSource interface (defined in Waher.Things). This interface gives each data source an identity, a localizable name, references to root nodes and child sources, as well methods to do access control.

 Localization support is provided by Waher.Runtime.Language. It provides a means to return and process translated strings in different languages.

Defining embedded nodes

Each embedded node in the concentrator implements the INode interface (defined in Waher.Things). Apart from node identity, a localizable name, references to child nodes, and basic access control, it also provides a means for publishing editable, and localizable properties, commands, and more.

The INode interface, however, only defines a generic embedded node. It allows the ConcentratorServer object to manage the embedded nodes. To make an embedded node into a sensor or an actuator respectively, you should implement the ISensor or IActuator interfaces correspondingly (also defined in Waher.Things). These interfaces will allow the ConcentratorServer object to read sensor data and to get access to control parameters.

The following diagram shows the basic object model for nodes in a concentrator:

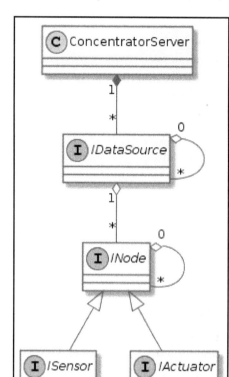

Concentrator object model

Redirecting node requests

When the `ConcentratorServer` object is instantiated, it creates its own `SensorServer` and `ControlServer` instances. There is no need to instantiate these separately. When a request is received on these objects, it checks that the request is properly made, and that references, data sources and nodes exist, and are correctly defined.

If a sensor data request is received, for instance, the ConcentratorServer object checks that the node exists and that it implements the ISensor interface. If the IsReadable property is true, it proceeds by calling the StartReadout method, defined by ISensor, on the node. Similarly, if a control operation is received, the ConcentratorServer object checks that the node implements the IActuator interface. If the IsControllable property is true, it can access its controllable parameters by calling the GetControlParameters method defined by IActuator. All other types of processing, including error management, are managed by the ConcentratorServer object.

Implementing a concentrator

We are now ready to implement our first concentrator. The goal will be to create a concentrator that includes both our sensor and our actuator into a single physical device. It will work seamlessly with the controller application developed in Chapter 10, *The Controller*, since each embedded node registers itself as a separate thing. The details of this implementation can be found in the ConcentratorXmpp project, in the *Mastering Internet of Things* GitHub repository.

Instantiating the concentrator

Instantiating the concentrator is easy. We first add a reference to the Waher.Networking.XMPP.Concentrator.UWP NuGet package to our project (if we're not doing an UWP app, we add the Waher.Networking.XMPP.Concentrator NuGet). We then simply create the object, with a reference to the XMPP client object we use, and reference to all the root data sources we define. We will define only one data source, the MeteringTopology data source. It is the default data source for embedded nodes that can be used for metering applications or cyber-physical systems. Nodes are arranged in a network topology, defining how they are connected and how to communicate with them:

```
this.concentratorServer = new ConcentratorServer(this.xmppClient,
    new MeteringTopology());
```

 Note that we do not need to instantiate the SensorServer and ControlServer classes, since the ConcentratorServer does this for us.

Defining the data source

Defining the metering topology data source is a straightforward process. We begin by stating that it implements the `IDataSource` interface:

```
public class MeteringTopology : IDataSource
{
    public MeteringTopology()
    {
    }
```

We define some basic properties of the source, such as its identity, that it does not have any child sources, and that it does not change over time:

```
public const string ID = "MeteringTopology";
public string SourceID => ID;
public bool HasChildren => false;
public DateTime LastChanged => DateTime.MinValue;
public IEnumerable<IDataSource> ChildSources => null;
```

We also need to make sure to give the data source a localizable human-readable name. Localizable strings are divided into namespaces. These namespaces can be defined as strings or as types, in which case the namespace becomes the full name of the type. Localizable strings are then identified and numbered using positive integer's values. A default value is also provided, in case the string is not defined yet. In that case, the default string is persisted for the corresponding namespace and identity number:

```
public Task<string> GetNameAsync(Language Language)
{
    return Language.GetStringAsync(typeof(MeteringTopology), 1,
        "Metering Topology");
}
```

 Check the `Waher.Runtime.Language` NuGet and the `Translator` class for more information about how to browse, export, and import dynamic localizable strings.

Providing basic access control

The `IDataSource` defines a method called `CanViewAsync`, which allows the data source to decline access to the source unless certain prerequisites are met. For our first implementation, we will assume that anyone who has been granted access to the concentrator, also has access to the data source:

```
public Task<bool> CanViewAsync(RequestOrigin Caller)
{
    return Task.FromResult<bool>(true);
}
```

The `RequestOrigin` object will contain the XMPP address (or JID) of the entity making the request to access the data source. It also contains any service, device, or user tokens used in the call. Access can be granted or rejected based on any of these identities.

Publishing our nodes

Our data source will only contain two static embedded root nodes. We add these in code:

```
public static ActuatorNode ActuatorNode = new ActuatorNode();
public static SensorNode SensorNode = new SensorNode();

public IEnumerable<INode> RootNodes =>
    new INode[] { ActuatorNode, SensorNode };
```

Access to all nodes in the source is provided through the `GetNodeAsync` method. Since our implementation only contains two static nodes, we do a simple if-then-else sequence to check for the identities. In a more dynamic setting, some form of look-up procedure would be used:

```
public Task<INode> GetNodeAsync(IThingReference NodeRef)
{
    if (SensorNode.SameThing(NodeRef))
        return Task.FromResult<INode>(SensorNode);
    else if (ActuatorNode.SameThing(NodeRef))
        return Task.FromResult<INode>(ActuatorNode);
    else
        return Task.FromResult<INode>(null);
}
```

Defining our embedded sensor node

To define a node class, we need to determine which of the interfaces, ISensor or IActuator, to implement. Implementing ISensor and IActuator automatically implements INode, which is a requirement. But the node can also choose to implement both. For our sensor node, we will only implement the ISensor interface, however. We base our class on the ThingReference class, defined in Waher.Things. The sensor node will have a static identity. And we do not use partitions in our example:

```
public class SensorNode : ThingReference, ISensor
{
    public const string NodeID = "Sensor";

    public SensorNode()
        : base(NodeID, MeteringTopology.ID, string.Empty)
    {
    }
```

The ThingReference class defines the NodeId property, which we define in the constructor. The INode interface provides two alternative identities that can be used in certain cases: a LocalId, which is unique only among siblings, and a LogId, which is used when logging events relating to the node. For our purposes, we let these be identical to the NodeId property:

```
public string LocalId => this.NodeId;
public string LogId => this.NodeId;
```

Defining basic properties

Our example model is static, as we mentioned before. We will not support editing of nodes:

```
public DateTime LastChanged => DateTime.MinValue;
```

Our sensor will always be readable and never controllable. While the ISensor and IActuator interfaces define the methods for these actions, a class implementing the ISensor interface, for example, might not always be readable. It might depend on settings or timing:

```
public bool IsReadable => true;
public bool IsControllable => false;
```

Our nodes will not define any commands either:

```
public bool HasCommands => false;
public Task<IEnumerable<ICommand>> Commands => null;
```

We need to define a localizable human-readable name for the node class:

```
public Task<string> GetTypeNameAsync(Language Language)
{
    return Language.GetStringAsync(typeof(MeteringTopology), 4,
        "Sensor Node");
}
```

Defining the node topology

The node topology is basically the way nodes are connected, or related, to each other in the data source. There are two typical relations that need to be defined: a node's parent and a node's children. If the node does not have a parent, it's a **root node**. If it lacks children, it's a **leaf node**. All nodes with the same parent node, are called **sibling nodes**. In our example, our nodes are both parent nodes and leaf nodes:

```
public IThingReference Parent => null;
public bool HasChildren => false;
public bool ChildrenOrdered => false;
public Task<IEnumerable<INode>> ChildNodes => null;
```

The topology is managed using a set of methods defined by `INode`. Since we have a static topology, these methods will respond in the negative, or throw a `NotSupportedException`.

Method	Description
AcceptsChildAsync	If the node, from its perspective, accepts a new node as a child node.
AcceptsParentAsync	If the node, from its perspective, accepts a parent node as a parent.
CanAddAsync	If the caller (RequestOrigin) can add child nodes to the current node.
AddAsync	Adds a child node to the node.
CanDestroyAsync	If the caller (RequestOrigin) can destroy the current node.
DestroyAsync	Destroys the node.

UpdateAsync	Is called when the node properties have been updated.
CanEditAsync	If the caller (RequestOrigin) can edit the current node.
CanViewAsync	If the caller (RequestOrigin) can view the current node.
MoveDoXwnAsync	Moves the node up one step among its sibling nodes.
MoveUpAsync	Moves the node down one step among its sibling nodes.
RemoveAsync	Removes a child node from the current node, without destroying it.

Editing of properties in nodes is done dynamically by the ConcentratorServer class. All you need to do, is to publish the corresponding properties as public fields or properties on the node class, and to provide them with Get and Set methods in case they are made properties. You can also annotate the fields or properties with attributes defined in the Waher.Networking.Things.Attributes namespace, to give the resulting control form a better GUI.

Providing displayable parameters

Apart from editable properties of the node, you can also define a set of readable properties named **displayable parameters**. These displayable parameters are displayed together with the node, whenever the node is presented in a detailed list view. For our sensor, we simply display the current sensor values:

```
public async Task<IEnumerable<Parameter>>
    GetDisplayableParametersAsync(Language Language,
    RequestOrigin Caller)
{
    LinkedList<Parameter> Parameters =
        new LinkedList<Parameter>();

    if (App.Instance.Light.HasValue)
        Parameters.AddLast(new DoubleParameter("Light",
            await Language.GetStringAsync(
                typeof(MeteringTopology), 2, "Light (%)"),
            App.Instance.Light.Value));

    if (App.Instance.Motion.HasValue)
        Parameters.AddLast(new BooleanParameter("Motion",
            await Language.GetStringAsync(
                typeof(MeteringTopology), 3, "Motion"),
```

```
            App.Instance.Motion.Value));

    return Parameters;
}
```

Providing status feedback

It is possible to return textual feedback to the administrator for each node. This feedback might include important events, statuses, and error messages. We will make it easy for us, and assume the node works fine:

```
public NodeState State => NodeState.None;

public Task<IEnumerable<Message>> GetMessagesAsync(
    RequestOrigin Caller)
{
    return Task.FromResult<IEnumerable<Message>>(null);
}
```

As an exercise, make the node state reflect the status of the sensor. If there are problems connecting to the Arduino board, let the node state reflect this.

Performing readout of a sensor

The last thing we need to do for our sensor node is to implement the StartReadout method, which will perform the actual readout. Its details conform to the sensor readout example in the SensorXmpp project:

```
public async void StartReadout(ISensorReadout Request)
{
    try
    {
        Log.Informational("Performing readout.", this.LogId,
            Request.Actor);
        ...
    }
    catch (Exception ex)
    {
        Log.Critical(ex);
    }
}
```

Defining our embedded actuator node

Our actuator node will be defined in much the same way as the sensor node. The key difference is that it will implement the IActuator interface as well as the ISensor interface:

```
public class ActuatorNode : ThingReference, ISensor, IActuator
{
    public const string NodeID = "Actuator";

    public ActuatorNode()
        : base(NodeID, MeteringTopology.ID, string.Empty)
    {
    }
```

We also need to explicitly state that it is always controllable:

```
public bool IsReadable => true;
public bool IsControllable => true;
```

Defining control parameters for embedded nodes

Each embedded node is assumed to have a different set of control parameters. The ConcentratorServer therefore calls the GetControlParameters method defined by the IActuator interface, when necessary. All we need to do is implement this method. The definition of the control parameters otherwise conforms to the definition of the control parameters in the ActuatorXmpp project:

```
public ControlParameter[] GetControlParameters()
{
    return new ControlParameter[]
    {
        ...
    };
}
```

Registering our embedded nodes

We are now almost ready to try our concentrator with our controller application. For the controller to find our sensor and actuator, we need to register them in the Thing Registry. To do this, we need to make two different registrations. We create a registration method that takes generic metadata for the concentrator, and then add node-specific information for each node:

```
private void RegisterDevice(MetaDataTag[] MetaInfo)
{
    Log.Informational("Registering device.");

    MetaDataTag[] SensorTags = this.GetSensorMetaInfo(MetaInfo);
    MetaDataTag[] ActuatorTags = this.GetActuatorMetaInfo(
            MetaInfo);

    this.registryClient.RegisterThing(true, ActuatorNode.NodeID,
            MeteringTopology.ID, ActuatorTags,
            this.RegistrationResponse, ActuatorNode.NodeID);
    this.registryClient.RegisterThing(true, SensorNode.NodeID,
            MeteringTopology.ID, SensorTags,
            this.RegistrationResponse, SensorNode.NodeID);
}
```

Where the sensor node metadata is modified as follows, for example:

```
private MetaDataTag[] GetSensorMetaInfo(MetaDataTag[] MetaInfo)
{
    List<MetaDataTag> SensorTags = new List<MetaDataTag>(MetaInfo)
    {
        new MetaDataStringTag("CLASS", "Sensor"),
        new MetaDataStringTag("TYPE", "MIoT Sensor")
    };

    return SensorTags.ToArray();
}
```

Trying your concentrator

You should now be ready to try your concentrator with the controller application. While some details have been left to the reader, they are available in the ConcentratorXmpp project in the GitHub repository. When it runs, it makes the necessary registrations in the Thing Registry. The controller application will now be able to find both registrations and use them, if necessary. The controller application is already prepared for handling node identities, data sources, and partitions, as described in Chapter 10, *The Controller*.

You can also use the simple IoT Client presented in Chapter 9, *Social Interaction with Your Devices Using XMPP* to interact with your concentrator. A concentrator will be expandable. You can expand it to view available data sources. Data sources with nodes (or with other child sources) will in turn be expandable, as will nodes with child nodes. You interact with the embedded nodes as you would any other type of sensor or actuator:

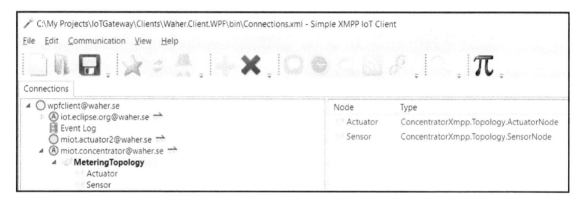

Concentrator in the simple IoT Client

Adding provisioning support to the concentrator

If you're familiar with the concepts of provisioning, as described in the previous chapter, and concentrators as described in this chapter, adding provisioning support to a concentrator is straightforward and will be left to the reader. The details are available in the ConcentratorXmpp2 project in the *Mastering Internet of Things* GitHub repository. The outline of the implementation is as follows:

- After finding a provisioning server, you create an instance of the ProvisioningClient class pointing to the provisioning server, with a reference to the XMPP client being used. This action will provision presence subscription requests (or friendship requests) for your device.
- If you want each embedded node to be provisioned as well, you provide a reference to the provisioning client to the ConcentratorServer instance when you create it. It will pass it on to the SensorServer and ControlServer instances it creates.
- If you provision embedded nodes, you must manage owner identities and ownership states separately for each node, and separately for the concentrator itself. The owner of the concentrator might be different from the owner of each embedded node.

> If you create an instance of the ProvisioningClient class, without passing it on to the ConcentratorServer constructor, you need to make sure that presence subscriptions are provisioned (that is, friendships are managed). Anyone with an approved presence subscription will be granted read and control access to all embedded nodes.
>
> The concentrator at iot.eclipse.org@waher.se is provisioned in this manner: anyone with granted access to the concentrator will be able to read and write to any of the topics (just as they would with an MQTT connection to the iot.eclipse.org broker, except they would be using XMPP).

Summary

In this chapter, you've been shown the basic principles of how to create a concentrator to embed functionality as nodes. You've learned the fundamental use cases for concentrators, the basic object model for a concentrator, and how to publish data sources and nodes in a concentrator. You've also learned the basic principles of managing nodes in a concentrator, how to register embedded nodes in a Thing Registry, and the basic principles of provisioning for embedded nodes in a concentrator. You've seen how to interact with nodes in a concentrator as if they were standalone devices on the network. In the next chapter, we will analyze how an Internet of Things Service Platform can help you with many of the repetitive tasks required to implement services for the Internet of Things.

13
Using an Internet of Things Service Platform

As we have seen throughout the chapters of this book, developing services for the Internet of Things may often include many repetitive tasks. These relate to the architecture of the application, infrastructure, data persistence, manageability, communication framework, hosting, inter-connectivity, user interfaces, and so on. In practical applications, you also need to consider managing devices. When on a tight schedule or having limited resources, many of these tasks are omitted, or receive little attention, to cut corners.

In this chapter, you will learn how an Internet of things (IoT) service platform can help you with many of the repetitive tasks required to create a successful IoT application. This chapter covers:

- An introduction to the IoT Gateway project
- An overview of its architecture
- An introduction to its hardware abstraction layer
- Management through its XMPP architecture
- How to create services
- How to interface things
- Using its databases and persistence layer
- Understanding the hosting environment
- An introduction to its security infrastructure

Understanding the IoT Gateway project

An IoT service platform can help you with many of the repetitive tasks required when creating an IoT service or device. It also provides you with an abstraction layer for devices and gives you support for many IoT-related protocols. By using such a platform as the base for your application, many of those repeated programming tasks can be eliminated, or wholly or partially automated and solved. This leaves you to focus on what you really want to do: develop functionality. This approach drastically increases productivity and shortens development cycles, which can be used to either increase functionality or quality, or to decrease development costs. Furthermore, it improves interoperability, increases security, and makes it simpler to manage massive amounts of things in large networks, since many of these aspects are already integrated into the platform.

For these reasons, this chapter is dedicated to the study of one such IoT platform: the WaherIoT Gateway. We have already used parts of the gateway in earlier chapters, when we used some of its libraries for communication, persistence, and so on.

Running the IoT Gateway

The IoT Gateway can be run as a standalone application, without any modification. There are different encapsulations of the IoT Gateway already prepared. They are built using the same code, but have different properties and are aimed at different operating systems. Since all libraries used are based on .NET Standard, they are portable across platforms and operating systems. The encapsulations are then compiled into .NET Core 2 applications. These the ones being executed. Since both .NET Standard and .NET Core 2 are portable, the gateway can therefore be encapsulated for more operating systems than currently supported.

Check out this link for a list of operating systems supported by .NET Core 2:
https://github.com/dotnet/core/blob/master/release-notes/2.0/2.0 -supported-os.md

Available encapsulations such as installers or app package bundles are listed in the following table. For each one is listed the start project that can be used if you build the project and want to start or debug the application from the development environment:

Platform	Executable project
Windows console	`Waher.IoTGateway.Console`
Windows service	`Waher.IoTGateway.Svc`
Universal Windows Platform app	`Waher.IoTGateway.App`

The IoT Gateway encapsulations can be downloaded from the GitHub project page: `https://github.com/PeterWaher/IoTGateway#iot-gateway`

All gateways use the library `Waher.IoTGateway`, which defines the executing environment of the gateway and interacts with all pluggable modules and services. They also use the `Waher.IoTGateway.Resources` library, which contains resource files common among all encapsulations.

The `Waher.IoTGateway` library is also available as a NuGet: `https://www.nuget.org/packages/Waher.IoTGateway/`

Running the console version

The console version of the IoT Gateway (`Waher.IoTGateway.Console`) is the simplest encapsulation. It can be run from the command line. It requires some basic configuration to run properly. This configuration can be provided manually (see following sections), or by using the installer. The installer asks the user for some basic information and generates the configuration files necessary to execute the application.

The console version is the simplest encapsulation, with a minimum of operating system dependencies. It's the easiest to port to other environments. It's also simple to run from the development environment. When run, it outputs any events directly to the terminal window. If sniffers are enabled, the corresponding communication is also output to the terminal window.

This provides a simple means to test and debug encrypted communication:

IoT Gateway console application

Running the gateway as a Windows service

The IoT Gateway can also be run as a Windows service (`Waher.IoTGateway.Svc`). This requires the application be executed on a Windows operating system. The application is a .NET Core 2 console application that has command-line switches allowing it to be registered and executed in the background as a Windows service. Since it supports a command-line interface, it can be used to run the gateway from the console as well. The following table lists recognized command-line switches:

Switch	Description
`-?`	Shows help information.
`-console`	Runs the service as a console application.
`-install`	Installs the application as a Window Service in the underlying operating system.
`-displayname Name`	Sets a custom display name for the Windows service. The default name if omitted is `IoT Gateway Service`.
`-description Desc`	Sets a custom textual description for the Windows service. The default description if omitted is `Windows Service hosting the Waher IoT Gateway`.
`-immediate`	If the service should be started immediately.
`-localsystem`	Installed service will run using the *Local System* account.
`-localservice`	Installed service will run using the *Local Service* account (default).
`-networkservice`	Installed service will run using the *Network Service* account.
`-start Mode`	Sets the default starting mode of the Windows service. The default is `Disabled`. Available options are `StartOnBoot`, `StartOnSystemStart`, `AutoStart`, `StartOnDemand` and `Disabled`
`-uninstall`	Uninstalls the application as a Windows service from the operating system.

Running the gateway as an app

It is possible to run the IoT Gateway as a **Universal Windows Platform** (**UWP**) app (`Waher.IoTGateway.App`). This allows it to be run on Windows phones or embedded devices such as the Raspberry Pi running Windows 10 IoT Core (16299 and later). It can also be used as a template for creating custom apps based on the IoT Gateway:

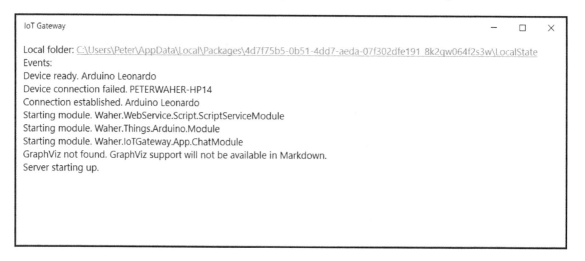

IoT Gateway UWP App

Configuring the IoT Gateway

All application data files are separated from the executable files. Application data files are files that can be potentially changed by the user. Executable files are files potentially changed by installers. For the Console and Service applications, application data files are stored in the `IoT Gateway` subfolder to the operating system's **Program Data** folder. Example: `C:\ProgramData\IoT Gateway`. For the UWP app, a link to the program data folder is provided at the top of the window. The application data folder contains files you might have to configure to get it to work as you want.

Configuring the XMPP interface

All IoT Gateways connect to the XMPP network. This connection is used to provide a secure and interoperable interface to your gateway and its underlying devices. You can also administer the gateway through this XMPP connection.

The XMPP connection is defined in different manners, depending on the encapsulation. The app lets the user configure the connection via a dialog window. The credentials are then persisted in the object database. The Console and Service versions of the IoT Gateway let the user define the connection using an `xmpp.config` file in the application data folder. The following is an example `configuration` file:

```
<?xml version='1.0' encoding='utf-8'?>
<SimpleXmppConfiguration
xmlns='http://waher.se/Schema/SimpleXmppConfiguration.xsd'>
    <Host>waher.se</Host>
    <Port>5222</Port>
    <Account>USERNAME</Account>
    <Password>PASSWORD</Password>
    <ThingRegistry>waher.se</ThingRegistry>
    <Provisioning>waher.se</Provisioning>
    <Events></Events>
    <Sniffer>true</Sniffer>
    <TrustServer>false</TrustServer>
    <AllowCramMD5>true</AllowCramMD5>
    <AllowDigestMD5>true</AllowDigestMD5>
    <AllowPlain>false</AllowPlain>
    <AllowScramSHA1>true</AllowScramSHA1>
    <AllowEncryption>true</AllowEncryption>
    <RequestRosterOnStartup>true</RequestRosterOnStartup>
</SimpleXmppConfiguration>
```

Most of the elements in this configuration file should be familiar to you if you have read the `Chapter` 9, *Social Interaction with Your Devices Using XMPP* on XMPP. The following is a short recapture:

Element	Type	Description
Host	String	Host name of the XMPP broker to use.
Port	1-65535	Port number to connect to.
Account	String	Name of XMPP account.
Password	String	Password to use (or password hash).

ThingRegistry	String	Thing registry to use, or empty if not.
Provisioning	String	Provisioning server to use, or empty if not.
Events	String	Event long to use, or empty if not.
Sniffer	Boolean	If network communication is to be sniffed or not.
TrustServer	Boolean	If the XMPP broker is to be trusted.
AllowCramMD5	Boolean	If the CRAM-MD5 authentication mechanism is allowed.
AllowDigestMD5	Boolean	If the DIGEST-MD5 authentication mechanism is allowed.
AllowPlain	Boolean	If the PLAIN authentication mechanism is allowed.
AllowScramSHA1	Boolean	If the SCRAM-SHA-1 authentication mechanism is allowed.
AllowEncryption	Boolean	If encryption is allowed.
RequestRosterOnStartup	Boolean	If the roster is required, it should be requested on start up.

Securing the password

Instead of writing the password in clear text in the configuration file, it is recommended that the password hash be used instead, if the authentication mechanism supports hashes. When the installer sets up the gateway, it authenticates the credentials during start up, and writes the hash value in the file instead. When the hash value is used, the mechanism used to create the hash must be written as well. In the following example, new-line characters are added for readability:

```
<Password type="SCRAM-SHA-1">
    rAeAYLvAa6QoP8QWyTGRLgKO/J4=
</Password>
```

Setting basic properties of the gateway

The basic properties of the IoT Gateway are defined in the `Gateway.config` file in the program `data` folder. For example:

```
<?xml version="1.0" encoding="utf-8" ?>
```

```xml
<GatewayConfiguration
xmlns="http://waher.se/Schema/GatewayConfiguration.xsd">
<Domain>example.com</Domain>
<Certificate configFileName="Certificate.config"/>
<XmppClient configFileName="xmpp.config"/>
<DefaultPage>/Index.md</DefaultPage>
<Database folder="Data" defaultCollectionName="Default"
   blockSize="8192" blocksInCache="10000" blobBlockSize="8192"
   timeoutMs="10000" encrypted="true"/>
<Ports>
<Port protocol="HTTP">80</Port>
<Port protocol="HTTP">8080</Port>
<Port protocol="HTTP">8081</Port>
<Port protocol="HTTP">8082</Port>
<Port protocol="HTTPS">443</Port>
<Port protocol="HTTPS">8088</Port>
<Port protocol="XMPP.C2S">5222</Port>
<Port protocol="XMPP.S2S">5269</Port>
<Port protocol="SOCKS5">1080</Port>
</Ports>
<FileFolders>
<FileFolder webFolder="/Folder1" folderPath="\ServerPath1"/>
<FileFolder webFolder="/Folder2" folderPath="\ServerPath2"/>
<FileFolder webFolder="/Folder3" folderPath="\ServerPath3"/>
</FileFolders>
</GatewayConfiguration>
```

Element	Type	Description
Domain	String	The name of the domain, if any, pointing to the machine running the IoT Gateway.
Certificate	String	The configuration file name specifying details about the certificate to use.
XmppClient	String	The configuration file name specifying details about the XMPP connection.
DefaultPage	String	Relative URL to the page shown if no web page is specified when browsing the IoT Gateway.
Database	String	How the local object database is configured. Typically, these settings do not need to be changed. All you need to know is that you can persist and search for your objects using the static Database defined in Waher.Persistence.

Ports	Port	Which port numbers to use for different protocols supported by the IoT Gateway.
FileFolders	FileFolder	Contains definitions of virtual web folders.

Providing a certificate

Different protocols (such as HTTPS) require a certificate to allow callers to validate the domain name claim. Such a certificate can be defined by providing a `Certificate.config` file in the application data folder, and then restarting the gateway. If providing such a file, different from the default file, it will be loaded and processed, and then deleted. The information, together with the certificate, will be moved to the relative safety of the object database. For example:

```xml
<?xml version="1.0" encoding="utf-8" ?>
<CertificateConfiguration
xmlns="http://waher.se/Schema/CertificateConfiguration.xsd">
<FileName>certificate.pfx</FileName>
<Password>testexamplecom</Password>
</CertificateConfiguration>
```

Element	Type	Description
FileName	String	Name of certificate file to import.
Password	String	Password needed to access private part of certificate.

Providing web content

The IoT Gateway includes a web server. It allows service modules to publish dynamic content and web APIs. But it also allows you to publish file-based web content. The root folder of the web server resides in the `Root` subfolder to the application data folder. It contains the default start page `Index.md`, which is a `Markdown` file. Markdown is by default converted to HTML automatically by the web server, unless Markdown is explicitly requested by the client. Since browsers do not request Markdown by default, browsing to the resource will result in a HTML page. After starting the gateway, you can browse its domain (or IP address), and the default start page is displayed, as shown in the following screenshot:

Default first page

Note that the `localhost` interface is not available in UWP apps. You must browse pages hosted by the gateway from another machine in the network.

You should examine the contents of the `Root` folder and its subfolders. This will allow you to better understand how the web content is built up.

Publishing network folders

Any subfolders to the `Root` folder will be available as web folders under your domain (or IP address). The IoT Gateway also allows you to publish network folders as web folders on the Gateway. This allows you to access distributed content on the network through a single web server. You do this by defining each network folder in a `FileFolder` element in the `Gateway.config` file described earlier. You must make sure the user account used to host the IoT Gateway has network access to the corresponding folders.

Using Markdown

While you can publish any type of content using the IoT Gateway web server, the default web page is defined using Markdown stored in `.md` files. Markdown has been shown to be a very efficient way to publish content on the web. Through the automatic rendering to HTML, it is relatively easy to create web pages with a consistent look and feel. And since HTML can be embedded in Markdown, it does not limit the content provider. The IoT Gateway contains a Markdown reference in the `Root` folder. You access it by browsing `/Markdown.md`.

> If you don't have access to the Gateway, you can also find the reference here:
> https://waher.se/Markdown.md

Using metadata for Search Engine Optimization

The first paragraph in a Markdown document can optionally consist of metadata about the document. This metadata is used, among other things, to generate information that search engines can use to better index the corresponding page. The following are examples of metadata tags that you could include in pages that you want indexed:

Tag	Description
Alternate	Link to alternate page.
Author	Name of author.
Copyright	Link to a copyright statement.
Date	Date when document was created.

Description	Description of the contents of the document.
Help	Link to help page.
Icon	Link to icon for page.
Keywords	Set of keywords describing the contents.
Next	Link to next page in series.
Previous	Link to previous page in series.
Prev	Same as Previous.
Subtitle	Subtitle of the page.
Title	Title of the page.
Web	Link to web page.

For a complete list of supported metadata tags, see https://waher.se/Markdown.md#metadata.

Providing menus using the Master/Detail model

The Markdown engine supports a Master/Detail model when rendering HTML output. Content is typically provided in the **Detail** pages. Menus on the other hand are provided in the **Master** pages. The Master pages are shared between multiple Detail pages and can therefore act as placeholders for a menu system. When writing a content page, define the Master page using the Master metadata tag:

```
Master: Master.md
```

In the Master page, define where the Detail page is to be introduced, by referring to the Details metadata tag using the [%Details] construct. Master pages can complement the metadata provided by Detail pages, by providing their own set of metadata tags.

The following shows the default menu in `Master.md` in the `Root` folder:

```
<header>
<nav>

*  [Home] (/Index.md)
*  [Markdown] (/Markdown.md)
*  [Script] (/Script.md)
*  [Calculator] (/Calculator.md)
*  [License] (/Copyright.md)
*  [IoT Gateway] (https://github.com/PeterWaher/IoTGateway)
*  [Waher Data] (http://waher.se/)

</nav>
</header>
<main>

[%Details]

</main>
```

Note that empty rows have syntactical meaning in Markdown. They separate blocks (or paragraphs) of text.

The bullet list is rendered as a series of `<li>` elements inside an `<ul>` tag. If the link inside the bullet refers to the current page, the `<li>` element will be annotated with the class attribute `active`. This allows you to display the item differently.

Customizing the user experience

There are metadata tags that you can use to customize the experience users have when visiting your page:

Tag	Description
AudioAutoplay	If audio content is provided on the page, this metadata element specifies if the content is to be played automatically when the page has loaded.
AudioControls	If controls are to be displayed for playing audio content on the page.
CSS	Includes a reference to a *Cascading Style Sheet* (**CSS**) document on the page.
JavaScript	Includes a reference to a **JavaScript** document on the page.
Parameter	Defines one query parameter that should be made available to underlying server script. By default, parameter values are strings unless they can be parsed as double or Boolean values. Metadata tags can be used multiple times on each page, one for each parameter being defined.
Refresh	Tells the browser to refresh the page after a given number of seconds.
VideoAutoplay	If video content is provided on the page, this metadata element specifies if the content is to be played automatically when the page has loaded.
VideoControls	If controls are to be displayed for playing video content on the page.

Adding security headers

The HTML generator recognizes certain HTTP headers that could be collectively named **security headers**. If metadata tags with the same names as these are used, they are copied into the generated HTML verbatim. This includes:

Tag	Description
Access-Control-Allow-Origin	Allows you to define a **Cross-origin resource sharing** (**CORS**) header.

Cache-Control	Overrides the default Cache-Control header generated by the renderer. Together with the `Vary` meta-tag they provide a means to control how the generated page will be cached.
Content-Security-Policy	Defines the expected behavior of the page.
Public-Key-Pins	Tells clients to pin a specific public key, decreasing the risk of **Man-In-The-Middle** (**MITM**) attacks.
Strict-Transport-Security	Forces clients to connect to the page using HTTPS.
Sunset	Flags content for removal at a given (future) time.
Vary	Together with the Cache-Control header, defines how the page can be cached.

Authorizing user privileges

The Markdown engine supports authorization of authenticated user privileges. The following metadata tags can be used to protect your content:

Tag	Description
Login	Link to login page, if a valid user has not been authenticated. The login page in turn should contain a method for users to authenticate themselves. The simplest method might be a form with a post back to a web service, which authenticates the given credentials and stores the corresponding user object in the given user variable (see below).
Privilege	Privileges required by the authenticated user, before the user is allowed to view the page. The metadata tag can be used multiple times, once for each privilege. If no privileges are provided, all authenticated users are allowed to view the page. Unauthenticated users are still not allowed.
UserVariable	Name of the variable that holds the authenticated user object. The object must implement the `IUser` interface, defined in `Waher.Security`. For each privilege required, the `IUser.HasPrivilege` method is called to assure the user has the correct privileges.

Customizing content using server-side script

You can provide links to files containing server-side script by using the Script metadata tag. This script will be loaded and executed before the HTML page is generated. You can also embed script in your Markdown page by placing it between single braces { and }. The results of executing the script will be output in rendered results instead of the expression and the braces. If the result is an image such as a graph, the corresponding image will be inserted in its place.

For more information about embedding script in Markdown, including how to output graphs, see:
https://waher.se/Markdown.md#script

Using pre-processed script

There's also a pre-processing stage being performed before the HTML page is generated. You can embed script to be executed during the pre-processing stage between double braces {{ and }}. Outputting Markdown from pre-processed script is done by embedding the text between double brackets [[and]] inside the pre-processed script. Script to be executed inside Markdown text inside pre-processed script is embedded between double parenthesis ((and)).

The results of pre-processed script can change the structure of the document. It is assumed that the result will be output in string format. The result will be inserted in the in-memory text representation of the Markdown document, before the Markdown itself is parsed. For this reason, pre-processed script can be used to output data from dynamic data sources, for instance.

For more information about pre-processed script, see:
https://waher.se/Markdown.md#preProcessedScript

Interacting with .NET code from script

Through script you can interact with .NET code in your .NET modules. This includes accessing namespaces, types, creating and destroying objects, as well as calling methods, including static methods. Results will be available to the script. This feature allows you to provide logic in your custom .NET code modules that you can access through script on pages.

 For more information about how to interact with .NET code in your modules, see:
`https://waher.se/Script.md#interactionWithNetCodeBehindClasses`

Testing script

If you want to test your script live, the IoT Gateway comes with a script sandbox called the **Calculator**. It's available from the mail menu. In it, you can type any script you like, and see the results as you press *ENTER*.

 For a complete script reference, see the local resource `/Script.md` hosted by your IoT Gateway. You can also access it here:
`https://waher.se/Script.md`.

 Before deploying a solution based on the IoT Gateway, you should either protect the sandbox by requiring users to log in before they can access the sandbox, or you should remove it completely by removing the page and the web service `Waher.WebService.Script`.

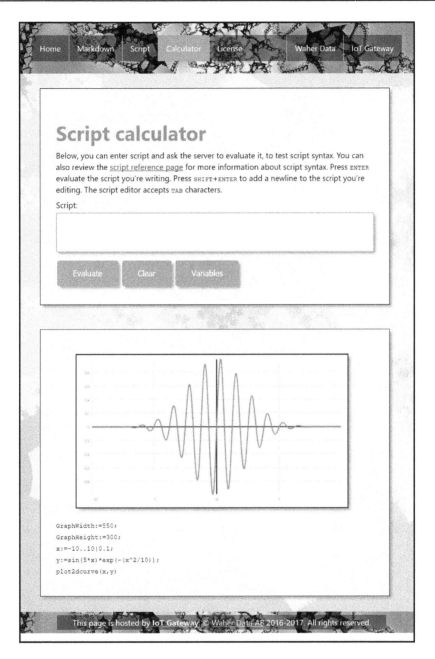

Script calculator

Below, you can enter script and ask the server to evaluate it, to test script syntax. You can also review the <u>script reference page</u> for more information about script syntax. Press ENTER evaluate the script you're writing. Press SHIFT+ENTER to add a newline to the script you're editing. The script editor accepts TAB characters.

Script:

Evaluate   Clear   Variables

```
GraphWidth:=550;
GraphHeight:=300;
x:=-10..10|0.1;
y:=sin(5*x)*exp(-(x^2/10));
plot2dcurve(x,y)
```

This page is hosted by **IoT Gateway**. © Waher Data AB 2016-2017. All rights reserved.

Script sandbox

Customizing code visualization

Code in Markdown can either be in-lined in text by embedding it between back-ticks ` and `, or placed in a separate block whose first and last rows begin with three back-ticks ` ` `, where the first can be suffixed by the name of the language used by the code. Visualization of such block-level code can be customized by specific code content handlers. The default behavior is to present the code verbatim, adding syntax highlights represented by the language if provided. But if there exists a class in the system implementing the ICodeContent interface defined in Waher.Content.Markdown.Model, which recognizes the language provided, the presentation of such code can be completely customized.

Visualizing Graphviz graphs

As an example, the IoT Gateway provides a code visualization of Graphviz diagram code. Instead of presenting the actual code, the code is converted to an image, and the image is presented. This requires Graphviz to be installed on the machine. The following example is taken from the Graphviz reference documentation. The following diagram shows how the code is presented in the rendered HTML output:

```
```dot: Fancy graph
digraph G {
    size ="4,4";
    main [shape=box]; /* this is a comment */
    main -> parse [weight=8];
    parse -> execute;
    main -> init [style=dotted];
    main -> cleanup;
    execute -> { make_string; printf}
    init -> make_string;
    edge [color=red]; // so is this
    main -> printf [style=bold,label="100 times"];
    make_string [label="make anstring"];
    node [shape=box,style=filled,color=".7 .3 1.0"];
    execute -> compare;
}
```
```

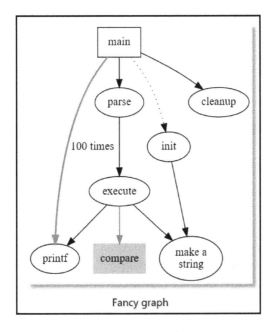

Customized code presentation

Graphviz and reference documentation can be found at:
`https://graphviz.org`

Customizing multimedia presentation

Multimedia can also be included in Markdown documents. The same syntax used for inserting images is used for all types of multimedia. The Markdown processor checks the system for classes implementing the `IMultimediaContent` interface defined in `Waher.Content.Markdown.Model`. Available classes analyze the URL, provided and grade their ability to handle the content. The best one is selected and gets to render the content. By default, there are multi-media renderers for images, video, and audio files, but also YouTube videos, external web pages, table of contents generation, and Markdown inclusion. You can provide any number of your own multimedia renderers to customize presentation of multimedia content by the gateway.

For more information on multimedia in Markdown, see:
https://waher.se/Markdown.md#multimedia

Pushing information to web clients

The IoT Gateway includes a mechanism to push information to connected web clients. Pages that accept information pushed to them, should include the `Events.js` JavaScript file in a JavaScript metadata reference. For example:

```
JavaScript: /Events.js
```

Each such page will include JavaScript that creates a `TabID` and registers itself with the server-side `ClientEvents` class, defined in `Waher.IoTGateway`. The `ClientEvents` class can then be used to check which tabs are registered with it, and for which resources. It can also be used to push data to the page. Methods available are:

Method	Description
GetOpenLocations()	Returns an array of locations (relative URLs) currently being viewed.
GetTabIDsForLocation()	Returns the Tab IDs of clients currently viewing a given page. The pages can be filtered based on query parameters.
GetTabIDsForLocations()	Returns the **Tab** IDs of clients currently viewing any of a given set of pages.
GetTabIDs()	Gets an array of connected clients. Each tab in a browser has a separate **Tab** ID.
PushEvent()	Pushes a type and corresponding data to a set of Tab IDs. The data can be JSON. The type should correspond to a JavaScript function taking one parameter. The `Event.js` JavaScript running in the clients with the corresponding Tab IDs will receive the event and call the corresponding function with the data provided.

Monitoring performance

There are various methods to monitor the performance of the IoT Gateway and its services. Apart from monitoring performance counters provided by the operating system, you can also monitor event logs and sniffer output, if enabled.

Monitoring event logs

In the application data folder, a subfolder called Events is created. In it, XML files will be output when events are logged from anywhere in the system. Old XML files will be deleted automatically. The XML files reference XSL transforms in the Transforms subfolder to the application data folder. This makes it possible to view finished XML files in browsers in a user-friendly manner.

 Events are also persisted in the object database. These events can be searched and accessed via the XMPP interface.

 You can output events from your code by accessing the static Log class defined in Waher.Events.

Monitoring communication sniffers

By default, sniffers are disabled. If you enable sniffers in the network configuration, the application data subfolders, HTTP, UPnP, XMPP, and so on, will be created. XML files will be created containing any communication taking place. As with events, references to XSL transforms will be available, making it easy to read the contents in a browser. Old files will be automatically deleted.

 Sniffers are useful when troubleshooting communication. But sniffers provide a way to access otherwise secured communication. Therefore, make sure to disable sniffers when they are not needed.

Developing services for the IoT Gateway

You can easily develop your own service modules for the IoT Gateway. You just create a *.NET Standard 2.0 Class Library* and add the code you want to include. You add references to the libraries you wish to use. If you want to access Gateway functionality, add a reference to the `Waher.IoTGateway` library.

Creating a service module

It is the `Waher.Runtime.Inventory` module that keeps track of all modules, classes, and types in the runtime environment. You don't have to initialize it yourself, as you did in the earlier chapters. The IoT Gateway makes sure to initialize it with all available assemblies. However, it defines an interface `IModule` that might be of importance to you. By implementing it, you will get notified when the Gateway starts and stops. This is done through calls to the `Start()` and `Stop()` methods defined by the interface. By implementing this interface, you can make sure to initialize and terminate your service module properly.

 Most of the architecture in the IoT Gateway is loosely coupled. This means there are no hard connections between classes defining properties and functionalities. Instead, an inventory of all available classes and which interfaces they implement is maintained.

 You can call the `GetTypesImplementingInterface()` method on the static `Types` class, defined in `Waher.Runtime.Inventory`, to learn which types are available supporting a given functionality.

Understanding the basic architecture

The IoT Gateway project contains different libraries and components, many of which we have already used in previous chapters. They are grouped together and named according to a naming convention that makes it easy to identify the function of each component. The following diagram contains a simple overview of the libraries used:

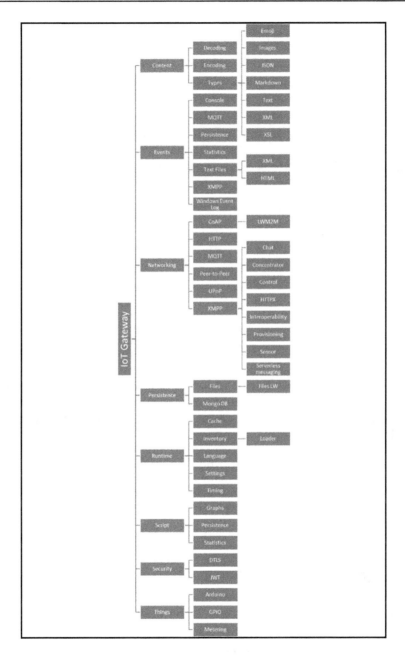

IoT Gateway component overview

Creating a manifest file

The Console and Service encapsulations of the IoT Gateway support standalone service modules. A standalone service module can be packaged and installed separately from the IoT Gateway. To be able to do this, you need to create a `manifest` file for your service. The `manifest` file describes which files are included in your services, and whether they are application files (assembly files) or content files. Note that you don't have to use libraries included in the IoT Gateway. The `manifest` file also describes the folder structure used. Create a manifest file with the extension `.manifest` and include it in your project as a content file. For example:

```
<Module xmlns="http://waher.se/Schema/ModuleManifest.xsd">
<Assembly fileName="YourCompany.Service.Module.dll"/>
<Folder name="Root">
<Content fileName="MainPage.md"/>
<Content fileName="MainCode.js"/>
<Folder name="Images">
<Content fileName="Image1.png"/>
<Content fileName="Image2.png"/>
</Folder>
</Folder>
</Module>
```

 The UWP app must be customized if you want to include your services in it. You should still create your services as standalone services. It allows you to test it using the console or Windows Service encapsulations of the IoT Gateway as well.

 You can view the schema for the manifest file here: https://github.com/PeterWaher/IoTGateway/blob/master/Utilities/Waher.Utility.Install/Schema/Manifest.xsd

Installing your service

In your installation folder of the IoT Gateway, there's a utility called `Waher.Utility.Install.exe`. It helps you with installation and uninstallation of your services. It accepts the following command-line switches:

Switch	Description
-?	Shows help information.

`-m MANIFEST_FILE`	Points to the manifest file describing the files in the module.
`-d APP_DATA_FOLDER`	Points to the application data folder.
`-s SERVER_EXE`	Points to the executable file of the IoT Gateway.
`-v`	Verbose mode.
-i	Install. This is the default. Switch is not required.
`-u`	Uninstall. Add this switch if the module is being uninstalled.
-r	Remove files. Add this switch if you want files removed during uninstallation. Default is to not remove files.

Testing and debugging your service

If you have the possibility, it's easier to develop, test, and debug on your local machine. One way to do this, is to use the console version of the IoT Gateway. To test and debug your service, follow these steps:

- Install the IoT Gateway with all files, including debug files
- Execute `Waher.Utility.Install` from a post-build command-line event in Visual Studio, to install your service after successful compilation
- In the debug settings, launch the `Waher.IoTGateway.Console` executable file in the installation working folder, instead of executing the project file

You should now be able to run and debug your service directly from the Visual Studio IDE.

 An alternative is to execute the `dotnet.exe` application instead (located in `C:Program Filesdotnet`) to execute a .NET application available as a `.dll` file. In that case, the name of the `.dll` file should be provided as a command-line argument to `dotnet.exe`.

Deploying your service to an embedded device

To deploy your service to an embedded device, you need to create a UWP app based on the `Waher.IoTGateway.App` template. You add a reference to your service project. You're then ready to run the UWP app. The app will automatically find your service module, as the Console and Service encapsulations did. You can both execute it locally, for testing purposes, and remotely, on an embedded device.

Extending communication capabilities

You're free to create and add any type of connectivity to the IoT Gateway in your services. If you want to extend existing capabilities, you can do so as well. The static `Gateway` class defined in `Waher.IoTGateway` defines properties you can use to access the web server, CoAP Endpoint, and XMPP network connection, and so on. You can extend these by registering resources or protocol extensions in the `Start` and `Stop` methods of your `IModule` implementation:

Member	Description
`Gateway.XmppClient`	XMPP client connection.
`Gateway.HttpServer`	Web server and available resources.
`Gateway.CoAPEndpoint`	CoAP Endpoint and available resources.

Interfacing things

The IoT Gateway implements a dynamic concentrator, where individual nodes can optionally be registered and provisioned. Management of nodes is done through the XMPP interface. It can be performed using the simple IoT client for instance.

`Waher.Things` defines the basic abstraction model for things in the gateway. Each node (`INode`) can have a parent and a set of children, forming a tree structure of nodes. Nodes reside in a data source (`IDataSource`). Data sources also form a tree structure. A node is considered a *thing* and is referenced (`IThingReference`) through the triple *Node ID*, *Source ID*, and *Partition*. Controllable nodes are called actuators (`IActuator`) and readable nodes sensors (`ISensor`). These interfaces, and how they are used to read data, perform control operations, and define displayable parameters, were introduced in the previous chapter. If the node should be able to support registration in a Thing Registry, and requires decision support from a *Provision Server*, it should implement `ILifeCycleManagement`:

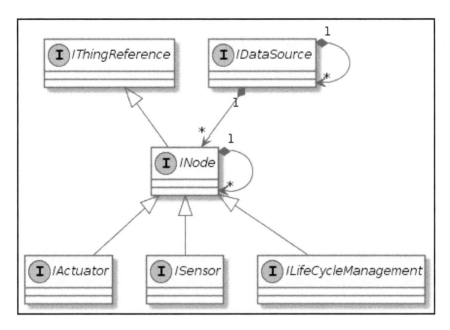

Basic abstraction model for things

Using the Metering Topology data source

In the previous chapter, we created a small static concentrator. The IoT Gateway defines a more flexible dynamic concentrator. It allows standalone modules to define new classes of nodes that can be administered through the concentrator interface. The Waher.Things.Metering library defines a data source called the **Metering Topology** (MeteringTopology). The Metering Topology has one root node (Root), representing the IoT Gateway itself. Nodes in this library are derived from the MeteringNode class. All nodes deriving from MeteringNode inherit certain important properties: they are all persisted in the local object database.

They also maintain persisted information about their current state, and it is possible to log different types of messages on them:

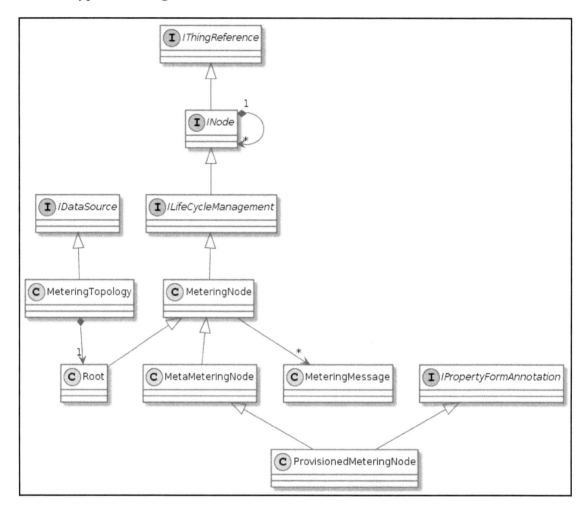

Basic abstraction model for the Metering Topology

Two specializations exist of the metering node: one that allows administrators to annotate it with metadata (`MetaMeteringNode`), and one that allows administrators to decide if its life cycle should be managed by a Thing Registry and provisioning server (`ProvisioningMeteringNode`).

Controlling node hierarchy

In the previous chapter, we created a static hierarchy of nodes. The IoT Gateway supports a dynamic hierarchy. While the concentrator infrastructure in the gateway performs most of the tasks required to manage your nodes, you need to provide some basic information that the gateway cannot guess. `INode` defines methods that allow the gateway to understand which node classes can be added where. It asks all available node classes, which it fetches from the inventory, and asks them who can be added to whom, and which nodes accept which nodes as children. If the response is positive to both these questions, the corresponding child type can be added to the corresponding parent type.

Method	Description
`AcceptsChildAsync`	If the node, from its perspective, accepts a new node as a child node.
`AcceptsParentAsync`	If the node, from its perspective, accepts a parent node as a parent.

Editing node properties

Properties that need to be persisted only need a get and a set method defined, and the object database used by `Waher.Persistence` will persist the property according to its type. But allowing administrators to edit properties requires human interfaces. It is not sufficient to know the name of the property and the data type of the value.

To enable the IoT Gateway to create human readable interfaces for editing node properties, you must annotate each editable property with information suitable for human interaction. The `Waher.Things.Attributes` namespace contains a series of attributes that can be used to annotate properties and classes with such information. If these attributes are not sufficient, you can customize the property dialog by implementing the `AnnotatePropertyForm()` method defined in the `IPropertyFormAnnotation` interface, available in the `Waher.Networking.XMPP.DataForms` namespace. Available attributes include:

Method	Type	Description
`AlphaChannel`	Property	Enables editing of the alpha channel of a color property.
`DateOnly`	Property	Only the date part of a `DateTime`-valued property is editable.

`DefaultLanguage`	Class	Defines the default language code for human readable texts in the class.
`Header`	Property	Defines a localizable header string for the property.
`Masked`	Property	Makes sure input for the property is masked.
`Open`	Property	Defines an open parameter. Open parameters accept values outside of given options, as long as the input conforms to the underlying data type.
`Option`	Property	Defines an option for the property and its corresponding localizable human-readable label. The attribute can be used multiple times.
`Page`	Property	Defines the page (or tab) with a localizable label in the dialog for the property.
`Range`	Property	Defines the valid input range for the property.
`ReadOnly`	Property	Defines a property as read-only (in property dialogs).
`RegularExpression`	Property	Provides a regular expression for validation of user input.
`Required`	Property	Tells the system the property is required.
`Section`	Property	Defines a section with a localizable label inside a page (or tab) where the property will be displayed.
`Text`	Property	Adds a localizable text paragraph before or after the property. The attribute can be used multiple times.
`ToolTip`	Property	Defines a localizable tool-tip text for the property.

Interacting with your things

The best way to understand how these attributes and properties work to create a dynamic concentrator is to spend some time and examine the `Waher.Things.Arduino` project, available in the IoT Gateway repository. It defines an object structure for what we did in the previous chapter, with the difference that this time objects are generalized. This means that depending on which objects we choose to create at runtime and how we configure them, we can change the functionality of our concentrator. We can choose to add different types and numbers of sensors and actuators, and all in runtime, using our administrative client:

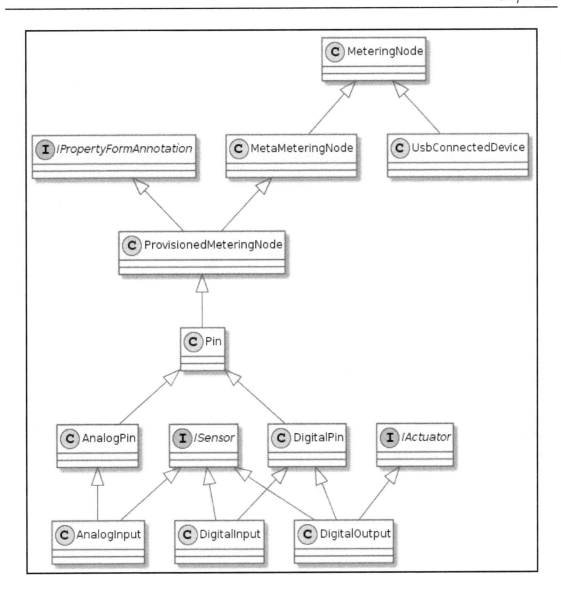

Architecture of the Arduino project

The Arduino project contains three classes that represent the sensors and actuator: `AnalogInput`, `DigitalInput`, and `DigitalOutput`. These contain properties and logic related to their function. They derive from `AnalogPin` and `DigitalPin` correspondingly.

These contain logic and displayable parameters common for all pins of the corresponding type. These in turn are derived from `Pin`, which contains properties common to all pins. By deriving from `ProvisionedMeteringNode`, all pins can be provisioned. This is managed automatically by the IoT Gateway for you. The `UsbConnectedDevice` node will act as the parent node for all pin nodes. It corresponds to the Arduino and USB serial *Firmata* connection.

When implementing a class such as the `UsbConnectedDevice`, you must take into consideration that the underlying resource (the USB serial port) is **singular**. This means, only one instance of the USB serial interface can be open at once. But the `UsbConnectedDevice` class can be instantiated multiple times for various reasons. Since it is persisted in the object database, it can be loaded as the result of simply scanning the database, generating a report, or browsing the data source. It is therefore important to separate the node logic from the communication logic, and make sure at most one instance of the communication logic class is active at once. You can check the `Waher.Things.Arduino` implementation of the `UsbConnectedDevice` class for an idea on how to do this.

Managing your things

If you run the `Waher.IoTGateway.App` UWP app with the Arduino connected to your PC or device, the `Waher.Things.Arduino` service (located in the `Module` class) will find the Arduino automatically and add a `UsbConnectedDevice` node to the Metering Topology **Root** node. You can select it in the **Simple IoT Client** and press the **Add** icon. Since there are multiple node classes that can be added to the Arduino node, you'll be presented with a list of possible choices, as shown in following screenshot:

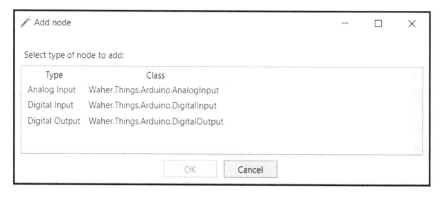

Adding node

In the property dialog that appears, see the following screenshot, available properties are ordered and displayed in tabs (or pages). The first three tabs contain the identity of the new node, a required property, and metadata about the node. The fourth tab contains information about provisioning, if provisioning is to be used, the `IoTDisco` URI if not claimed, and the owner JID if claimed. In the last tab, you can set properties controlling which pin to use, how to configure the pin, what is being read or controlled, and how to scale and report the data:

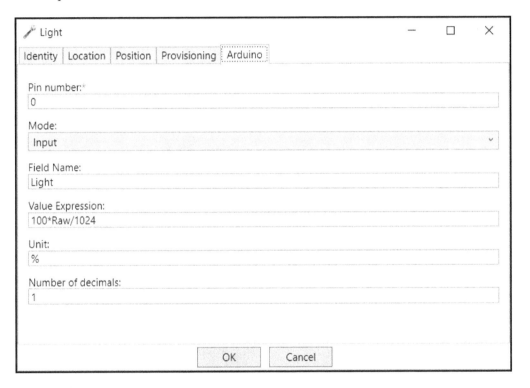

Property pages

After adding an analog input node for pin **A0**, a digital input for pin **D8**, and a digital output for pin **D9**, we should have a setup that is like we had earlier. The main difference is that we have two sensor nodes for the light input and the motion detector. You can get an overview of your configuration by viewing the displayable parameters in the list view in the **Connections** tab, as shown in the following screenshot.

You can also select the individual nodes and read and configure them (if you have permissions).

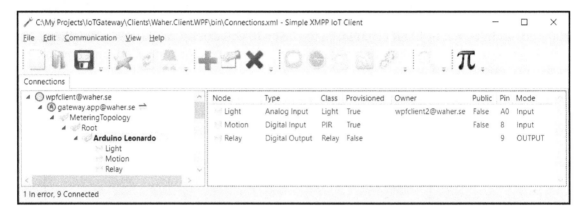

Configuring the Arduino board

Packaging your service

When your service has reached a sufficient level of quality, you will want to distribute it to others. Depending on the encapsulation of the IoT Gateway you've chosen, you have different options.

Creating an installer

The IoT Gateway has a Windows **WiX** MSI installer project (**Waher.IoTGateway.Win32**). This MSI can install the IoT Gateway in a customized manner.

> The WiX toolset is an open source set of tools to create Windows installers. More information about the WiX toolset can be found here: `http://wixtoolset.org/`.

You don't have to customize the Wix MSI project to include your service. Instead, there's a WiX Burn project called `Waher.IoTGateway.Setup`. It has the capacity to install multiple MSI packages, as well as make sure .NET is installed.

To create an installer for your service, follow these steps:

1. Create a Burn project mimicking `Waher.IoTGateway.Setup`.
2. From the Burn project, call the `Waher.IoTGateway.Win32` MSI package to install the IoT Gateway.
3. Create a WiX MSI installer project, which will install your service files.
4. Reference the `Waher.IoTGateway.Installers` project in your Wix MSI project. It includes custom actions that you will need to install your service.
5. Copy your files appropriately.
6. Call the `InstallManifest` custom action to install your installed service using its manifest file into the IoT Gateway.
7. Call the `UninstallManifest` or `StopServiceAndUninstallManifest` custom action to uninstall your service using its manifest file.
8. You can call the `StartService` and `StopService` custom actions to start and stop the Windows service.
9. Call the `OpenLocalhost` custom action to open a browser displaying the main page of the IoT Gateway.

Summary

In this chapter, you've been shown the principles of how the IoT Gateway works, and what you can do with it. You've learned about the different execution models and how to configure and run the gateway. You've been shown how to provide and customize dynamic web content using the gateway, how to develop services for the gateway, and how to monitor gateway performance. You've also learned how to interface and manage things using the gateway abstraction layer, and how to package your finished service. In the next chapter, we start the third part of the book by looking at how to harmonize different IoT technologies.

14
IoT Harmonization

In the previous chapters of this book, we just got a taste of the different methods and technologies used to create IoT applications. From simple to complex, using different patterns of communication, some secure others less so, the variety of technologies in use is enormous. In this chapter, we will take some steps back and review the original goal of why we want to create a Smart City, and what a Smart City really might be. Considering what we now know, this will result in some important conclusions. This chapter covers the following topics:

- A review of the vision of a Smart City
- Driving forces for the development of Smart Cities
- Requirements for reaching these goals
- An overview of required new standards
- An introduction to the IEEE IoT Harmonization project
- A presentation of new business roles

Envisioning the Smart City

At the beginning of this book, we presented the following vision of what a Smart City is in a *Smart Society*; there are the following access:

- The ubiquitous access to interoperable sensors and actuators
- The ubiquitous access to data and information from society's authorities
- Access to smart services in all niches of society

Simply put, a Smart Society will be open and **transparent**, and there will be sensors and actuators everywhere that you can interact with through a multitude of services tailored for the needs of the society.

Deriving some immediate consequences

From the preceding vision, we can derive a set of keywords immediately:

- **Interoperability (as opposed to proprietary or bespoke)**: Without interoperability based on standards, there can be no ubiquitous access to devices.
- **Openness (as opposed to closed off or sealed)**: The members of the society collectively pay for its authorities to perform its duties. The data they collect must be accessible by members of the society. If not, any decisions they make will be made using sub-standard information that is not smart. Access to devices also means devices must be open in the sense that they can be reutilized by different parties. Requiring service providers to install duplicate devices in the same areas where existing devices doing the same thing already exist, just to get the same type of data, is not smart.

 Open does not mean free. A restaurant can be open to the public, but it does not mean you can go there and eat for free. It means, the restaurant cannot deny you entry if you want to go there based on your identity. The internet is open, but you pay to access it.

- **Localization (as opposed to globalization)**: Globalized efforts can never respond to local needs. A society cannot be smart unless it can organize itself at a local level and adapt to local challenges. Technology must meet this need, not work against it.
- **Identity (as opposed to anonymous access)**: Openness on the internet places a lot of responsibility on the shoulders of those publishing information. As we have seen, strongly authenticated identities protect the publishers of information, by allowing them to make proper security decisions on who to allow access (authorization). Anonymous access protects malicious users. Strong identities protect publishers. A Smart City must protect those that publish devices and data. Therefore, it must support strongly authenticated identities.

Strong identities do not imply privacy intrusion

Using strong identities means you must authenticate yourself before you can participate in a meaningful conversation. A privacy intrusion occurs when somebody else uses information about you without your knowledge or consent (or some other legal basis). Anonymous communication gives a false promise of protecting you against such intrusions, it doesn't. Privacy legislation does (more on this in a later chapter). You don't protect your privacy by forcing everyone, including yourself, to wear blindfolds when you communicate with them. Privacy means you have the right to choose with whom you communicate and have confidential communication with. You can only do that if you know who the other party is. It also means that others are not allowed to listen in on confidential conversations. Only good privacy legislation together with strong identities can help you protect your privacy.

- **Ownership**: Why would somebody investing in producing data or installing devices let somebody else access them? Unless there is some form of compensation, it would only increase load and degrade system performance, while others would be able to deliver the same kind of service you provide, at a lower cost. To incentivize parties to open access to data and things, Smart Cities must be based on *ownership of data and things* and have an *economic feedback model* where consumers of data and things compensate owners for access:

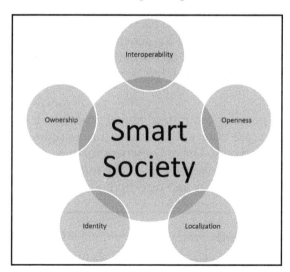

Smart City foundation

Avoiding the lure of the dark side

There are other visions of the Smart City, compared to the vision presented in this book, several bordering on the dystopic. They are often pushed by global big businesses, and often for reasons of self-interest, advancing their positions and trademarks. These ideas are then repeated, without realizing the underlying reasons, by a large audience hoping to be noticed or hoping to be able to jump on the *buzz word* bandwagon and earn money in start-up companies looking for venture capital. The common denominator in these visions (or deliriums) is often an all-intrusive collection (or hoarding) of data from everywhere, everyone, and everything. This data is then to be processed ("mined") centrally in "the cloud". The belief (or hope) is that advances in computing performance and Artificial Intelligence will allow these companies to extract valuable information from the dataset, information that would not be possible without the large-scale hoarding they hope to implement. Supposedly, this valuable information will allow us to live longer, cure incurable diseases, be more beautiful, and live in peace (for some reason, it's mostly marketing, economic, and political profiling that occurs in these supposedly humanistic data centers. Altruism is good, as long as somebody else pays for it).

Be it as it may, saving the world from dangerous diseases and pestilence is an important use case. But it is just one of many important use cases. To protect privacy and ownership of data and things, an open *decentralized architecture* respecting ownership is required. Such an architecture does not inhibit centralized processing of data. Centralized collection and processing would still be possible, but only *with the permission* of the corresponding owners. And through this permission, and an economic feedback model, the owners have a chance to *take part of the profits* from the data and the conclusions they contribute to. The reverse is not true, however: an architecture based on centralized hoarding of information cannot be used to provide localized services on the edge, respecting the privacy and rights of its owners.

Currently, big businesses push for centralized global proprietary solutions that cement their trademarks. These solutions are often antithetical to the concepts of interoperability, openness, localization, and privacy. The only ownership they are concerned about is their own. They risk becoming the new *robber barons* of the information age, due to lack of legislation and government incentives and direction:

Once centralized, you cannot go back

Understanding the driving forces

While today's robber barons try to push their information domination schemes on the world disguised as *Smart City* solutions, a decentralized open infrastructure for a true Smart City, respecting ownership and privacy is inevitable. Why? The following are a set of driving forces that will help break the big business monopoly on infrastructure in different domains, and make an open infrastructure a reality:

- **Reuse of existing resources**: This is logical and the only cost-effective way to provide smart services. It's not feasible that service providers must install their own set of equipment, if existing equipment is available. Buyers of equipment will require manufacturers to provide open standardized interfaces. It will not be possible to seal off and control everything from devices, infrastructure, backend, and services.

- **Cross-fertilization of domains**: It will be the source for most new types of services in a Smart Society. It's in the intersection of domains that most innovations occur (e-Health services can benefit greatly from home automation and security services, for instance). A single domain cannot envision everything that can be done with their technology. Inventiveness will require openness and interoperable access.

- **Local requirements**: It will not be satisfied by global efforts not supporting or understanding local needs. The requirement to optimize every aspect of society will force underlying infrastructure to support local efforts.

- **Privacy legislation**: It will force companies to respect owner rights. Not doing so will be exceedingly costly.

- **Representational government**: This, albeit slow, will understand their role, and help create legislation protecting the rights and freedoms of its citizens. They have done so in the past every time robber barons have appeared. Finally, if everything else fails, anti-trust legislation will break monopolies, forcing the parts to become interoperable.

Dividing responsibilities

Very few companies are able to provide complete vertical solutions, taking into consideration the creation of devices, hosting of infrastructure, and development of backend and frontend software. And those that do, must often cut corners, resulting in faulty or insecure solutions, or in dead ends. And while complexity and requirements increase, demand for lower costs and efficiency increase, making it even more difficult. **Vertical segmentation** is not sustainable, except for the largest companies. For big businesses, vertical segmentation is a means to control its customer base and defend its market share. But as we have seen, even for big businesses, vertical segmentation is not sustainable. They will be forced to open their solutions, allowing others to compete on their markets. This makes it unnecessary even for them to strive for market domination through vertical segmentation. A better option is **Horizontal Segmentation**, as is illustrated in the following image. If you specialize, you can reach a broader audience than if you would have to solve all problems in a vertical stack, using the same effort. Each rectangle in the following image is approximately of the same area, representing the effort and resources you have. You can do more if you specialize:

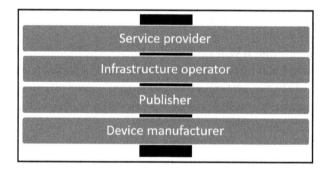

Vertical versus horizontal segmentation

Consider a temperature sensor manufacturer. They want to deliver connected temperature sensors. Can they imagine all types of applications that would benefit from integrating a temperature sensor? Are they experts in backend development and internet security? Surely not. It would therefore make sense for them to publish their sensors using interoperable interfaces, and let others invent the applications, people who do not know how to create temperature sensors. Service providers are better at creating services, operators better at hosting infrastructure, data providers better at publishing data, and device manufacturers better at creating devices. They shouldn't have to do the work of others. And most often, there's no benefit from trying. It is often more cost effective to use existing products that do not lie within your core business than it is to develop similar products yourself.

Proposing a solution

So, if our model of representational government is kept intact, a decentralized interoperable infrastructure respecting ownership of data and things is inevitable. It is just a question of time. But how much time, and what technology should such an infrastructure be based on? There's a plethora of devices and communication protocols in use already. Do they have to be updated or become obsolete?

To solve some of these questions, IEEE formed a working group called the *IEEE Devices and Systems Harmonization Working Group*, which hosts a project named *Standard for Harmonization of Internet of Things (IoT) Devices and Systems*. The objectives of this group and project is to find the underlying common denominator between different technologies and propose a means to harmonize these technologies so they can interact in one unified network.

Developing standards

To provide a truly interoperable infrastructure, all aspects of it need to be standardized. Nothing can be proprietary or bespoke open source, which can be changed at any minute. A recognized standards body must publish reviewed interfaces that everyone can use, and that are guaranteed to be maintained and responsibly updated to avoid breaks in compatibility. Standards must be available in the following areas:

- Communication
- Representation
- Operation
- Security
- Privacy
- Discovery
- Decision Support
- Economic feedback models (or contracts)

Using abstractions

When harmonizing devices communicating using different technologies, the question of complexity arises. If you have only two technologies, only one bridge is required. If you need to bridge three technologies, three bridges would be required. But how about four technologies? Do you need to create six bridges? Or 10 bridges between five technologies? 15 bridges for six technologies? For N technologies, you would need N(N - 1) / 2 bridges, at least if you bridge them directly between each other, as is shown in the following image. This process has an order of complexity of N2, which is clearly not maintainable as technologies grow. If somebody introduces a new technology, either that party needs to create bridges to every other technology that exists, or each technology provider needs to create a bridge to the new technology:

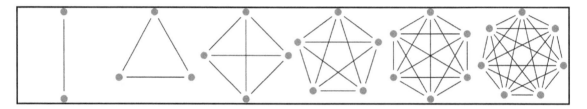

Bridging between technologies directly

A more fruitful method is to create an **abstraction layer** that can act as an intermediary between each technology. In such a case, the complexity of the system would be linear. Any technology provider would only have to provide a bridge to that abstraction layer, to be able to participate in the harmonized network, as is shown in the following image:

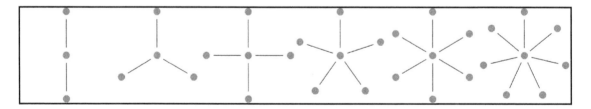

Bridging between technologies using an abstraction layer

Choosing XMPP

Due to the versatile nature of XMPP compared to other protocols, XMPP is proposed to work as a backend protocol, interconnecting islands of devices communicating using other means. Since it supports the common communication patterns used in other technologies, standardized as well as legacy technologies, it can also bridge seamlessly between XMPP and the corresponding underlying technology. The federated aspect of XMPP makes it possible to seamlessly integrate islands into a whole.

The proposal also aims at creating standardized interfaces for a decentralized open, secure, and interoperable infrastructure for the Smart City. These interfaces will act as the proposed *abstraction layer*, facilitating harmonization between technologies. They must define loosely coupled interfaces that contain sufficient room for metadata to allow for any imaginable use case. It proposes to do this by standardizing the extensions presented earlier in this book:

- Sensor data (representation)
- Control operations (operation)
- Protocol Bridging (concentrators)
- Discovery (thing registries)
- Decision support (provisioning, security, privacy)

You can access the current state of the interfaces by viewing the IEEE GitLab repository at: `https://gitlab.com/IEEE-SA/XMPPI/IoT`. Since the URL of a repository might change to a subdomain of ieee.org, a current link will be available at the Mastering IoT repository at GitHub: `https://github.com/PeterWaher/MIoT`, other links of interest: `https://standards.ieee.org/develop/wg/DASH.html` and `https://standards.ieee.org/develop/project/1451-99.html`.

Defining economic feedback models

One of the goals of the IoT Harmonization working group is to define a method to publish and accept contracts for usage of things in the network. Discovery and provisioning interfaces already exists. But an infrastructure for contracts that can be accepted would allow for the creation of economic feedback models based on usage. This would permit the creation of open markets for the Smart City. It would complete the requirements of standards and allow the creation of true Smart Cities.

Defining new roles

The proposed model creates room for several new business roles that companies can specialize in. Apart from device manufacturers and service providers, it also defines business models for the following:

- **Smart City Operators**: who provide infrastructure, monitor compliance of contracts, and enforce economic feedback
- **Device publishers**: who install, monitor, and publish things
- **Data publishers**: who maintain and publish datasets

The last two are particularly important. By creating open markets for data and things, actors will find it lucrative to publish these. This will also drive competition, which in turn will generate access to better and cheaper things and data, which in turn will drive the development of the Smart Society.

Summary

In this chapter, you've been introduced to the IEEE IoT Harmonization effort. You've been presented with a vision of the Smart Society, what its driving forces are, and some of its perils. You've been given an overview of the standardization effort required, how XMPP plays a role in future Smart Societies and the need for economic feedback models to make the Smart Society a reality, and what new business roles will appear. In the next chapter, we will discuss security for the IoT.

15
Security for the Internet of Things

Unfortunately, security is one of those things that is seldom considered sufficiently, if at all. Security is invisible and, therefore, difficult to measure. Functionality is much more entertaining, and it is visible and demonstrable. It can turn heads, raise money, and give positive feedback. Security, on the other hand, cannot give positive feedback. And it is difficult to raise money for it, since it is difficult to prove security claims are valid. Lack of security, however, can give negative feedback, but only when it is too late.

If security problems are grave on the internet as a whole, for things on the internet, it's even worse. Devices, not operated by human, and supposed to work for years, perhaps without being able to be updated, are at great risk of being compromised and utilized for malicious purposes. The goal of this chapter is to motivate the reader to take security for the Internet of Things into account from the very beginning, integrating it into the fabric of the design and architecture, and not adding it later as an add-on, in case it is needed. It covers:

- An introduction to the problem
- A review of common attack surfaces
- An introduction to common counter measures

Understanding the risks

James Clapper, former director of National Intelligence of the USA, told Popular Science in 2016 that *America's Greatest Threat is the Internet of Things*. And the list of threats to America is not small.

The reason for this statement is that our society is so automated and optimized. Vulnerabilities in things make it possible to disrupt services, logistics, communication, energy, and the economy. It is possible to paralyze a modern society, using vulnerabilities in the systems used to make it run.

Today, hospital equipment, health devices, utilities, transport, trains, ships, cars, vans, airplanes, power plants, nuclear facilities, grocery stores, railways, motorways, harbors, and so on are to some extent automated. And they will be more so in the future, some even becoming autonomous, running without human intervention. And many of these systems contain serious vulnerabilities, sometimes known, but most often unknown to the creators, but not to cyber warriors. Many of the items on which people will depend, will become susceptible to attacks and remote control. Some recent accidents and incidents already bear witness to apparent hacker activity.

When connecting yourself, or a device to the internet, you must understand what the internet is, who else is connected, and what they do. It is not a safe laboratory, office, or home network. Your neighbors on the internet will include criminals, murderers, pedophiles, teenage hackers, profiling companies, government agencies, and so on, and then you and your devices. If you lived in a neighborhood with such neighbors, would you leave your door to the house unlocked?

You can do an experiment to find out who's monitoring you on the internet, and how long it takes for them to find your machine. If you publish a server on the internet and log all access to it on common ports, and enable audit logs, you will find all types of entities prowling the internet trying to find a way in into your server. *Hacking is automated.* Finding your server can be done in minutes. It doesn't take many minutes to find available servers using IPv4 on the internet on a given port. Scanning IPv6 takes a little more time, but is doable. On HTTP you can check the `From` header, to distinguish legitimate scanning made by research institutes and search engines from illicit ones. Remember to compare the presented domain name with the IP address being used to send requests. Known vulnerabilities are tested, from communication level to application level. Common passwords are automatically tested. Don't rationalize away the risk by asking yourself *who's interested in my service anyway?* with the purpose of not having to do anything because your service or data is not interesting enough. Perhaps they're not interested in your service, data, or devices. Perhaps they're only interested in using your equipment to perform attacks on others, or store illegal information such as child pornography, or just destroy your devices because it's fun, or for the reason of blackmailing you.

Getting to a bad place

When the internet was created and especially the web, much effort was invested into the interconnection of machines, transmission of messages, and publication of information, and little effort was made concerning the problem of how to avoid malicious users sabotaging the network and published information. Good people will not consider the fact that bad people will share the network with them. Resilience was defined as the ability to recover from faults. This would typically mean infrastructure losses and breakdowns, which were imagined to be random events, natural disasters, or wars, which were large scale local area events. Malicious attacks, however, do not affect components randomly, or locally, but systematically and globally, and in a much more sophisticated manner. Attacks exploit vulnerabilities in the design or code, to make it do things that were never intended or imagined. As such, protection mechanisms have not naturally developed. It is difficult to develop a protection mechanism for something you have not imagined would occur. Simple redundancy and routing provide little protection against such attacks. And what is worse: data protection mechanisms contain vulnerabilities that can be exploited. They increase complexity and, therefore, also the risk of introducing new vulnerabilities.

The lack of proper security measures gave rise to a plethora of methods to hijack content, machines, and users. Instead of learning from past mistakes, much of the same errors are repeated today in the development of the Internet of Things, as enthusiastic engineers quickly create things that publish new information on the internet, paying little attention to the more boring aspects of security and protection. As security is invisible, it doesn't turn the heads of investors or journalists. So, it is one of the things that is being left for later, when there is time. As it happens, there just never is sufficient time...

But things are much more vulnerable than personal computers. While users can install software that protects personal computers, albeit not 100%, and keep their operating systems updated, things installed in the field often do not have the same possibilities. They might have to run years in the field unchanged, and resist hijacking and hacking attempts. And if vulnerabilities are found and exploited, things in the field might not even be updateable to counteract the attack and repair the vulnerability.

Understanding the root causes

So, how do we avoid repeating the same mistakes? Are these vulnerabilities and security threats an intrinsic part of the internet that we cannot counteract, and therefore we do not even try? Or are there methods that can be used to significantly improve the security in communication?

The major problem was that solutions were devised before the whole problem was understood. They wanted to find a method to transmit messages between computers in interconnected networks. They managed to do that exceedingly well. They did not consider, however, how to avoid the **injection** of fraudulent messages, or **eavesdropping** on transmitted messages. So, these were left out in the underlying protocols. As it became evident that these problems existed and posed a threat, solutions were added to solve them. But as these were aggregates, they became optional additions. They were never integrated into existing technology and made mandatory, since that would break *compatibility*. And the more technologies that existed, the more the paradigm was cemented owing to the inability to break compatibility; the more additions and aggregations that were made increased the amount of optional data protection measures available. But as they were optional, they required expert knowledge, which was not uniformly available, leaving the internet work to grow uncontrolled, unsecured, and very vulnerable.

And, as if that was not enough, problems got worse with the introduction of the World Wide Web, and the use of the HTTP protocol. It is an exceedingly popular protocol, and the very good at what it was designed to do: transporting open documents. But the complete absence of integrated and distributed security in the protocol and lack of capabilities when it comes to communication patterns have created an impressive library of technologies and extensions that complement the missing parts, extending it beyond the wildest dreams of its originators. But as has been mentioned earlier, these are all optional aggregates, requiring expert knowledge not readily available. Creating secure web platforms today is a very challenging task, even though the technology was introduced close to three decades ago.

Looking at alternative options

At some point in time, you must realize that continuing this path is not a good idea. Sometimes, you must throw away the old, even though it has served you well, and begin anew. When the weight of the legacy outweighs the benefits of continuing as usual, it's time to look at new options. And with the introduction of the Internet of Things, this is happening.

We have looked at several of the new options in this book. We've looked at new communication patterns and introduced new protocols. When designing a solution, you have the option of using a new type of technology. But take care to avoid repeating the same mistakes that others have done before you: don't be satisfied with a technology only because it solves your immediate problem quickly and rapidly and hope you can always do adjustments as requirements appear. Even though modern development processes encourage this mode of thinking, erroneously calling it **agile**, it is not a wise choice for the long run. Important design considerations with critical security implications for the future should be carefully reviewed before decisions are made that can only be changed with difficulty later. Try to envision the entire life cycle of the product, service, or system, before you set the first stone. Functionality built on top can be developed *ad hoc*, but intrinsic architectural decisions are more difficult to change.

A building is not more robust than its foundation. If the foundation is weak, it doesn't matter how much effort you plough into building additions on top. It will never be a solid building. For that reason, the creation of the foundation is the most important step when erecting a building, even if it is not visible. The same holds true for information systems. Without a robust foundation with sound architectural decisions, the system will always be vulnerable. Therefore, spend time and consideration to make a good foundation that will support your solution over time.

Getting to a better place

Regardless of whether you want it or not, if you're designing something for the Internet of Things, you must lay the foundation for it at the beginning. At the core of the foundation lies communication (among other things). Throughout the chapters, we've seen that protocols such as MQTT and HTTP, while they are easy to use, form a very bad foundation for interconnected things on the internet. While there are applications where they can be used, such as secondary web interfaces (HTTP) and local distributions of data (MQTT), for interoperability and exchange of data between devices on the internet, they are poor options. The amount of vulnerabilities you need to protect against, as well as the lack of communication pattern support, greatly outweighs using another protocol. CoAP with LWM2M might be a good choice, but only if the topology remains fixed, and if data collection and centralized processing is your main (or only) mode of communication. It's also a very poor choice, if interconnectivity between devices is on your feature wish list, or any form of secure formation of *ad hoc* networks.

If you, on the other hand, see a value in being able to create secure interoperable ad hoc networks of things and services, XMPP will provide you with a solid foundation to build upon. If you are not sure you need these things, assume you will, since it helps you avoid building yourself into a corner that you can only escape from with great difficulty. Since XMPP was originally built for instant messaging, it has intrinsic support for ad hoc networks. It is also the only protocol that has an intrinsic (inescapable) pluggable (SASL) distributed (federated) authentication mechanism coupled with an authorization mechanism (presence subscription negotiation) and encryption. It always forwards the authenticated identity of communicating parties in telegrams, making it easier for devices to make security decisions. Brokers make **spoofing** (pretending to have an address you don't have) more difficult by overriding senders claimed addresses, and checking that brokers forward messages they have a right to forward. Brokers also help solve the topology problem. And the rich support for communication patterns and scalability permits you to design virtually any communication model you might need. For this reason, you will find XMPP at the core of many of the world's most renowned communication infrastructure products. And if high intensity communication between nodes is required, server-less communication is a possibility if the network topology allows it.

 Brokers can help things with security issues, as in the case of XMPP, or make it harder to cope with all vulnerabilities, as in the case of MQTT. For this reason, MQTT might be a good option to transport information in controlled environments where its vulnerabilities can be checked. XMPP is a better option in uncontrolled networks, such as the internet, where brokers help participants reduce their vulnerability.

Mastering data protection technologies

It is difficult to master all the technologies that exist concerning data protection. It is furthermore, a field that is in constant flux as new vulnerabilities are found. By choosing a good underlying foundation for your project, such as XMPP, you get a technology that helps you with many of the underlying risks — *but not all*. You will still need to understand the basics of data protection and cyber security. To cover this field meaningfully would require multiple books and is beyond the scope of this book. In this chapter, however, you will be presented by a very brief overview of technologies you should be familiar with, to the point of knowing how they work, what problems they solve, and when to use them.

Skimming the basics of encryption

Encryption algorithms are often divided into **symmetric** and **asymmetric** ciphers. Encryption algorithms often use multiple algorithms together to achieve the expected properties. Such ciphers are called **hybrid**. But understanding the distinction between symmetric and asymmetric ciphers is important.

Symmetric ciphers are typically faster and have smaller keys. **AES** is an example of a symmetric cipher that has hardware support on most modern machines. *Elliptic curve cryptography* is also symmetric. These ciphers are called symmetric since both encryption and decryption use the same key. Since these ciphers often are faster, they are preferred when encrypting a large bulk of data, for example, when transferring content, or when the sender and receiver are the same, such as when encrypting local storage or personal information. Since the key must be the same, if two (or more) entities partake in the conversation, cryptographic **key exchange** becomes important. **Diffie-Hellman** is a set of algorithms for key exchange. Note that the cipher is not stronger than the weakest link.

Asymmetric ciphers on the other hand are slower. They have one key for encryption and another for decryption. In a **Public Key Infrastructure** (**PKI**) based on asymmetric ciphers, the **public key**, which can be known by everybody, is used for encryption and for validating signatures. The **private key**, known only to the holder of the key, is used for decryption and the creation of signatures. Given the public key, it's considered hard to derive the private key. PKI has the advantage of not requiring key exchange. **RSA** is an example of a popular asymmetric cipher.

Hybrid ciphers typically combine the features of different ciphers. It's common to use an asymmetric cipher, such as RSA, to encrypt symmetric keys, for instance, in the key exchange phase, and then use the corresponding symmetric cipher, such as AES or an elliptic curve, to encrypt the bulk of the message.

Encryption can provide you with a false sense of security. Normally, when discussing encryption, merely node-to-node encryption, such as **TLS**, is discussed. Since transport typically makes multiple jumps between nodes, such as brokers, proxies, middleware, or malicious middlemen, data is decrypted at each node, and then re-encrypted before being passed on, if the next step is also encrypted. Data is not secured when it has been decrypted. Transport layer security protects against **sniffing** (eavesdropping) and **injection** of false messages, but it is only as secure as the underlying cipher, many of which can be broken today. **Downgrade attacks** trick the other party to use a cipher that can be broken.

A stronger form of encryption is **end-to-end encryption** (**E2E**) where data is decrypted when it reaches its intended destination. E2E is performed on the application layer and not on the transport layer.

Protecting data integrity

Hash algorithms are deterministic, unstable cryptographic functions that produce a *short* value, or a **hash**, given a set of data. Unstable means that a small change in the input produces a very large change in the output. This makes it very difficult to reverse the calculation; such that given a hash, it is very difficult to find a dataset that generates that same hash. Doing so is called finding a collision. **SHA** is a set of well-known hash algorithms.

Hashes can be used to create signatures or maintain the integrity of a data item, such as a file. Since the hash is small, it's easy to transmit and store. Computing the hash multiple times gives the same value, unless something has been changed in the file. The hash, therefore can be used to protect the integrity of the file, meaning you can detect if somebody has tampered with the information.

Hashes can also be used to protect user credentials. Instead of transmitting or storing passwords, hashes of passwords, combined with some **salt**, can be transmitted and stored. When a user provides a password, the hash is calculated and compared, instead of the password itself. This produces the same result. But if a malicious user gets access to the database, or listens to the communication, and retrieves a hash, the original password will be very difficult to extract. And the use of the salt (a random number unique to the context) makes sure the hash cannot be used somewhere else.

Understanding key sizes

When using different algorithms, it might be difficult to evaluate the relative strengths of each, since the key sizes vary (counted in bits). The NSA has made some recommendations for commercial enterprises on the relative strengths of different methods. These can be used as a guideline for how secure the corresponding cipher is, or how "easy" it is to break it (for, or according to, the NSA). They can therefore be considered comparatively of similar strength.

Algorithm	Key size	Usage
RSA	3072	Keys, signatures
Diffie-Hellman	3072	Key exchange
Elliptic Curve	NIST P-384	Key exchange, signatures
SHA	384	Integrity
AES	256	Confidentiality

You can find the NSA recommendations here:
`https://cryptome.org/2016/01/CNSA-Suite-and-Quantum-Computing-FAQ.pdf`

Using certificates

X.509 certificates are containers of cryptographic algorithm references and keys, as well as metadata, or claims that the certificate is supposed to make. These claims might be related to a name such as a domain name, email address, and so on. The claims are only valid for a given amount of time. A certificate contains an **expiration date**. After that date, the certificate automatically becomes invalid.

The algorithm references constitute an example of a *loosely coupled architecture*, making algorithms *pluggable*. As algorithms become obsolete, they can be exchanged for newer ones, without having to change the overlying architecture.

Certificates define a PKI. The **public** part of the certificate can be transmitted to others, who can use it to **validate** the claims made, and that the certificate is valid. The public part can also be used to validate signatures made by the holder of the **private** part and encrypt information to it. The holder of the private part can use it to **sign** information, and to **decrypt** information sent to it. The private part of the certificate is typically protected by a password. Certificates also have a **thumbprint**, a hash value that can be used for integrity checks to identify that certificate.

Certificates also have a mechanism to protect against losses or compromises of the private part of the certificate: most certificates are issued by a **Certificate Authority**, or **CA**. You can **revoke** a certificate with its **issuer**. The CA maintains a list of certificates that have been revoked. When validating a certificate, its **chain** is also validated to check a certificate has not been revoked. The chain is formed by fetching the certificate of the issuer, validating it, checking its issuer, and so on, until reaching a **root certificate**. A root certificate does not have an issuer. The root certificate must be **installed** in the system, for the chain to be valid. The list of installed root certificates is typically maintained by the operating system or the system administrator.

When connecting to a domain on the internet, the domain name is first resolved into one or more IP addresses by your DNS server. When connecting to these addresses, you don't really know if the IP addresses are correct. A malicious user might have introduced their own IP addresses into the server to perform a **Man-In-The-Middle** attack (**MITM**). This is called **DNS spoofing**. As you connect to the server using TLS, the server presents a certificate to prove it is who it says. The client validates the certificate and reads the name (or **subject**) on it and compares it with the name originally resolved. If they match, communication can continue, since only the holder of the private part of the certificate can generate the appropriate signature.

When validating certificates, consider **pinning** the CA certificate. This means that you explicitly check the identity of the CA certificate, or its thumbprint, and make sure it is one that you know. This pin must be updated, as the CA needs to update its certificates too. But the lifetime of a CA certificate is often longer than a normal certificate. And pinning the CA certificate in your validation routine makes sure an impostor is not able to present you with a valid certificate made from another CA that has been compromised (or a self-signed certificate that somebody has installed, see the following section).

Avoiding self-signed certificates

One of the most common certificate-related errors developers commit is to create **self-signed** certificates, instead of creating proper certificates. Perhaps it is to be able to create certificates with an apparent long lifetime, to avoid having to update them in the field, or to avoid the cost of creating a proper certificate. Both arguments are invalid. You can easily create valid certificates for free today.

Using self-signed certificates is a great risk in itself. Apparent security is not true security. First, you must disable security features to allow such certificates to be validated. Either you do that in code or you install the certificate everywhere where the certificate is to be validated. Both create severe vulnerabilities. In the first case, disabling such features in code, often results in these features being forgotten and ending up in production environments. This in turn results in the system being vulnerable against MITM attacks. Installing self-signed certificates in the system can be even worse. Having access to the private part of a certificate you can create other certificates, having the self-signed certificate as an issuer. These will automatically validate. You can then perform successful MITM attacks using DNS spoofing of well-known services, and you would not notice, since the fraudulent certificates used would validate everywhere where the self-signed certificate was installed.

You can easily automate the creation of valid certificates for free, by using an **ACME** client, such as **certbot**, and a CA such as **Let's Encrypt**: `https://letsencrypt.org/`

It might in some cases be better to not use encryption at all, than to use encryption based on self-signed certificates.

Also, a requirement to use TLS or DTL, does not require you to use certificates, even if it is the common use case. There are ciphers based on **pre-shared keys** (**PSK**) that you can use. In such case encryption is established. But you lose the ability to validate certificate chains and revoke compromised keys. But, it's preferable to use PSK in a responsible manner than it is to use self-signed certificates.

Use `https://www.ssllabs.com/ssltest/` to check your TLS servers and get tips on what you can do to improve their security. While you're at it, if you run Windows Servers, you can use the IIS Crypto tool to control cipher settings to improve your score: `https://www.nartac.com/Products/IISCrypto.`

Avoiding creating a Certificate Authority

Unless you are a big company with the goal of creating a proper certificate authority, don't create your own CA just because you need a method to create a lot of your own certificates:

- First, make sure you really need these certificates. If you're forced to use client-side certificates for things, just because the authentication mechanism in the underlying protocol is inherently insecure, such as is the case with MQTT, consider choosing another technology such as XMPP. If the underlying technology permits, such as in the case of CoAP and LWM2M, consider using PSK that you can generate easily yourself instead of certificates, rather than having to create your own CA. Certificates should only be used on high-value nodes due to their increased complexity and relatively short lifetime.
- Creating a CA requires you to maintain a redundant and resilient set of certificate servers that can respond to validation requests. If they go down, your system risks going down.
- If you need more certificates than can be created using the free options of CAs such as Let's Encrypt, consider getting a commercial account instead of creating your own CA.
- Creating your own CA requires you to install the CA certificate on all machines that will interact with your things and services. This is undesirable. It creates vulnerabilities in these systems and forces you to maintain your CA servers and corresponding certificates under stringent watch.

Don't create solutions that require the installation of root certificates. These must be maintained. Also, don't create long-lived certificates. Instead, use ACME to automate the creation of relatively short-lived certificates.

Using tokens to transport claims

Due to the complexity of using certificates and the need to be able to transport custom claims, technologies such as **JSON Web Tokens**, or **JWT**, have become popular. They allow the transmission of claims encoded into a simple text string that is easy to distribute and contains a HMAC SHA-256 signature. **HMAC** basically means that the claims are salted in a special way with a secret. This secret must be *shared* between the issuer of the token and all recipients. While JWT tokens are simpler to implement and maintain, they induce a vulnerability compared to certificates in distributed systems, since the secret must be distributed between all entities. Therefore, only use such tokens where such a distribution can be made in a controlled manner. The simplest example is if the issuer is the same as the receiver. This is the case when an application on a web server issues a token to a web page, whose JavaScript uses the token in subsequent API calls to the server, as we did in Chapter 6, *Creating Web Pages for Your Devices*.

Enforcing ubiquitous encryption

It is easier to just encrypt everything than it is to analyze how sensitive different aspects of the system are and encrypt only that which is sensitive enough. Hardware support for encryption has made the performance loss of using encryption negligible in most cases. And selecting and making choices just increases the risk of making the wrong choices. Therefore, just enforce **ubiquitous encryption**: encrypt all data at rest (storage) and data in transit (communication) by default.

If you process sensitive data, especially sensitive personal data, you should consider end-to-end encryption as well. Normal transport-level encryption, such as that provided by **TLS**, only encrypts data between nodes in the network. To avoid data leaking through compromised nodes, end-to-end encryption can be used.

 Simple is often better and more secure, since it is easier to maintain an overview. Complexity increases the risk of making mistakes. Simplify your processes and reduce unnecessary decisions where you can, to increase security. Ubiquitous encryption is an example of this.

Creating checklists

The chain is not stronger than the weakest link. And in many cases, the **human factor** is the weakest of them all. Even experienced and knowledgeable people forget things. And if it is not your human factors playing a trick, it might be one of your co-workers... To avoid forgetting important steps during development, quality assurance, deployment, and production, create mandatory **checklists** to follow, just as in aviation. Using checklists is a great support in stressful moments, and for people with good, albeit short, memories. Execute these checklists at important milestones in your project, to make sure you haven't forgotten anything important. Items you could include in these checklists, but should not be limited to:

- Run security-related unit tests
- Check certificates are valid and not set to expire soon
- Make sure ubiquitous encryption is enforced
- Check TLS endpoints using `https://www.ssllabs.com/ssltest/`
- Check security headers with `https://securityheaders.io/`
- Execute validation checks
- Execute penetration tests to make sure unauthenticated and unauthorized access is never granted at any level of the system to any data, service, or device
- Scan the network for open ports that should be closed, unauthenticated access points, and use of standard passwords
- Update software and operating systems
- Update documentation
- Make sure your Data Protection Impact Assessment (see the next chapter) is updated
- Configure **key stores** and usage of **Trusted Platform Modules** (**TPM**) to manage cryptographic keys
- Update keys and passwords where necessary

The checklists or corresponding tests should be updated as new vulnerabilities are found and data protection measures added.

Also remember that a checklist is a tool to help you remember important steps in stressful situations. It is not a replacement for *critical thought*. Just because you've completed your checklist doesn't mean your system is secure. And don't avoid creating checklists, just because you can't figure out *everything* you have to do. Partial checklists are better than non-existing checklists.

Updating your firmware

Just as operating systems must be updated regularly, and software running on PCs need frequent updates, things need to be updated as vulnerabilities are found and protected against. New proposed legislation, beginning in the USA, will require things to be updateable. Otherwise, government authorities will not be allowed to buy them. Such legislation is sure to be implemented in other countries as well, as time passes. This will put pressure on manufacturers to include this in their products. The result will be that products that do not support this feature will find it difficult to find a market place. For that reason, plan to make your things updateable remotely. Care must be taken, however, to make sure only you can update your things, and nobody else.

Distributing your risks

Centralized processing is not only bad for privacy, scalability, and responsiveness. It is bad for security reasons as well. Centralized nodes easily become vulnerable in **Denial of Service (DoS)** attacks, especially **Distributed Denial of Service (DDoS)** attacks. The point of a DoS attack is to flood a central node with requests to deplete its processing power, effectively denying access to the server to its rightful owners. But just as distributing the attack among multiple attacking machines makes the DoS more efficient, distributing the processing makes the system less vulnerable and more resilient to such attacks. **Edge computing** is based on processing information as close to the source (the edge) as possible. This is the ultimate form of distributed processing, even though intermediate nodes can be used as well. As the loads on central nodes decrease, it's easier to scale organically. Processing power can be dedicated to the main task at hand, instead of solving complex scalability issues centrally. It also helps maintain privacy and integrity, since data is processed close to the people concerned.

This can be used by the owners of the equipment to enforce ownership of the information as well. Since data is not stored at central points, illicit access to all the information is also made more difficult. This decreases the risk of it being abused or leaked in bulk.

Centralized	Distributed (federated)
Expensive	Inexpensive
Inefficient	Efficient
Difficult to scale	Scales organically
Unsecure	Secure
Loss of integrity	Maximal integrity
Easy to abuse	Difficult to abuse
User cannot control information	User owns information

Note that a distributed architecture for processing does not prohibit centralized processing of certain information under certain conditions. Such can always be made, but with adequate permissions. The opposite is not true, however. Once you've centralized processing, it's very difficult to go back and perform distributed processing of the information.

Avoiding leaking data unintentionally

Many data leaks that occur in systems are unintentional. Developers publish data in an accessible format because they want it to be easy for them to access the data. It might not occur to them that their APIs or data sources will be found, and attempted, by others. Always add a layer of **authentication** and **authorization** to your data sources and APIs as well. It is not sufficient to add such layers in user interfaces. So much should be clear by now.

But there are other unintentional data leaks that are more difficult to find: do you use **third-party services**? Every time you call such a service, you leak information to them, through the parameters you use in your API calls. Whether it be position information through a map API, or IP addresses through a log API, information is leaked, and can be collected and processed to analyze your service, your users, and their behavior. Make sure you have confidentiality agreements signed with every third party you communicate with that regulate which data can be collected, and for which purposes.

Search features and the use of **wildcards** in searches and subscriptions are other sources of leaks. While very useful to accomplish legitimate tasks, they can also be used by malicious users to extract too much information from your system. Make sure to log and monitor such use and put limits on how much freedom is allowed.

If you've used `Waher.Persistence.FilesLW` for persisting data locally in the examples in this book, you can easily protect that data from leaking unintentionally, by encrypting it, if you run the application on a platform that supports .NET Standard 1.5, such as .NET Core 2 or UWP 2. In that case, you simply use the `Waher.Persistence.Files` library instead. All data at rest, persisted using this library, will be seamlessly encrypted using AES-256 by default. The application interface is the same.

Summary

In this chapter, you've been introduced to some of the risks involved in creating solutions for the Internet of Things. The goal has not been to dissuade you from doing so, but to prepare you, so that you know how to protect your solutions from common forms of attack. You've learned why security for the IoT is so important, how vulnerable smart societies are, and how design choices affect the security of your solutions. You've also been given an overview of some common forms of attacks and how to protect your systems from common vulnerabilities. In the next chapter, we will discuss privacy and how it affects the Internet of Things.

16
Privacy

The last chapter of this book is dedicated to perhaps the most important subject of our time: privacy. Its importance is widely underestimated, and the design decisions we make for information systems we help build have a huge impact on our ability to protect the privacy of our users. The question of privacy is often completely omitted, simply because it is believed by many to be impossible to protect in the information society of today. I, as the author of this book, leave this chapter till last, because if there is anything I wish you to take with you in your professional career it is a heightened awareness of how important privacy is, that it is possible to protect, and what you can and must do to protect it. This chapter covers the following topics:

- An introduction to what privacy is and why it matters
- An introduction to new privacy legislation
- How technology can help protect privacy

Defining privacy

If you ask people on the street, at work, at home, or in class what privacy is, or what it means, you are normally met with blank stares. People have no clue. They are not even sure if it is important or not. It is too vague. You might even encounter people who claim that privacy is a bad thing. Only bad people require privacy. If you have nothing to hide, why hide? No wonder privacy has eroded fast, if people don't know what it is, see no value in it, and do nothing to defend it against those who profit from eliminating it.

Understanding the importance

In article 12 of UN's *Universal Declaration of Human Rights*, we can read: *No one shall be subjected to arbitrary interference with his privacy, family, home or correspondence, nor to attacks upon his honor and reputation. Everyone has the right to the protection of the law against such interference or attacks.* Simply put, **privacy** is a *fundamental human right*.

The fundamental human rights form the basis on which all legislation should be built, national as well as international. Without it, or parts of it, our society will degrade into something that is not pleasant. Each article is based on hundreds, or thousands, of years of experience and multitudes of failed examples, and each one is a requirement for building a society that gives a minimum of protection for its citizens.

Understanding what it means

As with all articles of the declaration, they contain few words to make the point clear. Perhaps too few words we might think, especially since technology has advanced so much since the declaration was written. But there are some following basic things that we can derive from the declaration:

- Correspondence originally referred to communication using letters. Today, it includes electronic communication such as email.
- The use of the words *arbitrary interference* means there are *non-arbitrary forms of interference* that are acceptable, without breaking the UN declaration. What could those be? Modern privacy laws provide the answer (see the following sections).
- The definition contains a double negation: You have a right to not be subject to arbitrary interference with your correspondence. Let's eliminate that double negation and write it as a positive statement: *You have the right to communicate confidentially*. This is a fundamental human right.
- You also have the right to *select with whom you communicate*. Others cannot do that for you, meaning eavesdrop arbitrarily.
- The article also states that you have the right to *not be subject to attacks on your honor or reputation*. This means you have the right to be legally protected from people *suggesting* (which is a form of attack) you might have something to hide, simply because you want to have confidential conversations with others. There are things we want to do in private, and only discuss with private friends or family, without it being suspicious, illicit, or immoral. It is our fundamental human right to do those things, as long as we do not limit other people's fundamental human rights.

Google represents one of the biggest threats to privacy in recent times. Their disregard for the items listed in this section should come as no surprise to the reader. That they seem to have complete disrespect for Article 12 of the Universal Declaration of Human Rights is perhaps best summarized by Eric Schmidt, a previous Google CEO, in his statement *If you have something that you don't want anyone to know, maybe you shouldn't be doing it in the first place*. The obvious extension to this is that he thought Google had the right to collect any personal information about everyone, since if anyone objected, it was due to morally suspicious activity. They are in the right; anybody objecting is in the wrong. Visit `https://www.eff.org/deeplinks/2009/12/google-ceo-eric-schmidt-dismisses-privacy`. For a search engine that respects privacy, see: `https://duckduckgo.com/`. For a social network that respects privacy, see Little Sister®: `https://littlesister.se/`. Also, make sure to follow the **Electronic Frontier Foundation**: `https://www.eff.org/`.

Being informed

The rights given to you state that you have the right to communicate in confidence with people and that you decide who they are. At the same time, you have the right to not be subjected to arbitrary interference. These statements together provide an important implication: *you have the right to be informed* about non-arbitrary interference with your privacy. Otherwise, you will not be able to select with whom you communicate, or not be able to communicate in confidence. If somebody interferes with your privacy, for instance, by collecting and processing your personal information, that party is obliged to inform you about it, so that you can take the corresponding steps to protect your rights.

Introducing the GDPR

The state of privacy of individuals in the world looked bleak until 2016. Most people were subjected to the pleasures of global internet companies, who abused their positions to collect and process the personal information of their users, without their informed consent, selling it on to third parties, and not always in the best interest of the original users. This uncontrolled state of affairs is only beneficial for a few robber barons who can exploit the fact that most people are unaware of what is happening, how the proposed technology works, what the alternatives are, what their rights are, who is benefitting from it all, and who bears the long-term consequences.

To provide authorities with effective means to regulate the processing of personal information and give some of the lost rights back to people, the European Union managed to create perhaps the first effective and good legislation in this field in May 2016: the **General Data Protection Regulation**, or the **GDPR**. It gives companies two years to adapt their processing activities before the law comes into full effect in May 2018. This legislation is good for everybody except those who want to exploit the personal information of unsuspecting individuals. It provides effective means to regulate the processing of personal information, it provides and defines proper rights for individuals, and it gives companies a means to compete using privacy as a quality measurement, instead of having to compete breaking privacy. For the first time, companies have an efficient means to earn money, by providing solutions that protect the privacy of people, instead of invading it.

If you talk to lawyers about the GDPR, some might object, saying that much of the GDPR existed previously, and that the GDPR is not much of a difference to earlier legislation. This might be true in some regards, and in theory alone. Much of the regulation existed in various forms of legislation earlier. What is different is that the GDPR not only harmonizes the legislation across member states in the EU, but that it also extends its reach to any service in the world being offered to European citizens. It also provides an efficient means to regulate it with heavy sanctions and fines if you don't comply. This difference makes the law something every company must consider, even global giants. Earlier legislation, you could pretty much ignore. In theory, the GDPR might not be much different; it is based on previous work. But in practice, it implies a drastic paradigm shift in how the processing of personal information can be performed. Anyone interested in privacy can read the source material directly on the internet. It is available in 24 languages, all with the same status as law: `http://eur-lex.europa.eu/legal-content/EN/TXT/?uri=OJ:L:2016:119:TOC`.

Balancing rights

The first thing the GDPR recognizes is that there are many different human rights and that no right is absolute. While individuals have a right to privacy, people also have the right to associate with companies for the purposes of industry, creating solutions and providing services that process personal information. One of the goals of the GDPR is to **balance** these rights, as well as the provisions set up in other existing laws.

Another goal is to *facilitate the free flow of information*. This might sound nefarious, or counter-intuitive, but it is not. It means that companies complying with the regulations set forth in the GDPR are allowed to share this information with others that also follow the regulations, as long as this flow of information complies with the requirements, and without having to apply for a permission to do so. We will outline what these requirements are in the following sections, and what happens if you do not follow these requirements.

It is interesting to note that some countries have enacted legislation prohibiting the free flow of personal information by requiring data to be stored and processed within the boundaries of the same nation. In comparison, the GDPR does facilitate the free flow of information since it focuses on rights of the data subjects, rather than technical solutions and limitations.

Measuring proportionality

It is difficult to establish a balance between two incompatible measurements. Privacy is subjective, profit or public value can be measured objectively. How do you balance these two?

The GDPR outlines some sort of a minimum and a maximum effort you must make to protect the privacy of individuals. The minimum effort is called: **state of the art**. The *state of the art* is a fluid term, popular in patent law. It refers to the highest level of *general development* in each field, and it is known to people *skilled in the craft*, or *skilled in the art*. Simply put: while there might exist plenty of more advanced solutions to different topics, sorting under specialized developments, **professionals in the field** know what the best practices are, that is, the highest level of general development. This is also what is expected of you, by the GDPR. Lack of knowledge is not an acceptable excuse in the GDPR. If something is complicated or hard, just because you're inexperienced in the field of inquiry does not make it a valid argument for not having to enforce it. It is not a measurement of the true complexity of the problem. What is valid is what people that are *skilled in the art* think.

The maximum effort the GDPR requires of you is that you're not required to do more than what is **proportional** to the risks faced by all participants, or data subjects. This includes a measurement of the cost.

A data subject is a natural person about whom personal data is being processed.

Defining personal data

The GDPR concerns the processing of personal data. So, it is important to know exactly what is meant by personal data. **Personal Data** is *any information* relating *directly*, or *indirectly*, to an *identified* or *identifiable* natural person called a **data subject**. Let's think about what this very broad definition means:

- Information that not only directly, but also indirectly, relates to a person is also personal. Number of references is not limited.
- It does not matter if the processing activity has the person identified or not. It is sufficient that a person can be identified even, by an external party, for the data to be personal.
- It does not even matter, if this process of identification is possible for all records, or to what degree this possibility exists. If the data is indirectly related to *an identifiable person*, the data is personal.
- The GDPR goes on to provide a non-exclusive list of artefacts considered personal data: names, identification numbers, location data (such as positions), online identifiers (such as MAC, IP and email addresses, keys, account names, and so on), one or more factors specific to the physical, physiological, genetic, mental, economic, cultural, or social identity.

Personality is contagious: Data relating to personal data automatically becomes personal data.

It might just be easier for you to process your information as if it all was personal. Sensor data is often personal. There are various relations that might make the sensor data personal: one might be the indirect relationship with its owner. Another might be related to what the sensor measures. If the sensor is in a home, in a vehicle, at the office, in a wearable device, and so on, it's personal. If it is a public sensor with the ability to measure information that can be used to identify people, it's also personal.

Anonymizing data

If you manage to anonymize data, the GDPR no longer applies to that data. Unfortunately, the term is often used erroneously. **Anonymization** of data means that it is *no longer possible* to identify a natural person from the data. This requires stringent proof. Replacing the identity of persons in a dataset with numbers, GUIDs, or hashes does not satisfy this requirement, since it is still possible to reverse engineer and identify the original set of persons, especially if you have a list of possible persons to compare against. This process is called **pseudonymization** and is still considered personal data, according to the GDPR. Pseudonymized data is defined as data where it is possible to identify a person given external data. Pseudonymization is still considered a data protection mechanism.

While anonymization is difficult, valid methods still exist. One example is **statistical aggregation**. Operations as sums, averages, variance, standard deviations, and so on eliminate the possibility to say anything about individuals, if the population is sufficiently large. Another method is **data obfuscation**, or **data masking**. This means you destroy certain details in the dataset, which accomplishes the same thing as aggregation. An example can be to destroy one of the four bytes in an IPv4 address. From the three remaining bytes, you can deduce the region, but not the individual performing an action, for instance.

Defining processing

Now that we have a better understanding of what constitutes personal data, we also need to know what "processing" means. As with personal data, the definition is very broad. The GDPR defines **processing** to mean *any operation* or set of operations that is performed on personal data or on sets of personal data, regardless if the processing is done using automatic or manual means. It limits manual operations to those that are made for the purposes of filing. There are very few loopholes.

Doing as little as possible

If you want to find a one-word definition for what the GDPR is, it is: **minimalism**. You can say it's a minimalistic definition. What it means is that the GDPR allows you to:

- Do *as little as possible*.
- For *as short a time as possible*. Old data must be deleted.
- For *as few purposes as possible*.
- *As correctly as possible*. You are obliged to update erroneous data.

- *Share with as few as possible.* You must also assure their datasets are kept up to date.
- And always with *proportional data protection mechanisms* in place.

Informing the data subjects

But it is you who defines what these limits are. You must also **inform** the data subjects of what you are doing. This information must be provided in a **transparent** manner. Transparent does not mean open, since you can hide relevant information by providing too much information. This is normally what happens in legal agreement texts. Under the GDPR, long complicated texts such as those do not constitute transparent information. Instead, transparency means the text must be informative, easy to understand, clear, and concise. It must use plain language, and special consideration must be made if the processing activity involves children. It must be relevant to the audience (the receivers), not the sender, which is typically the case with legal documents.

 There might be cases where processing of personal data does not require informing data subjects. Such cases include processing activities mandated by law that require secrecy. Another exception might be if it is impossible to inform the subjects. In such cases, general statements should be made available publicly by other means.

Once you've defined your boundaries and informed the data subjects, you can commence processing. You are then not allowed to go outside of the boundaries you've set up and informed the data subjects about, without informing the data subjects about that fact. And you are only allowed to perform the new processing activity on data collected after the time you informed the subjects. You are not allowed to execute it on old data retroactively.

 This minimalistic requirement implies a paradigm shift on how data can be processed. The traditional statement made by proponents of centralized big data solutions that *the more you collect, the more potential value you have* is no longer true, considering the GDPR. Since you are not allowed to retroactively process the data you've collected in new processing activities, hoarding the data "just in case" makes no sense. The old paradigm is no longer true. In the new paradigm, the more data you collect, the more risk you have and the greater your responsibility. But the potential value stays the same. The new paradigm states that *you should only collect data to which you can assign a value.*

Finding your legal grounds

To be allowed to process personal data in the first place, you must have a legal foundation for doing so. The GDPR provides you with the following six options to choose from:

- The most recognized form is based on **consent**. This means that you get an approval from each data subject after having informed them of what you are going to do. After getting the approval, you're allowed to perform the processing that you've described. Each subject must be allowed to withdraw their consent at any time. And doing so should be as easy as it was to give it. And when they do, you're no longer allowed to process their personal data and must remove it.

- You are also allowed to process personal data if it is your **legal obligation** to do so. You are still required to inform the data subjects (unless the law explicitly states you're not allowed to), but do not need their consent.

- If you have a **legitimate interest** that outweighs the rights and freedoms of the data subjects, you are also allowed to perform the processing, after informing the data subjects of what you're intending to do. The data subjects have the right to **object** to the processing. In such cases, you are only allowed to continue processing such data for which you have *compelling reasons* to continue. This means that you are not able to continue the processing without such data. Data for which there are no compelling reasons to maintain, must be deleted. Processing based on legitimate interest does not require consent, but still requires information being provided to data subjects. An example of legitimate interest might be to monitor employees at work to optimize production, for instance. Another example might be processing to facilitate research and development of new and better products and services.

- If you have a **contract** with a data subject, you can perform the corresponding processing for the time specified. You must, as always, provide transparent information about the processing activities to the data subject.

 Note that the processing of personal information of employees based on a contract with the employer does not constitute a legal ground based on that contract. Instead, the processing must be based on a *legitimate interest*.

- If the processing activity can save lives somehow, it is of **vital interest**. Such processing is allowed, always with proportional data protection mechanisms, and always with a requirement of transparent information being given to the data subjects.

- Other types of processing that are for the common good, or **public interest**, can also be allowed, given the requirements of proportionality and transparency.

Avoiding certain topics

There are certain things that you should stay away from. Unless you have explicit consent or are otherwise explicitly permitted, you are not allowed to do any of the following processing activities, considered **high-risk** activities:

- Processing of **special categories** of data. This includes data related to *racial or ethnic origin, political opinions, religious or philosophical beliefs, or trade union membership, and the processing of genetic data, biometric data for the purpose of uniquely identifying a natural person, data concerning health or data concerning a natural person's sex life or sexual orientation.*
- Perform **profiling** of data subjects such that automatic decisions are made that have negative consequences (in a legal sense) for the data subjects. You can grade people and reward the people the algorithm finds are good. But you are not allowed to punish the bad.

 People are still allowed to make mistakes, but not algorithms. Since it is difficult to prove if an algorithm is fair or just, it cannot be made an arbiter, and decisions should not be made solely on the outcomes of automatic profiling. If you involve at least one human that weighs in, in the loop, you're safe, at least from the perspective of the GDPR.

- **Monitoring publicly accessible areas** on a large scale. You need a special permit to be the big brother...

If you are at risk of exposing data subjects to a high risk, you must perform a **Data Protection Impact Assessment (DPIA)**. If such an assessment concludes there is such a high risk, you must *consult* with authorities, who will euphemistically give you *advice* on the subject. I suggest you follow that advice. It is not called advice because it's optional for you to do anything. It is called advice because you can do something else, if you can show it is better. They still have their eyes on you and can give you any number of sanctions if they find you're doing something you shouldn't be.

Distributing responsibilities

The GDPR defines a top-down approach of assuring privacy is protected. At the top, you will find the European Council. It issued the GDPR. Under it, you find the European Data Protection Authority. It consists of the presidents of each national data protection authority. The goal of the European authority is to harmonize the interpretation of the GDPR across national boundaries. Each national authority controls the activity of each controller within the confines of the corresponding national border. It can get help from certification authorities, who help certify compliance from companies, organized by domain. *Certificates* and *codes of conduct* simplify audits for both companies and national authorities. **Controllers** determine the *purposes and means of processing* personal data. They have all the responsibilities and are hit hardest with sanctions if something is not done according to the requirements of the GDPR. **Processors** process personal data on behalf of a controller. They require *documented instructions* from the controller to be allowed to process data and are not allowed to contract other processors without the explicit permission from the controller. Any processing activity outside of what is permitted for a processor makes them a controller by default:

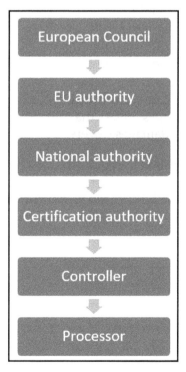

Authorities

GDPR does not concern itself where companies are registered, but where the main decisions are taken. If a controller makes its main decisions inside the EU, the GDPR applies to all processing of all personal data, regardless where in the world the data subject resides. If the controller resides outside of the EU, the GDPR still applies to all processing that involves European citizens.

Avoiding sanctions

So, what are the data protection authorities allowed to do? Well, their arm is indeed long. They can:

- Perform **audits**. Controllers and processors are required to give authorities access to all premises, equipment, data, and any information regarding the processing the auditors require.
- Issue **warnings**. Perhaps the lightest form of sanction.
- Issue **reprimands**, forcing companies to act within a given time.
- Give **orders**. They can basically order you to restrict your processing or turn the entire system off.
- Issue **fines**, up to 4% of total worldwide annual turnover (or 20,000,000 EUR, whichever is *higher*).
- Require **compensations** from the controller or processor, covering any damages, including indirect damages, unless the controller or processor can prove they are not responsible for the damages (reverse burden of proof).

Controllers are required to report personal data breaches within 72 hours of becoming aware of them. Not doing so, without providing proper justification, can also be a reason for sanctions.

Assisting controllers and processors

Any controller and processor that processes personal data on a large scale or as a core activity must designate a **Data Protection Officer**, or **DPO**. The DPO works together with management and advises them with regards to privacy legislation. The DPO is a protected resource. Management cannot issue instructions to the DPO, nor can they penalize the DPO for performing its tasks. They must also choose the DPO based on merits and expert knowledge. The DPO also helps instruct and advise the employees of the company. It is also the natural point of contact for the authorities, as well as the public. If they have any requests, they are free to contact the DPO.

Protecting personal data

The GDPR refers to specific data protection mechanisms only through the term **state of the art**. It does this, to make sure the legislation does not become obsolete as technology advances. But the term includes all aspects of authentication, authorization, encryption, signatures, hashes, penetration tests, monitoring, logging, and so on, discussed throughout this book. But the GDPR makes an important requirement: data protection must be implemented *by design* and *by default*.

Data protection by design means that it is not sufficient to add security as a varnish, or as a layer on top of an otherwise unprotected solution. Adding a login page is not sufficient, if the underlying APIs or database layers are unprotected.

Data protection by default means that security is not something you activate. Instead, all security features should be enabled by default. Instead of restricting access rights, you should provide access rights.

Consider a **white-list** and a **black-list** as two examples of authorization mechanisms. The white-list provides data protection by default. Nothing is permitted, except the items available on the white-list. The black-list is an example that does not provide data protection by default. From the start, when the list is empty, everything is permitted. Only items on the list are prohibited.

Giving individual rights

The GDPR also defines a set of rights that every natural person has. This list is what makes the GDPR a good legislation. Everyone has the right to:

- **Be informed** about processing activities processing its personal data. The information must be transparent.
- **Get access** to any personal data being processed.
- **Export** any personal data that the person has provided to a portable format.
- **Correct** any erroneous data.
- **Delete** its data (or be *forgotten*).

This right is not absolute. It depends on the legal foundation of the processing activity. For activities based on consent, the right is absolute. For processing activities based on legitimate interest, all data that the controller does not have compelling reasons to maintain must be deleted. For processing activities based on a contract or legal obligation, no right to delete data exists.

- **Object to** and **restrict** any processing of personal data while the status of the data is disputed.
- **Withdraw consent** from any processing activity based on consent. It must be *as easy* to withdraw consent, as it was to give it.
- Avoid being subject to automatic decisions having negative consequences (in a legal sense) based on automatic profiling.

If a data subject corrects, objects to, restricts, or deletes any personal data, the controller must make sure this is propagated to everyone with whom the data has been shared, as long as this is technically possible.

Solving the puzzle

The design choices you make not only affect the security of your solution, but also how difficult it will become to make the solution GDPR compliant. Centralized big data solutions are difficult to make compliant, while decentralized edge solutions are easier to make compliant. The reason is that decentralized solutions lend themselves naturally to the wills of the corresponding owners. For centralized solutions, you must build a lot of data protection mechanisms manually, to safeguard the privacy of its data subjects.

In this book, we have studied multiple protocols for use with the Internet of Things. Among these, XMPP provides the following several features that can help you build solutions that protect the privacy of your data subjects:

- The distributed, federated authentication and authorization model lends itself perfectly to making security decisions in distributed ad hoc networks.
- Presence negotiation required to communicate efficiently provides an efficient means to model a crude binary form of consent. It's also easy to withdraw.
- Provisioning provides a method for modeling a detailed form of consent. The owner of the devices can control in detail who can access them and what they do with them.
- XMPP allows you to outsource much of the administration of privacy to the data subjects themselves. Since many processing activities do not require centralized processing and can be processed equally well on the edge, there's no need to provide support for correction, deletion, restriction, and so on, explicitly in the backend. The owner controls the data completely.
- Using XMPP is an example of data protection by default. You need to negotiate presence subscription before you can have a meaningful interaction using the `iq` and `presence` stanzas. The roster is always at hand, as are the identities of senders of messages, so you can always easily determine the validity of an incoming message.

Summary

In this chapter, you've been introduced to the basic definition of privacy and why it is important. You've also been introduced to the new privacy legislation GDPR and how it relates to the basic definition of privacy. You've learned what rights individuals have, what obligations companies that want to process personal data have, what might happen if you do not comply with the GDPR, and how certain technologies can help you to comply with the GDPR.

This chapter concludes this book. It is my hope that this book has provided you with valuable insights into the world of the Internet of Things and some of the technologies involved. If you have any comments, suggestions, or questions, please don't hesitate to contact the author. Contact details can be found at `https://waher.se/`.

Other Books You May Enjoy

If you enjoyed this book, you may be interested in these other books by Packt:

Internet of Things for Architects
Perry Lea

ISBN: 978-1-78847-059-9

- Understand the role and scope of architecting a successful IoT deployment, from sensors to the cloud
- Scan the landscape of IoT technologies that span everything from sensors to the cloud and everything in between
- See the trade-offs in choices of protocols and communications in IoT deployments
- Build a repertoire of skills and the vernacular necessary to work in the IoT space
- Broaden your skills in multiple engineering domains necessary for the IoT architect

Practical Internet of Things with JavaScript
Arvind Ravulavaru

ISBN: 978-1-78829-294-8

- Integrate sensors and actuators with the cloud and control them for your Smart Weather Station
- Develop your very own Amazon Alexa integrating with your IoT solution
- Define custom rules and execute jobs on certain data events using IFTTT
- Build a simple surveillance solutions using Amazon Recognition and Raspberry Pi 3
- Design a fall detection system and build a notification system for it
- Use Amazon Rekognition for face detection and face recognition in your Surveillance project

Leave a review - let other readers know what you think

Please share your thoughts on this book with others by leaving a review on the site that you bought it from. If you purchased the book from Amazon, please leave us an honest review on this book's Amazon page. This is vital so that other potential readers can see and use your unbiased opinion to make purchasing decisions, we can understand what our customers think about our products, and our authors can see your feedback on the title that they have worked with Packt to create. It will only take a few minutes of your time, but is valuable to other potential customers, our authors, and Packt. Thank you!

Index

www.ingramcontent.com/pod-product-compliance
Lightning Source LLC
Chambersburg PA
CBHW060651060326
40690CB00020B/4594